TRUE BASIC
PROGRAMS AND SUBROUTINES

TRUE BASIC
PROGRAMS AND SUBROUTINES

JOHN CLARK CRAIG

TAB BOOKS Inc.
Blue Ridge Summit, PA 17214

IBM PC® is a registered trademark of International Business Machines Corporation.
True BASIC® is a registered trademark of True BASIC, Inc.

FIRST EDITION

FIRST PRINTING

Library of Congress Cataloging in Publication Data

Craig, John Clark.
True BASIC—Programs and Subroutines.

Includes index.
1. BASIC (Computer program language) I. Title.
QA76.73.B3C72 1985   005.26   85-27635
ISBN 0-8306-0990-3
ISBN 0-8306-1990-9 (pbk.)

Contents

Introduction

BASIC is by far the most successful computer language in existence, if judged by the number of users. Since its creation in 1963 at Dartmouth College, BASIC has found its way into almost every small- to medium-sized computer on the market today. Unfortunately, common BASIC has some problems.

The first versions of BASIC for microcomputers had to be squeezed into just a few thousand bytes of memory. Sacrifices were made in the syntax and construction of the language. There were no standards or guidelines; implementors were free to modify the language as necessary, and they did.

Today, personal computers commonly have hundreds of thousands of bytes and speed greater than the mainframes of 20 years ago. BASIC also has changed, but not for the better. Sure, it has grown more powerful, and statements are available to do just about anything desired with your computer. However, the language designers took the easy route, adding the new statements in a piecemeal manner to the existing sloppy language. The result is that today we have many different versions of BASIC, each providing similar capabilities, and each requiring many, many hours of study to master.

Things are starting to get better. The original inventors of BASIC, John Kemeny and Thomas Kurtz, have introduced True BASIC to the world. This version of the language closely adheres to the *Draft Proposed American National Standard for BASIC*, which should become the standard for the BASIC language in the near future. Every complaint that I have ever heard about BASIC— and most of the complaints have been valid—are now satisfied. This is a truly fantastic language!

True BASIC is a compiled language. Programs operate several times faster than with the "other" BASIC, yet the compilation process is completely automatic. You simply type RUN to compile and run programs.

Computer-specific knowledge is unnecessary. You don't need to know the number of pixels on your screen, the internal storage requirements for different types of numbers, etc. In fact, programs written for your IBM PC will run just fine, without modification, on a Macintosh!

The full memory of your PC is available for True BASIC programs. Most other versions of BASIC limit program and data size to 64K bytes, which is piddling by today's standards.

You don't sacrifice capabilities. Commands are available that match or surpass just about anything that the "other" BASIC can do. For example, graphics commands are available to flood any irregularly shaped area of the screen with color, create animation effects by storing images in strings, fill rectangular areas with color, and so on. Plus there are new commands to fill polygonal areas with color, as well as to scale, rotate, and otherwise manipulate predefined images. The list goes on and on.

True BASIC is a modern, structured language. (You won't find a GOTO statement in any of the programs in this book.) If you are accustomed to programming in BASIC you'll discover that the structured programming techniques of True BASIC provide a new sense of freedom and creative power. You'll quickly discover that you can write much larger, more powerful programs with less strain and with greater understanding.

This book presents a collection of programs to help you "get your feet wet" with the True BASIC language. Subject areas are varied; there are programs of interest for just about everyone. Even more important than the overall programs are the many subroutines and functions used throughout this book. You will find many uses for these "program units" in programs of your own creation.

Chapter 1

Getting Started

This chapter presents a variety of True BASIC programs to get you started. The MENU program provides a way for you to run most of the other programs in this book from a menu. The other programs are short demonstrations to help you get a feel for the capabilities of True BASIC.

MENU

This program loads a list of programs and displays a menu for running any of them (Fig. 1-1). You simply type in the number of the program listed and that program will be run. When the chosen program terminates, control returns to this program and the menu will be redisplayed.

The **CHAIN** statement is demonstrated by this program. Often, the **CHAIN** statement can be used to break a large programming task into smaller, more manageable tasks.

You may wish to provide a different list of programs for the menu. Edit the file named **DIRLIST.TRU**, adding or subtracting any filenames you desire. The **MENU** program (Listing 1-1) will automatically accommodate any reasonable number of filenames in the **DIRLIST.TRU** file.

METRIC

This program (Listing 1-2) performs many of the more common metric conversions for length, area, volume, mass, force, energy, and power. All the conversion definitions are stored in a separate, editable file named **MCNVRSNS.TRU**. This allows

```
                              * MENU *

      1. BIN2HEX      16. FRACTION    31. PI          46. SIMULTAN    61. Z_SERIES
      2. CALENDAR     17. GETMANDL    32. PIECHART     47. SORTNUM     62. Z_WYEDEL
      3. CARDDECK     18. HEX2BIN     33. QUICKBAR     48. SORTSTR
      4. CIPHER       19. IMGFILES    34. QUICKPLT     49. SPIRAL
      5. CIRCLE3P     20. LIFE        35. RANDOM       50. STARS
      6. CLOCK_1      21. LOADPIC     36. RCTIMING     51. STAT
      7. CLOCK_2      22. LOGS        37. R_BRIDGE     52. TIMING
      8. CLOCK_3      23. MANDELBR    38. R_CLRCOD     53. VECTORS
      9. COMBPERM     24. MEANS       39. R_DELWYE     54. WNDCHILL
     10. COMPLEX      25. METRIC      40. R_MENU       55. Z_BRIDGE
     11. COORD3D      26. MOON        41. R_PARALL     56. Z_DELWYE
     12. DEC2FRAC     27. MORSE       42. R_SERIES     57. Z_MENU
     13. DISTRIBU     28. MUSIC       43. R_WYEDEL     58. Z_PARALL
     14. FACT         29. NEXTPLOT    44. SATELLIT     59. Z_POLREC
     15. FACT_BIG     30. OHMS_LAW    45. SIDEREAL     60. Z_RECPOL

      Enter the number of the program to be RUN ?
```

Fig. 1-1. Main menu screen display.

Listing 1-1. MENU.TRU main menu program.

```
! **********************************
! **  File:       MENU.TRU       **
! **  Date:       8/13/85        **
! **  Author:     John Craig     **
! **  Language:   True BASIC     **
! **********************************
!
! This program provides a menu driven system for running most
! of the programs on this disk.  This demonstrates one use of
! the CHAIN statement.

! Make room for all the possible program names
  DIM Prog$(200)

! Program names are stored in the file "DIRLIST"
  OPEN #1: NAME "DIRLIST"

! Read in the program names, counting them as they arrive
  DO WHILE MORE #1
      LET Count = Count + 1
      INPUT #1: Prog$(Count)
  LOOP
  CLOSE #1
```

```
! Repeat the rest of this program over and over
  DO

     ! Set video mode
       SET MODE "80"
       SET COLOR "white/black"

     ! Start with a clean slate
       CLEAR

     ! Display program name
       PRINT USING Repeat$("#",80): "* MENU *"
       PRINT

     ! Determine number of rows to display
       FOR Rows = 5 TO 5 STEP 5
           IF Rows * 5 > Count THEN EXIT FOR
       NEXT Rows

     ! Display the program names
       FOR I = 1 TO Count
           SET CURSOR Mod((I-1),Rows) + 4, 15 * Int((I-1) / Rows) + 1
           PRINT USING "###. <#######": I,Prog$(I)
       NEXT I

     ! Clear out the keyboard buffer
       DO WHILE KEY INPUT
           GET KEY And_forget_it
       LOOP

     ! Ask user for program number
       SET CURSOR 20,1
       INPUT PROMPT "  Enter the number of the program to be RUN ? ": N

     ! Go do it to it
       CLEAR
       SET CURSOR 12,30
       PRINT "CHAINing to ";Prog$(N)
       CHAIN Prog$(N),RETURN

     ! Next program, please
  LOOP

  END
```

Listing 1-2. METRIC.TRU metric conversion program (continued to page 6).

```
! *********************************
! ** File:      METRIC.TRU    **
! ** Date:      8/15/85       **
! ** Author:    John Craig    **
! ** Language:  True BASIC    **
! *********************************
!
! This program provides menu driven metric conversions

! Start with a clean slate
```

3

```
    CLEAR
    SET MODE "40"

! Display program name, centered in 40 columns
    PRINT USING Repeat$("#",39): "* METRIC *"
    PRINT
    PRINT

! Open the file containing the conversions
    OPEN #1: NAME "MCNVRSNS"

! Read in all the subject areas
    DIM Subject$(20)
    WHEN EXCEPTION IN
        DO
            LINE INPUT #1: X$
            IF Pos(X$,"=") = 0 AND Trim$(X$) <> "" THEN
                LET X$ = Lcase$(Trim$(X$))
                LET X$(1:1) = Ucase$(X$(1:1))
                IF X$ <> "End" THEN
                    LET Subs = Subs + 1
                    LET Subject$(Subs) = X$
                END IF
            END IF
        LOOP
    USE
        CLOSE #1
    END WHEN

! Display the subject menu
    FOR I = 1 TO Subs
        PRINT Tab(15);Str$(I);". ";Subject$(I)
    NEXT I
    PRINT

! Prompt user to select from the menu
    PRINT
    PRINT USING Repeat$("#",39): "Enter a number..."
    PRINT
    PRINT Tab(17);
    INPUT Choice

! Re-open the file to get the conversions of interest
    OPEN #1: NAME "MCNVRSNS"

! Read in and grab just the conversions wanted
    DIM Conversion$(100)

! First, input lines til we find the subject line of choice
    DO
        LINE INPUT #1: X$
    LOOP UNTIL Ucase$(X$) = Ucase$(Subject$(Choice))
! Next, input lines until blank line is discovered
    DO
        LINE INPUT #1: X$
        LET Count = Count + 1
        LET Conversion$(Count) = Trim$(X$)
    LOOP UNTIL Conversion$(Count) = ""

! Decrement the extra count
```

```
     LET Count = Count - 1

! Close up the file
  CLOSE #1

! Clear the display
  SET MODE "80"
  CLEAR

! Title the new screen
  PRINT Subject$(Choice);"..."
  PRINT

! Generate the menu display and grab conversion parts
  DIM A$(100),B$(100),Multiplier(100)
  FOR I = 1 TO Count
      IF I > 1 AND Mod(I,20) = 1 THEN
          PRINT
          PRINT "Press the space bar to continue..."
          DO
              IF KEY INPUT THEN
                  GET KEY Keycode
              ELSE
                  LET Keycode = 0
              END IF
          LOOP UNTIL Keycode = Ord(" ")
      END IF
      LET Work$ = Conversion$(I)
      LET Equal = Pos(Work$,"=")
      LET Aster = Pos(Work$,"*")
      LET A$(I) = Trim$(Work$(1:Equal-1))
      LET B$(I) = Trim$(Work$(Equal+1:Aster-1))
      LET Multiplier(I) = Val(Work$(Aster+1:Maxnum))
      PRINT Str$(I+I-1);". ";A$(I);" to ";B$(I)
      PRINT Str$(I+I);". ";B$(I);" to ";A$(I)
  NEXT I

! Ask user for conversion number
  PRINT
  INPUT PROMPT "Conversion number ? ": Conversion

! Calculate pointer to conversion information
  LET Ptr = Int((Conversion-1)/2)+1

! Ask for units to convert
  PRINT
  PRINT "Enter ";
  IF Mod(Conversion,2) = 1 THEN
      PRINT A$(Ptr);
  ELSE
      PRINT B$(Ptr);
  END IF
  INPUT PROMPT " ? ": X

! Convert
  IF Mod(Conversion,2) = 1 THEN
      LET Y = X / Multiplier(Ptr)
  ELSE
      LET Y = X * Multiplier(Ptr)
```

```
    END IF

  ! Display the result
    PRINT
    IF Mod(Conversion,2) = 1 THEN
        PRINT X;A$(Ptr);" = ";Y;B$(Ptr)
    ELSE
        PRINT X;B$(Ptr);" = ";Y;A$(Ptr)
    END IF

  ! Wait for user
    PRINT
    PRINT "Press any key to continue..."
    GET KEY Before_continuing

  ! End of the road
    END
```

you to add other conversions as desired.

The first display is of a menu for category selection. Enter a number for the type of conversion desired. For example, suppose you were to order concrete for a radio telescope mounting base and the volume of the base were given to you in cubic meters. Enter the number 3 to select the category of volume conversions:

* METRIC *

1. Length
2. Area
3. Volume
4. Mass
5. Force
6. Energy
7. Power

Enter a number . . .

? 3

The second display (Fig. 1-2) is a menu of conversions for the category chosen. Continuing with our example, enter the number 5 to select the "Cubic meters to Cubic yards" conversion. Finally, you will be asked to enter the number of cubic meters to be converted to cubic yards.

The contents of the file named **MCNVRSNS.TRU** (Fig. 1-3) define all the conversions and their categories. Edit this file as desired, following the same format. Notice that each conversion statement is used to define two conversions; the program determines if multiplication or division by the numerical constant is necessary for the conversion chosen. For example, the conversion statement

Cubic meters = Cubic yards * .764554857984

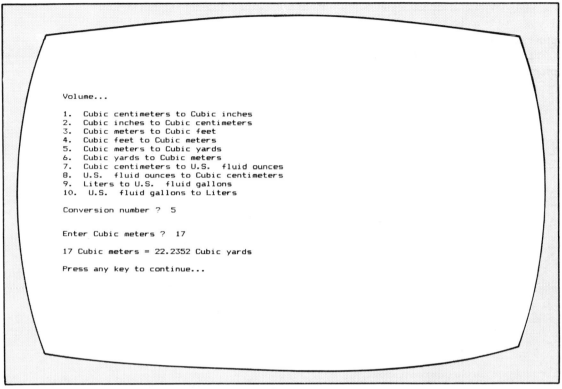

```
Volume...

1.   Cubic centimeters to Cubic inches
2.   Cubic inches to Cubic centimeters
3.   Cubic meters to Cubic feet
4.   Cubic feet to Cubic meters
5.   Cubic meters to Cubic yards
6.   Cubic yards to Cubic meters
7.   Cubic centimeters to U.S.  fluid ounces
8.   U.S.  fluid ounces to Cubic centimeters
9.   Liters to U.S.  fluid gallons
10.  U.S.  fluid gallons to Liters

Conversion number ?  5

Enter Cubic meters ?  17

17 Cubic meters = 22.2352 Cubic yards

Press any key to continue...
```

Fig. 1-2. Volume conversion submenu of metric conversion program.

is analyzed and used for converting cubic meters to cubic yards and also for converting cubic yards to cubic meters.

Feel free to edit the **MCNVRSNS.TRU** file as desired to add or remove conversion definitions. Be sure to leave a blank line before each category name (yes, you may add new categories), and make sure the **END** statement is the last line in the file.

SATELLIT

This program calculates the aiming instructions for a parabolic satellite antenna dish. The program prompts you for the latitude and longitude on the earth where the antenna is located and the longitude on the equator directly below the geosynchronous satellite. Output from the program consists of the azimuth and elevation to pivot the antenna to aim at the satellite.

The program is quite verbose but fairly self-explanatory. The initial screen display is shown in Fig. 1-4; following the entry of satellite longitude, the screen clears and the information in Fig. 1-5 appears. Listing 1-3 is the program code.

SORTNUM

This program demonstrates a simple, short, easy-to-program method of sorting an array of numbers. It is not as efficient as some of the more exotic methods, but for relatively small arrays it is quite sufficient for getting the job done. Figure 1-6 shows a typical screen display from SORTNUM, using 50 random numbers generated by the program itself.

The sorting task is performed by the subroutine named **Sortnum** at the end of the program listing (Listing 1-4).

SORTSTR

This program (Listing 1-5) demonstrates a simple, short, easy- to-program method

```
LENGTH
Centimeters = Inches * 2.54
Centimeters = Feet * 30.48
Microns = Mils * 25.4
Meters = Feet * .3048
Meters = Yards * .9144
Kilometers = Miles * 1.609344

AREA
Square centimeters = Square inches * 6.4516
Square meters = Square feet * .09290304
Square meters = Square yards * .8361273
Square kilometers = Square miles * 2.58998811
Hectares = Acres * .4046873

VOLUME
Cubic centimeters = Cubic inches * 16.38706
Cubic meters = Cubic feet * .028316846592
Cubic meters = Cubic yards * .764554857984
Cubic centimeters = U.S. fluid ounces * 29.57353
Liters = U.S. fluid gallons * 3.785412

MASS
Kilograms = Pounds (avdp.) * .45359237
Tons (metric) = Ton (short) * .90718474

FORCE
Dynes = Ounce (force) * 27801.3851
Newtons = Pounds (force) * 4.448221615
Pascals = Psi * 6894.757293
Millibars = Inches of Hg * 33.864

ENERGY
Calories = BTU (IST) * .2521644007
Watt-hours = BTU (IST) * .2930710702
Joules = BTU (IST) * 1055.055853
Joules = Ft-lbs * 1.355817948

POWER
Watts = BTU (IST) per hour * .2930710702
Watts = Horsepower (mechanical) * 745.6998716
Watts = Horsepower (electrical) * 746
Watts = Ft-lbs/sec * 1.355817948

END
```

Fig. 1-3. Contents of file MCNVRSNS.TRU.

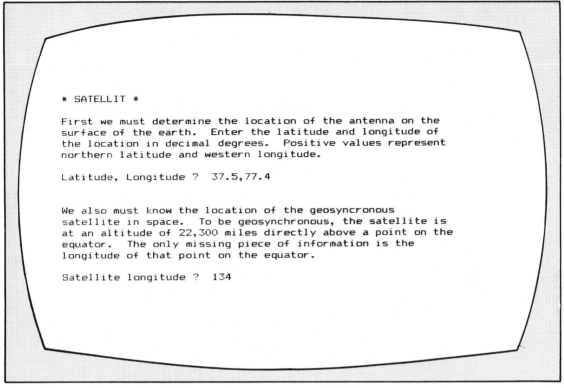

```
* SATELLIT *

First we must determine the location of the antenna on the
surface of the earth.  Enter the latitude and longitude of
the location in decimal degrees.  Positive values represent
northern latitude and western longitude.

Latitude, Longitude ?  37.5,77.4


We also must know the location of the geosyncronous
satellite in space.  To be geosynchronous, the satellite is
at an altitude of 22,300 miles directly above a point on the
equator.  The only missing piece of information is the
longitude of that point on the equator.

Satellite longitude ?  134
```

Fig. 1-4. First screen of satellite positioning program.

of sorting an array of strings. It is not as efficient as some of the more exotic methods, but for relatively small arrays it is quite sufficient for getting the job done.

The sorting task is performed by the subroutine named **Sortstr** at the end of the program listing. True BASIC string manipulations are quite efficient. It appears that when two strings are swapped, only the addresses of the strings are actually swapped in memory, rather than the actual string data. The result of this method is faster string manipulation.

Figure 1-7 is a typical screen display from **SORTSTR**. The sample strings shown in the left column are read from **DATA** statements beginning about 30 lines into the program; the right column consists of the same strings sorted into ascending alphabetic order.

WNDCHILL

This program uses the standard formula for computing the wind chill index, given the wind speed in miles per hour and air temperature in degrees Fahrenheit.

This program serves as a short, simple example of a True BASIC program, complete with prompted inputs, a short function definition, displayed output of results, and a scan of the keyboard to wait for a keypress before terminating the program. Figure 1-8 is the screen display, and Listing 1-6 shows the program code.

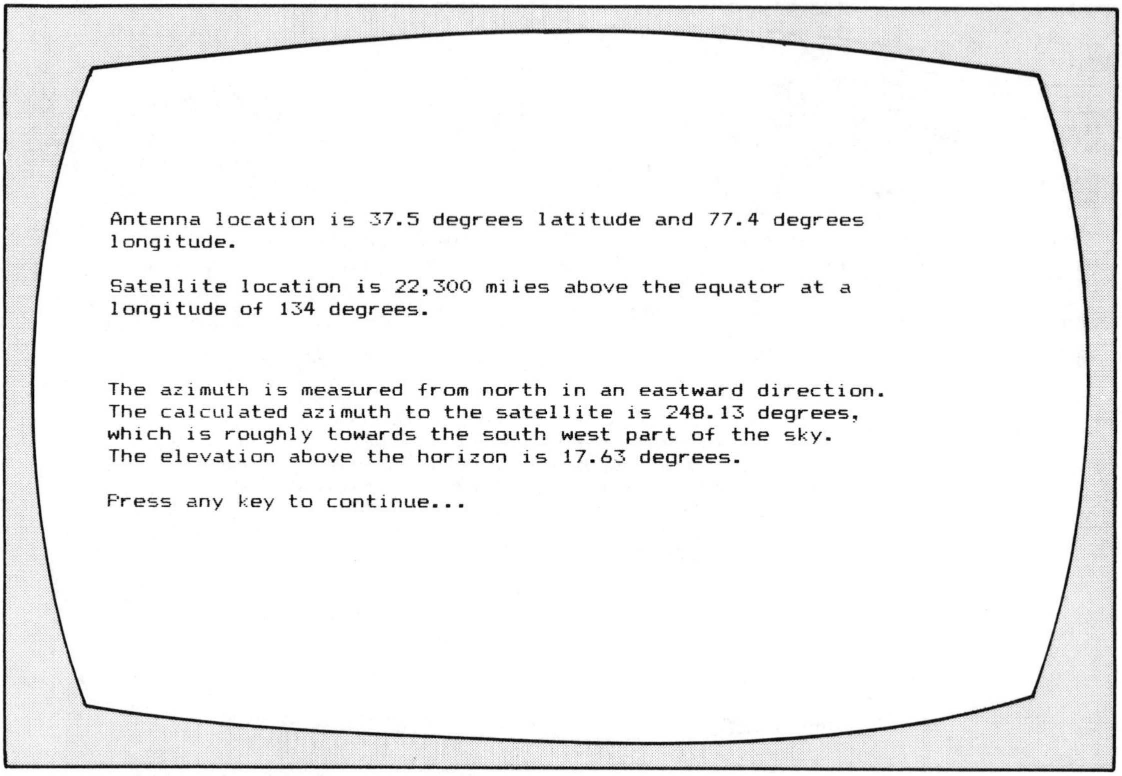

```
Antenna location is 37.5 degrees latitude and 77.4 degrees
longitude.

Satellite location is 22,300 miles above the equator at a
longitude of 134 degrees.


The azimuth is measured from north in an eastward direction.
The calculated azimuth to the satellite is 248.13 degrees,
which is roughly towards the south west part of the sky.
The elevation above the horizon is 17.63 degrees.

Press any key to continue...
```

Fig. 1-5. Second screen of satellite antenna positioning program.

Listing 1-3. SATELLIT.TRU satellite antenna positioning program.

```
! *********************************
! **   File:       SATELLIT.TRU   **
! **   Date:       7/27/85        **
! **   Author:     John Craig     **
! **   Language:   True BASIC     **
! *********************************
!
! This program calculates where to aim a
! geosynchronous satellite dish antenna
! given the antenna's location on the earth
! and the satellite's location in space.

! Declare the library of trigonometric functions
  LIBRARY "\tbfiles\fntdlib.trc"

! DECLARE FUNCTION cot, sec, csc, asin, acos, acot, asec, acsc
  DECLARE FUNCTION Acos
  OPTION ANGLE DEGREES

! Start with a clean slate
  CLEAR

! Display program name
```

```
    PRINT "* SATELLIT *"
    PRINT

!  Ask user for the antenna location
    PRINT "First we must determine the location of the antenna on the"
    PRINT "surface of the earth.  Enter the latitude and longitude of"
    PRINT "the location in decimal degrees. Positive values represent"
    PRINT "northern latitude and western longitude."
    PRINT
    INPUT PROMPT "Latitude, Longitude ? ": Latitude,Longitude
    PRINT
    PRINT

!  Ask user for the satellite location
    PRINT "We also must know the location of the geosyncronous"
    PRINT "satellite in space.  To be geosynchronous, the satellite is"
    PRINT "at an altitude of 22,300 miles directly above a point on the"
    PRINT "equator.  The only missing piece of information is the"
    PRINT "longitude of that point on the equator."
    PRINT
    INPUT PROMPT "Satellite longitude ? ": Satlong

    CLEAR
    PRINT "Antenna location is";Latitude;"degrees latitude and";Longitude;
    PRINT "degrees longitude."
    PRINT
    PRINT "Satellite location is 22,300 miles above the equator at a"
    PRINT "longitude of";Satlong;"degrees."
    PRINT
!  Calculate the aim azimuth and elevation
    LET Longdiff = Satlong - Longitude
    LET Tmp1 = 1821378689 - 537374800 * Cos(Latitude) * Cos(Longdiff)
    LET Elevation = Acos((Tmp1-1740301311) / (12734 * Sqr(Tmp1))) - 90
    LET Azimuth = Atn(Tan(Longdiff) / Sin(Latitude)) + 180

!  Tell user the azimuth for aiming at the satellite

    IF Elevation < 0 THEN
        PRINT "This satellite is below the horizon. Sorry."
    ELSE
        PRINT "The azimuth is measured from north in an eastward direction."
        PRINT "The calculated azimuth to the satellite is";
        PRINT Round(Azimuth,2);"degrees,"
        PRINT "which is roughly towards the ";
        IF Azimuth > 290 OR Azimuth < 70 THEN PRINT "north ";
        IF Azimuth > 110 AND Azimuth < 250 THEN PRINT "south ";
        IF Azimuth > 20 AND Azimuth < 160 THEN PRINT "east ";
        IF Azimuth > 200 AND Azimuth < 340 THEN PRINT "west ";
        PRINT "part of the sky. ";
        PRINT "The elevation above the horizon is";
        PRINT Round(Elevation,2);"degrees."
    END IF
!  Wait for key press
    PRINT
    PRINT "Press any key to continue..."
    GET KEY Before_continuing

!  All done
    END
```

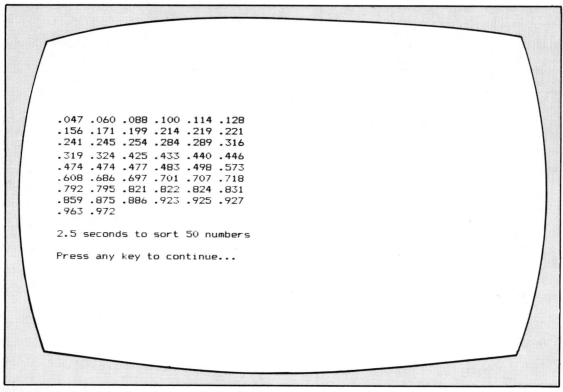

```
.047 .060 .088 .100 .114 .128
.156 .171 .199 .214 .219 .221
.241 .245 .254 .284 .289 .316
.319 .324 .425 .433 .440 .446
.474 .474 .477 .483 .498 .573
.608 .686 .697 .701 .707 .718
.792 .795 .821 .822 .824 .831
.859 .875 .886 .923 .925 .927
.963 .972

2.5 seconds to sort 50 numbers

Press any key to continue...
```

Fig. 1-6. A typical screen from the numeric sort program.

Listing 1-4. SORTNUM.TRU program, demonstrating a numeric sort subroutine.

```
!  **********************************
!  **   File:       SORTNUM.TRU    **
!  **   Date:       8/10/85        **
!  **   Author:     John Craig     **
!  **   Language:   True BASIC     **
!  **********************************
!
!  This program demonstrates a simple sorting subroutine
!  adequate for sorting relatively short numerical arrays.

!  Start with a clean slate
   SET WINDOW 0,1,0,1
   SET COLOR "yellow/blue"
   CLEAR

!  Display program name
   PRINT "* SORTNUM *"
   PRINT


!  Build the array for the sorting
   DIM Array(50)

!  Fill the array with 50 random numbers
```

12

```
    RANDOMIZE
    FOR I = 1 TO 50
        LET Array(I) = Rnd
    NEXT I

! Sort it all
    LET Time_start = Time
    CALL Sortnum(Array)
    LET Elapsed = Time - Time_start

! Display the results
    FOR I = 1 TO 50
        PRINT USING " #.###": Array(I);
        IF Mod(I,6) = 0 THEN PRINT
    NEXT I
    PRINT
    PRINT
    PRINT USING "##.# seconds to sort 50 numbers": Elapsed
    PRINT

! Wait for a key press
    PRINT "Press any key to continue..."
    GET KEY Before_continuing

! All done
    END

! Subroutine to sort an array of numbers
    SUB Sortnum(A())
        FOR I = 1 TO Size(A)-1
            FOR J = I+1 TO Size(A)
                IF A(I) > A(J) THEN
                    LET Tmp = A(I)
                    LET A(I) = A(J)
                    LET A(J) = Tmp
                END IF
            NEXT J
        NEXT I
    END SUB
```

Listing 1-5. SORTSTR.TRU program, demonstrating a string sort subroutine.

```
! **********************************
! **   File:       SORTSTR.TRU   **
! **   Date:       8/10/85       **
! **   Author:     John Craig    **
! **   Language:   True BASIC    **
! **********************************
!
! This program demonstrates a simple sorting subroutine
! adequate for alphanumerically sorting short string lists.

! Start with a clean slate
    SET WINDOW 0,1,0,1
    SET COLOR "yellow/blue"
    CLEAR

! Display program name
```

```
    PRINT "* SORTSTR *"
    PRINT

! First, scan the number of string items
    WHEN EXCEPTION IN
        DO
            READ Dummy$
            LET Count = Count + 1
        LOOP
    USE
    END WHEN

! Build the string arrays for the sorting
    DIM Unsorted$(1),Sorted$(1)

! Read in all the string items
    RESTORE
    MAT READ Unsorted$(Count)

! Here's the sample string DATA to be sorted
    DATA One,Two,Three,Four,Five
    DATA Six,Seven,Eight,Nine,Ten
    DATA Eleven,Twelve,Thirteen,Fourteen,Fifteen
    DATA Sixteen,Seventeen

! Sort it all
    MAT Sorted$ = Unsorted$
    LET T0 = Time
    CALL Sortstr(Sorted$)
    LET Elapsed = Time - T0

! Display the results
    FOR I = 1 TO Count
        PRINT Unsorted$(I),Sorted$(I)
    NEXT I

! Show the elapsed sort time
    PRINT
    PRINT "Sorting time was";Elapsed;"seconds."
    PRINT

! Wait for a key press
    PRINT "Press any key to continue..."
    GET KEY Before_quitting

! All done
    END

! This subroutine sorts an array of strings
    SUB Sortstr(A$())
        FOR I = 1 TO Size(A$)-1
            FOR J = I+1 TO Size(A$)
                IF A$(I) > A$(J) THEN
                    LET Tmp$ = A$(I)
                    LET A$(I) = A$(J)
                    LET A$(J) = Tmp$
                END IF
            NEXT J
        NEXT I
    END SUB
```

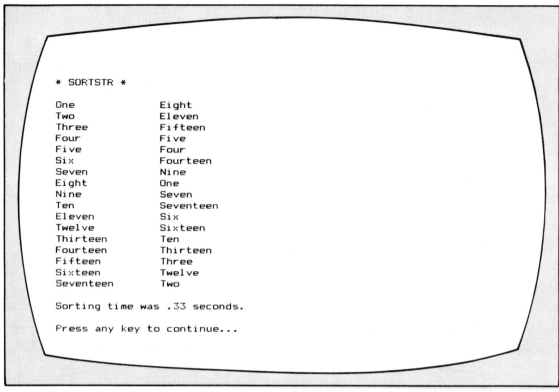

```
* SORTSTR *

One              Eight
Two              Eleven
Three            Fifteen
Four             Five
Five             Four
Six              Fourteen
Seven            Nine
Eight            One
Nine             Seven
Ten              Seventeen
Eleven           Six
Twelve           Sixteen
Thirteen         Ten
Fourteen         Thirteen
Fifteen          Three
Sixteen          Twelve
Seventeen        Two

Sorting time was .33 seconds.

Press any key to continue...
```

Fig. 1-7. Typical screen display from string sorting program SORTSTR.

Listing 1-6. Program to calculate wind chill factor.

```
! **********************************
! ** File:      WNDCHILL.TRU    **
! ** Date:      7/25/85         **
! ** Author:    John Craig      **
! ** Language:  True BASIC      **
! **********************************
!
! This program calculates the wind chill index
! given the air temperature in Fahrenheit and
! the wind velocity in miles per hour.

! Declare external function
  DECLARE FUNCTION Wind_chill

! Start with a clean slate
  CLEAR

! Display program name
  PRINT "* WNDCHILL *"
  PRINT

! Ask user for the temperature
  PRINT "What is the temperature outside (F) ";
```

```
    INPUT Temperature

! Ask user for the wind speed
  PRINT "What is the wind speed          (mph) ";
  INPUT Wind
  PRINT

! Tell 'em how cold it's gonna feel
  PRINT "Then the wind chill index is ";
  PRINT Wind_chill(Temperature,Wind);
  PRINT "degrees Fahrenheit."
  PRINT

! Wait for key press
  PRINT "Press any key to continue..."
  GET KEY Before_continuing

! All done
  END

! This function calculates wind chill index
! given the temperature and wind speed.
!
  FUNCTION Wind_chill(Fahrenheit,Mph)
      LET Tmp = .474266 + .303439 * Sqr(Mph) - .0202886 * Mph
      LET Wind_chill = Int(91.9 - (91.4 - Fahrenheit) * Tmp)
  END FUNCTION
```

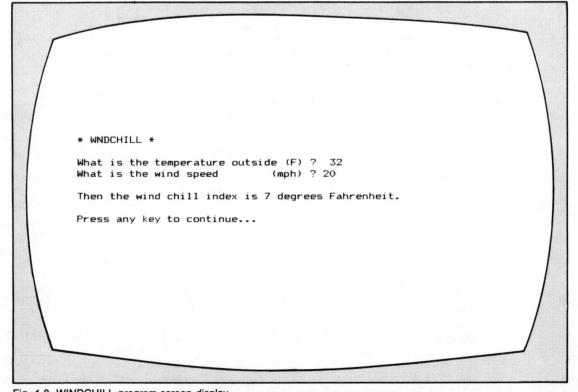

```
    * WNDCHILL *

    What is the temperature outside (F) ?  32
    What is the wind speed          (mph) ? 20

    Then the wind chill index is 7 degrees Fahrenheit.

    Press any key to continue...
```

Fig. 1-8. WINDCHILL program screen display.

Chapter 2

Just for Fun

These programs highlight some of the more enjoyable aspects of programming with True BASIC. They provide starting points for creating your own games, entertain with some good old-fashioned folk tunes, and fascinate with the ever-changing graphics of "Life" and "Mandelbrot plots."

CARDDECK

This program (Listing 2-1) demonstrates some techniques you might find useful next time you're programming blackjack, poker, rummy, or any other card game. A deck of 52 cards is stored as an array of 52 numbers. After the array is shuffled, up to 52 cards are selected without repetition. The program asks you for the number of hands and the number of cards per hand; it then proceeds to "deal" each hand, giving a verbal description of each card.

The function named **CARD$** builds a string containing the name of any of the cards from 1 to 52. You might try your hand at adding in the capability of returning the string "joker" for cards numbered 53 and 54.

The subroutine named **Shuffle** is not only useful for shuffling an array of 52 cards, but for shuffling the contents of any array into a pseudorandom sequence quickly and efficiently. The method used makes one pass through the array, swapping each arrray element with any other, chosen at random. This technique shuffles the array with as much randomness as the random number generator provided by True BASIC.

As a sample run, have your computer deal two hands of five cards each (Fig. 2-1).

Listing 2-1. CARDDECK.TRU program.

```
! *********************************
! **   File:       CARDDECK.TRU    **
! **   Date:       8/10/85         **
! **   Author:     John Craig      **
! **   Language:   True BASIC      **
! *********************************
!
! This program demonstrates subroutines and functions
! useful for programming card games

! Declare external functions
  DECLARE FUNCTION Card$

! Start with a clean slate
  CLEAR

! Display program name
  PRINT "* CARDDECK *"
  PRINT

! Ask user for the number of hands and the cards per hand
  INPUT PROMPT "How many hands to be dealt ? ": Hands
  INPUT PROMPT "How many cards per hand ?    ": Cards
  PRINT

! Display the hands using graphics mode
  SET WINDOW 0,1,0,1

! Open a brand new deck of cards
  DIM Card(52)
  FOR I = 1 TO 52
      LET Card(I) = I
  NEXT I

! Shuffle the deck
  CALL Shuffle(Card)

! Deal 'em
  FOR I = 1 TO Hands
      PRINT
      PRINT "Hand number";I
      PRINT
      FOR J = 1 TO Cards
          LET Ptr = Ptr + 1
          IF Ptr > 52 THEN
              PRINT
              PRINT "End of the deck"
              STOP
          END IF
          PRINT Card$(Card(Ptr))
      NEXT J
      PRINT
      PRINT "Press any key to continue..."
      GET KEY Before_continuing
  NEXT I

! All done
  END
```

```
! Subroutine to shuffle an array
  SUB Shuffle(A())
      RANDOMIZE
      LET Count = Size(A)
      FOR I = 1 TO Count
          LET J = Int(Rnd * Count + 1)
          LET Tmp = A(I)
          LET A(I) = A(J)
          LET A(J) = Tmp
      NEXT I
  END SUB

! Function to convert a number from 1 to 52 to a card name
  FUNCTION Card$(Card)

      SELECT CASE Mod(Card,13)
      CASE 0
          LET Number$ = "ace"
      CASE 1
          LET Number$ = "king"
      CASE 2 TO 10
          LET Number$ = Str$(Mod(Card,13))
      CASE 11
          LET Number$ = "jack"
      CASE 12
          LET Number$ = "queen"
      END SELECT

      SELECT CASE Int((Card - 1) / 13)
      CASE 0
          LET Suit$ = "hearts"
      CASE 1
          LET Suit$ = "clubs"
      CASE 2
          LET Suit$ = "diamonds"
      CASE 3
          LET Suit$ = "spades"
      END SELECT

      LET Card$ = Number$ & " of " & Suit$
  END FUNCTION
```

MUSIC

There are two methods of making sounds in True BASIC. The **SOUND** statement provides the mechanism for creating precisely controlled beeps and noises. The **PLAY** command helps you make beautiful music. This program (Listing 2-2) plays a few folk tunes to demonstrate the **PLAY** command.

LIFE

This program (Listing 2-3) runs a colorful simulation of "life," an interesting computer diversion about which whole books have been written. The rules are fairly simple. Each yellow square in the 10 × 10 grid is a "cell" which is dependent on its neighbors for survival. Neighboring cells are those in any of the positions around the faces and corners of a cell. At any given time a cell may then have anywhere from zero to eight

```
       * CARDDECK *

       How many hands to be dealt ? 2
       How many cards per hand ?    5

       Hand number 1

       4 of diamonds
       jack of hearts
       2 of clubs
       9 of hearts
       queen of hearts


       Press any key to continue...

       Hand number 2

       queen of diamonds
       10 of hearts
       ace of spades
       2 of diamonds
       6 of clubs

       Press any key to continue...
```

Fig. 2-1. Screen display for the CARDDECK program. The computer has selected two random five card hands.

Listing 2-2. Program demonstrating music capabilities of True BASIC (continued through page 23).

```
   ! *******************************
   ! **   File:      MUSIC.TRU      **
   ! **   Date:      8/17/85        **
   ! **   Author:    Jeanie Craig   **
   ! **   Language:  True BASIC     **
   ! *******************************
   !
   ! This program plays a few folk tunes, to demonstrate
   ! the PLAY statement.

   ! Declare external functions
     DECLARE FUNCTION Choose

   ! Set up first menu
     DIM Menu$(10)
     READ Question$
     FOR I = 1 TO 10
         READ Menu$(I)
     NEXT I
     DATA "Press the number for a tune... "
     DATA Skip To My Lou,"Oh, My Darling Clementine",On Top Of Old Smoky
     DATA "Long, Long Ago",Down In The Valley,Buffalo Gals
```

```
   DATA She'll Be Coming Round The Mountain,Red River Valley
   DATA Home On The Range,""

! Let's play as many songs as the user wants to
   DO

      ! Start with a clean slate
      CLEAR

      ! Display program name
      PRINT "* MUSIC *"
      PRINT

      ! Ask user for starting coordinate system
      LET Tune = Choose(Question$,Menu$)
      SELECT CASE Tune
      CASE 1
           CALL Skip
      CASE 2
           CALL Clementine
      CASE 3
           CALL Smoky
      CASE 4
           CALL Long
      CASE 5
           CALL Valley
      CASE 6
           CALL Buffalo
      CASE 7
           CALL Mountain
      CASE 8
           CALL River
      CASE 9
           CALL Range
      END SELECT

      ! Let's go back and maybe play another tune
   LOOP

! All done
   END

! Function to help user make a menu selection
   FUNCTION Choose(Question$,Menu$())

      ! Display the question
      PRINT Question$
      PRINT

      ! Show the choices
      FOR I = 1 TO 10
          IF Menu$(I) = "" THEN
              LET Count = I - 1
              EXIT FOR
          ELSE
              PRINT USING "#. ": I;
              PRINT Menu$(I)
          END IF
      NEXT I
      PRINT
```

```
       ! Tell 'em what to do
         PRINT "Press the key for your choice...";

       ! Build the test string
         LET Test$ = "123456789"(1:Count)

       ! Wait until one of the keys is pressed
         DO

            ! Wait for any key press
              DO
              LOOP UNTIL KEY INPUT

            ! Grab the key and check for appropriate choice
              GET KEY Keycode
              LET Choice = Pos(Test$,Chr$(Keycode))
              IF Choice = 0 THEN SOUND 55,.2

            ! Keep trying for an appropriate key press
         LOOP UNTIL Choice > 0

       ! Send the choice back to the caller
         PRINT Choice
         PRINT
         PRINT
         LET Choose = Choice

    END FUNCTION

! Skip To My Lou
  SUB Skip
      LET P$ = "mb ms t200 o4"
      LET P$ = P$ & "e4 e4 c4 c4 e4 e8 e8 g2 d4 d4 < b4 b4 > d4 d8"
      LET P$ = P$ & "d8 f2 e4 e4 c4 c4 e4 e8 e8 g2 d4 e8 f8 e4 d4 c2"
      LET P$ = P$ & "c4 r4"
      PLAY P$ & P$
  END SUB

! Oh my Darling Clementine
  SUB Clementine
      LET P$ = "mb mn t120 o4"
      LET P$ = P$ & "c8 c8 c4 < g4 > e8 e8 e4 c4 c8 e8 g4 g4 f8 e8 d2"
      LET P$ = P$ & "d8 e8 f4 f4 e8 d8 e4 c4 c8 e8 d4 < g4 b8 > d8 c2"
      PLAY P$ & P$
  END SUB

! On Top Of Old Smoky
  SUB Smoky
      LET P$ = "mb mn t180 o3"
      LET P$ = P$ & "c4 c4 e4 g4 > c2. < a2.. f4 f4 g4 a4 g2..."
      LET P$ = P$ & "c4 c4 e4 g4 g2. d... e4 f4 e4 d4 c2..."
      LET P$ = P$ & "c4 c4 e4 g4 > c2. < a2.. f4 f4 g4 a4 g2..."
      LET P$ = P$ & "c4 c4 e4 g4 g2. d2.. e4 f4 e4 d4 c2..."
      PLAY P$
  END SUB

! Long Long Ago
  SUB Long
      LET P$ = "mb mn t200 o4"
```

```
            LET P$ = P$ & "c2 c4 d4 e2 e4 f4 g2 a4 g4 e1 g2 f4 e4 d1 f2"
            LET P$ = P$ & "e4 d4 c1 c2 c4 d4 e2 e4 f4 g2 a4 g4 e1 g2 f4"
            LET P$ = P$ & "e4 d1 f2 e4 d4 c2."
            PLAY P$
        END SUB
    ! Down In The Valley
        SUB Valley
            LET P$ = "mb mn t120 o3"
            LET P$ = P$ & "g4 > c4 d4 e2. c2. e4 d4 c4 d2.. < g4 b4 > d4"
            LET P$ = P$ & "f2. d2. d4 e4 d4 c2.. < g4 > c4 d4 e2. c2."
            LET P$ = P$ & "e4 d4 c4 d2.. < g4 b4 > d4 f2. d2. d4 e4 d4"
            LET P$ = P$ & "c2.."
            PLAY P$
        END SUB

    ! Buffalo Gals
        SUB Buffalo
            LET P$ = "mb mn t200 o3"
            LET P$ = P$ & "c4 d4 e4 f4 a4 g4 e2 g4 f4 d2 f4 e4 c4"
            LET P$ = P$ & "< g4 > c4 d4 e4 f4 a4 g4 e4 e4 g4 g4"
            LET P$ = P$ & "d4 < b4 > c2. r > c4 < b4 a4 g4 a4 g8 g8 e2"
            LET P$ = P$ & "g4 f8 f8 d2 f4 e8 e8 c2 > c4 < b4 a4 g4 a4"
            LET P$ = P$ & "g8 g8 e4 e4 g4 g8 g8 d4 < b8 b8 > c2."
            PLAY P$
        END SUB

    ! She'll Be Coming Round The Mountain
        SUB Mountain
            LET P$ = "mb ms t240 o4"
            LET P$ = P$ & "d4 e4 g4 g4 g4 g4 e4 d4 < b4 > d4 g1."
            LET P$ = P$ & "g4 a4 b4 b4 b4 b4 > d4 < b4 a4 g4"
            LET P$ = P$ & "a1. > d4 c4 < b4 b4 b4 b4 a4 g4 g4"
            LET P$ = P$ & "g4 e4 e4 e4 e4 a4 g4 f+4 e4 d4 d4"
            LET P$ = P$ & "g4 g4 b4 a4 f+4 d4 g1"
            PLAY P$
        END SUB
    ! Red River Valley
        SUB River
            LET P$ = "mb mn t120 o3"
            LET P$ = P$ & "d4 g4 b2 b4 a4 g2 a4 g4 e4 g2. d4"
            LET P$ = P$ & "g4 b2 g4 b4 > d2 c4 < b4 a1 d4 g4 b2"
            LET P$ = P$ & "b4 a4 g2 a4 b4 > d4 c2. < e4 e4 d2 f+4"
            LET P$ = P$ & "g4 a2 b4 a4 g1 d4 g4 b2 b4 a4 g2"
            LET P$ = P$ & "a4 b4 > d4 c2. < e4 e4 d2 f+4 g4 a2"
            LET P$ = P$ & "b4 a4 g1"
            PLAY P$
        END SUB
    ! Home On The Range
        SUB Range
            LET P$ = "mb ms t120 o3"
            LET P$ = P$ & "d4 d4 g4 a4 b2 g8 f+8 e4 > c4 c4 c2 c8"
            LET P$ = P$ & "c8 d4 < g4 g4 g4 f+4 g4 a2. d4 d4 g4"
            LET P$ = P$ & "a4 b2 g8 f+8 e4 > c4 c4 c2 c8 c8 < b4 a4"
            LET P$ = P$ & "g4 f+4 g4 a4 g2.. > d2. c4 < b4 a4 b2.."
            LET P$ = P$ & "d8 d8 g4 g4 g4 g4 f+4 g4 a2.. d4 d4"
            LET P$ = P$ & "g4 a4 b2 g8 f+8 e4 > c4 c4 c2 c8 c8 < b4"
            LET P$ = P$ & "a4 g4 f+4 g4 a4 g2."
            PLAY P$
        END SUB
```

Listing 2-3. LIFE simulation program (continued to page 28).

```
! *********************************
! **   File:       LIFE.TRU      **
! **   Date:       7/22/85       **
! **   Author:     John Craig    **
! **   Language:   True BASIC    **
! *********************************
!
! This is the famous computer simulation called LIFE

! Initialization
  CLEAR
  SET WINDOW -.3,10.3,-.3,11
  DIM Life(10,10)

! Draw a border around edge of universe
  SET COLOR 1
  BOX LINES 0,10,0,10
  BOX LINES -.3,10.3,-.3,10.3
  FLOOD -.1,-.1
  SET COLOR 0
  BOX LINES 0,10,0,10

! Ask user to create some life
  CALL Edit(Life,Generation)

! Do each generation until "Esc" key is pressed
  DO
      LET Generation = Generation + 1

    ! Display generation information
      CALL Clear_line
      PRINT "LIFE - Generation";Generation

    ! Calculate next generation
      CALL Evolve(Life)

    ! Watch for any key presses
      IF KEY INPUT THEN
          GET KEY Keycode

        ! Anything but the Esc key then edit life forms
          IF Keycode <> Ord("Esc") THEN
              CALL Edit(Life,Generation)
          END IF

        ! Finished checking for key presses
      END IF

    ! Do it all again if Esc key hasn't been pressed
  LOOP UNTIL Keycode = Ord("esc")

! Tell user to press one more key
  CALL Clear_line
  PRINT "Press any key..."

! All done
  END
```

```
! Subroutine to let user play God
  SUB Edit(Life(,),Generation)

! Tell user what to press
  CALL Clear_line
  PRINT "Press Csr-keys, Space-bar, or Enter"

! Preset cursor location
  LET Xc = 5
  LET Yc = 5

! Draw starting marker
  SET COLOR 2
  DRAW Marker WITH Shift(Xc,Yc)

! Edit until the Enter key is pressed
  LET Enter_flag = Ø
  DO

     ! Wait for key stroke
     DO
     LOOP UNTIL KEY INPUT
     GET KEY Keycode

     ! What key was pressed?
     SELECT CASE Keycode

        ! Cursor up key?
        CASE 328
           IF Yc < 1Ø THEN
              SET COLOR Life(Xc,Yc)
              BOX AREA Xc-1,Xc,Yc-1,Yc
              LET Yc = Yc + 1
              SET COLOR 2
              DRAW Marker WITH Shift(Xc,Yc)
              LET Generation = Ø
           END IF

        ! Cursor down key?
        CASE 336
           IF Yc > 1 THEN
              SET COLOR Life(Xc,Yc)
              BOX AREA Xc-1,Xc,Yc-1,Yc
              LET Yc = Yc - 1
              SET COLOR 2
              DRAW Marker WITH Shift(Xc,Yc)
              LET Generation = Ø
           END IF

        ! Cursor left key?
        CASE 331
           IF Xc > 1 THEN
              SET COLOR Life(Xc,Yc)
              BOX AREA Xc-1,Xc,Yc-1,Yc
              LET Xc = Xc - 1
              SET COLOR 2
              DRAW Marker WITH Shift(Xc,Yc)
              LET Generation = Ø
           END IF
```

```
                    ! Cursor right key?
            CASE 333
                IF Xc < 10 THEN
                    SET COLOR Life(Xc,Yc)
                    BOX AREA Xc-1,Xc,Yc-1,Yc
                    LET Xc = Xc + 1
                    SET COLOR 2
                    DRAW Marker WITH Shift(Xc,Yc)
                        LET Generation = 0
                    END IF

                    ! Space bar?
                CASE 32
                    IF Life(Xc,Yc) = 0 THEN
                        LET Life(Xc,Yc) = 3
                    ELSE
                        LET Life(Xc,Yc) = 0
                    END IF
                    SET COLOR Life(Xc,Yc)
                    BOX AREA Xc-1,Xc,Yc-1,Yc
                    SET COLOR 2
                    DRAW Marker WITH Shift(Xc,Yc)
                    LET Generation = 0

                    ! Enter key?
                CASE 13
                    SET COLOR Life(Xc,Yc)
                    BOX AREA Xc-1,Xc,Yc-1,Yc
                    LET Edit_flag = 1
                    SET COLOR 1

                    ! Any other key?
                CASE ELSE
                    SOUND 500,.1
                END SELECT

            ! Edit some more, unless <enter> was pressed
            LOOP UNTIL Edit_flag = 1

        ! Finished editing life
    END SUB

! Subroutine to modify each generation
    SUB Evolve(Life(,))

        DECLARE FUNCTION Neighbors

        ! Count neighbors around each cell
        FOR X = 1 TO 10
            FOR Y = 1 TO 10
                LET Old_color = Life(X,Y)
                LET Count = Neighbors(X,Y,Life)

                ! Empty cell with 3 neighbors sprouts to life
                IF Life(X,Y) = 0 AND Count = 3 THEN
                    LET Life(X,Y) = 1
                END IF

                ! Life with 2 or 3 neighbors is ok, else die
```

```
                    IF Life(X,Y) > 1 THEN
                        IF Count < 2 OR Count > 3 THEN
                            LET Life(X,Y) = 2
                        END IF
                    END IF

                    ! Has there been a change in this cell?
                    IF Life(X,Y) <> Old_color THEN
                        SET COLOR Life(X,Y)
                        BOX AREA X-1,X,Y-1,Y
                    END IF

                    ! Do the rest of the cells
                NEXT Y
            NEXT X

        ! Change marked cells
          FOR X = 1 TO 10
              FOR Y = 1 TO 10

                  ! Sprouting to life?
                  IF Life(X,Y) = 1 THEN
                      LET Life(X,Y) = 3
                      SET COLOR 3
                      BOX AREA X-1,X,Y-1,Y

                    ! Marked to die?
                  ELSEIF Life(X,Y) = 2 THEN
                      LET Life(X,Y) = 0
                      SET COLOR 0
                      BOX AREA X-1,X,Y-1,Y
                  END IF

                  ! Check 'em all
              NEXT Y
          NEXT X

      ! Another generation has passed us by
    END SUB

! Subroutine to clear and prepare top text line
  SUB Clear_line
      SET COLOR 3
      SET CURSOR 1,1
      PRINT Repeat$(" ",40)
      SET CURSOR 1,1
  END SUB

! Draws the "X" for the life editing routine
  PICTURE Marker
      PLOT LINES: 0,0; -1,-1
      PLOT LINES: -1,0; 0,-1
  END PICTURE

! Function to count neighbors of a cell
! Eight places are checked, corners and faces
!
  FUNCTION Neighbors(X,Y,Life(,))

    ! Scroll around left if necessary
```

```
          IF X = 1 THEN
                LET Left = 10
          ELSE
                LET Left = X - 1
          END IF

     ! Scroll around right if necessary
          IF X = 10 THEN
                LET Right = 1
          ELSE
                LET Right = X + 1
          END IF

     ! Scroll through bottom if necessary
          IF Y = 1 THEN
                LET Down = 10
          ELSE
                LET Down = Y - 1
          END IF

     ! Scroll through top if necessary
          IF Y = 10 THEN
                LET Up = 1
          ELSE

                LET Up = Y + 1
          END IF

     ! Add up all the neighbors, alive or dying but not sprouting
          IF Life(Left,Up) > 1 THEN LET N = N + 1
          IF Life(X,Up) > 1 THEN LET N = N + 1
          IF Life(Right,Up) > 1 THEN LET N = N + 1
          IF Life(Left,Y) > 1 THEN LET N = N + 1
          IF Life(Right,Y) > 1 THEN LET N = N + 1
          IF Life(Left,Down) > 1 THEN LET N = N + 1
          IF Life(X,Down) > 1 THEN LET N = N + 1
          IF Life(Right,Down) > 1 THEN LET N = N + 1
          LET Neighbors = N

     ! Return to Mr. Evolve's neighborhood
     END FUNCTION
```

neighbors. With each passing generation the number of neighbors determines the fate of a cell. If an empty location has exactly three neighbors surrounding it, a new cell springs to life. If a living cell has two or three neighbors, it survives; any other number of neighbors causes it to perish.

The cells are dynamically colored to represent their state of existence. Yellow cells are healthy, living cells. Red cells have been marked to die, green cells are those just coming to life. This technique of coloring the cells adds a fascinating touch to the simulation.

When the program first starts, or when any key is pressed during the action, the program enters an editing mode that allows you to set up any pattern of cells desired. Move the "X" symbol around the grid with the cursor arrow keys and press the space bar to toggle any cell into or out of the "living" state (Fig. 2-2). When you are satisfied with the pattern you've created, press the Return key to start the action.

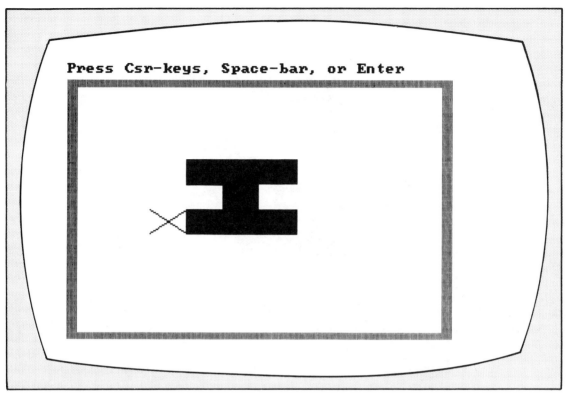

Fig. 2-2. Setting up a cell pattern for LIFE.

There are many fascinating clusters of cells that can evolve, depending on the initial state. Some "organisms" reach a stable condition where no change takes place with each generation, others oscillate between two states, and yet others slowly drift across the screen in a repeating pattern. Figure 2-3 shows a fifth-generation "life" screen. Your public library is a good place to find out more about this popular computer diversion if you get really hooked on the subject.

SPIRAL

This program (Listing 2-4) generates a wide variety of unusual and interesting graphics plots by calculating the path traced by a point fixed to a circle rolling around the edge of another. Figures 2-4 through 2-8 show some of the plots that may be created.

You may choose whether the rolling circle should roll on the inside or outside edge of the fixed circle, the number of teeth on each circle, and the radius from the center of the rolling circle to the point that will be traced in its motions. The actual radii of the two circles are calculated proportionally to the number of teeth on each.

The plot is scaled with the **WINDOW** statement to allow the curves to just brush the edges of the screen at their furthest points. This means that any choices made for the number of teeth, distance out to the trace point, etc., will still result in a plot that just fills the screen. Experiment with various numbers to get a feel for all the possibilities.

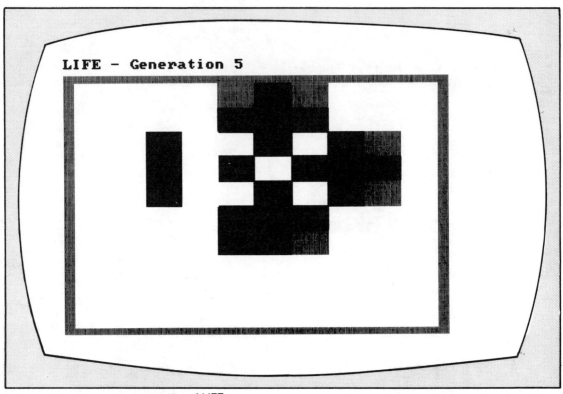

Fig. 2-3. One moment in the evolution of LIFE.

Listing 2-4. The SPIRAL program uses a variety of True BASIC's trigonometric functions (continued to page 32).

```
!  ********************************
!  **   File:       SPIRAL.TRU     **
!  **   Date:       7/24/85        **
!  **   Author:     John Craig     **
!  **   Language:   True BASIC     **
!  ********************************
!
!  The original concept for this program came from
!  Mark Erickson.  Thanks, Mark!
!
!  This program creates a variety of interesting graphics
!  plots and demonstrates some useful functions.

!  All trigonomtric functions will use degrees
   OPTION ANGLE DEGREES

!  Declare external function
   DECLARE FUNCTION Least_common_multiple

!  Start with a clean slate
   CLEAR

!  Display program name
```

```
      PRINT "* SPIRAL *"
      PRINT

   !  Describe the program to the user
      PRINT "This program creates the spiralling graph traced"
      PRINT "by a point on a circle that rolls around either"
      PRINT "the inside or outside edge of a fixed circle."
      PRINT

   !  Ask if circle is on inside or outside
      PRINT "Which way would you like the circle to roll around"
      PRINT "on the fixed circle..."
      PRINT
      PRINT "1. Inside edge"
      PRINT "2. Outside edge"
      PRINT

   !  Make sure user answers correctly
      DO
          INPUT Edge
          IF Edge <> 1 AND Edge <> 2 THEN SOUND 500,.3
      LOOP UNTIL Edge = 1 OR Edge = 2

   !  Ask for teeth numbers
      PRINT
      PRINT "Number of teeth on circles... fixed,rolling ";
      INPUT Fteeth,Rteeth
      PRINT

   !  Ask for location of 'pen' on rolling circle
      PRINT
      PRINT "One point on the rolling circle will be the 'pen'"
      PRINT "location for tracing the spiralling graph.  What"
      PRINT "distance would you like this point to be from the"
      PRINT "center of the rolling circle ? "
      PRINT

      INPUT Pradius

   !  Now the plot starts to thicken
      LET Lcm = Least_common_multiple(Fteeth,Rteeth)
      LET Ffraction = 360 / Fteeth
      LET Rfraction = 360 / Rteeth
      LET Rradius = Rteeth / Fteeth

   !  Scale the window so plot just fits
      IF Edge = 1 THEN
          IF Rradius < 1 THEN
              LET W = Pradius - Rradius + 1
          ELSE
              LET W = Pradius + Rradius - 1
          END IF
      ELSE
          LET W = 1 + Rradius + Pradius
      END IF
      SET WINDOW -W,W,-W,W

   !  Do the plotting
      FOR I = 0 TO Lcm
          LET Fixang = Mod(I,Fteeth) * Ffraction
```

```
              IF Edge = 1 THEN
                   LET Rotang = Mod(I,Rteeth) * Rfraction - Fixang
              ELSE
                   LET Rotang = Mod(I,Rteeth) * Rfraction + Fixang
              END IF
              LET Xtouch = Cos(Fixang)
              LET Ytouch = Sin(Fixang)
              IF Edge = 1 THEN
                   LET Xrcenter = Xtouch * (1 - Rradius)
                   LET Yrcenter = Ytouch * (1 - Rradius)
              ELSE
                   LET Xrcenter = Xtouch * (1 + Rradius)
                   LET Yrcenter = Ytouch * (1 + Rradius)
              END IF
              IF Edge = 1 THEN
                   LET Xpen = Xrcenter - Pradius * Cos(Rotang)
                   LET Ypen = Yrcenter - Pradius * Sin(Rotang)
              ELSE
                   LET Xpen = Xrcenter + Pradius * Cos(Rotang)
                   LET Ypen = Yrcenter + Pradius * Sin(Rotang)
              END IF
              PLOT LINES: Xpen,Ypen;
         NEXT I

     ! Wait for a key press
       GET KEY Before_quitting

     ! All done
       END

     ! Function to calculate the greatest common
     ! denominator of two numbers
     !
       FUNCTION Greatest_common_denominator(A,B)
            DO
                 LET C = Mod(A,B)
                 LET A = B
                 LET B = C
            LOOP WHILE C > 0
            LET Greatest_common_denominator = A
       END FUNCTION

     ! Function to calculate the least common
     ! multiple of two numbers
     !
       FUNCTION Least_common_multiple(A,B)
            DECLARE FUNCTION Greatest_common_denominator

            LET C = Greatest_common_denominator(A,B)
            LET Least_common_multiple = Abs(A * B / C)
       END FUNCTION
```

STARS

This program (Listing 2-5) creates the illusion of moving through a cluster of stars in space. The effect didn't turn out as spectacular as I had hoped, but the program does demonstrate the **PLOT POINTS** statement and the scanning of the keyboard during a running program.

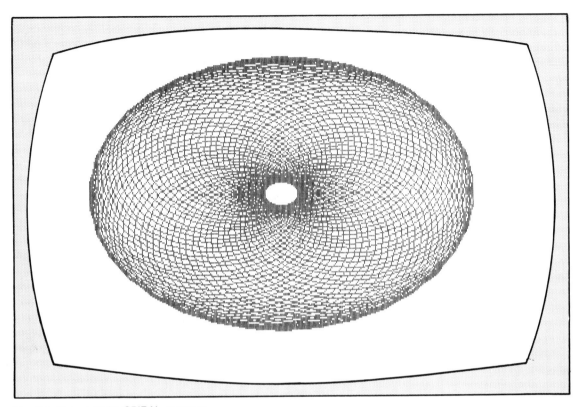

Fig. 2-4. Output of the SPIRAL program.

Listing 2-5. STARS.TRU demonstrates techniques for creating random graphics images.

```
!  **********************************
!  **    File:        STARS.TRU       **
!  **    Date:        8/10/85         **
!  **    Author:      John Craig      **
!  **    Language:    True BASIC      **
!  **********************************
!
!  This program creates a moving starfield

!  Shuffle the bag of stars
   RANDOMIZE

!  Initialize some variables
   LET Count = 20
   LET Acceleration = 1.03
   LET Velocity = 10 / 9

!  Create array of star coordinates
   DIM Star_x(1),Star_y(1)
   MAT Star_x = Zer(Count)
   MAT Star_y = Zer(Count)

!  Initialize graphics
```

```
    SET WINDOW -10,10,-10,10
    SET COLOR "white"

! Sprinkle some stars around
    FOR I = 1 TO Count .
        CALL Star_start(Star_x(I),Star_y(I))
        PLOT POINTS: Star_x(I),Star_y(I)
    NEXT I

! Main loop starts here
    DO
        FOR Range = 1 TO Count
            IF KEY INPUT THEN
                GET KEY Keycode
                SELECT CASE Chr$(Keycode)
                CASE "+"
                    LET Velocity = Velocity * Acceleration
                CASE "-"
                    LET Velocity = Velocity / Acceleration
                CASE ELSE
                    LET Quit_flag = 1
                END SELECT
                EXIT FOR
            END IF
            FOR Ptr = 1 TO Range
                CALL Process(Star_x(Ptr),Star_y(Ptr),Velocity)
                IF KEY INPUT THEN EXIT FOR
            NEXT Ptr
        NEXT Range
    LOOP UNTIL Quit_flag = 1

! Subroutine to pick a pseudorandom starting point for a star
    SUB Star_start(X,Y)
        LET Ang = Rnd * Pi * 2
        LET Radius = Rnd^2 * 10 + .01
        CALL Polar_rect(Radius,Ang,X,Y)
    END SUB

! Subroutine to shift a star out from center
    SUB Process(X,Y,Velocity)

        SET COLOR "background"
        PLOT POINTS: X,Y
        LET X = X * Velocity
        LET Y = Y * Velocity
        IF Abs(X) > 10 OR Abs(Y) > 10 THEN
            CALL Star_start(X,Y)
        END IF
        SET COLOR "white"
        PLOT POINTS: X,Y
    END SUB

! End of main program
    END

! Converts polar to rectangular
    SUB Polar_rect(Rho,Theta,X,Y)
        LET X = Rho * Cos(Theta)
        LET Y = Rho * Sin(Theta)
    END SUB
```

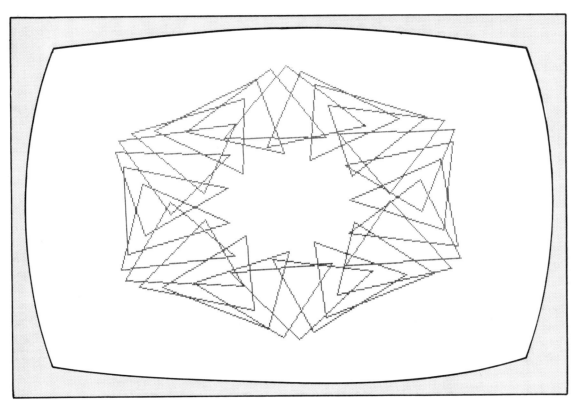

Fig. 2-5. Output of the SPIRAL program.

The star coordinates are kept in the arrays **Star__x** and **STAR__y**. Change the value assigned to the variable **Count** to create a different number of stars. **Count** is used to redimension the **Star__x** and **Star__y** arrays by use of the matrix function **Zer**.

While the main **DO LOOP** of the program is in operation, you may press either the plus (+) or minus (–) key to change the velocity of the stars. Pressing any other key will stop the program.

MANDELBR

The Mandelbrot set of complex numbers is described in detail in the August, 1985 issue of *Scientific American*. The cover and several illustrations for the article show beautiful, surrealistic, high-resolution graphics plots of these numbers. This program creates the same plots, in lower resolution but still fascinating.

A unique idea is presented here for allowing the IBM PC to show more shades of color than the four colors normally allowed. "Pixels," comprised of various combinations of four normal-size color pixels, are created and saved in strings by use of the **BOX KEEP** statement. The screen is scaled for a low-resolution mode of 160 × 100, and each large pixel is quickly plotted on the screen by use of the **BOX SHOW** statement.

The program (Listing 2-6) takes some time to complete each plot. Depending on

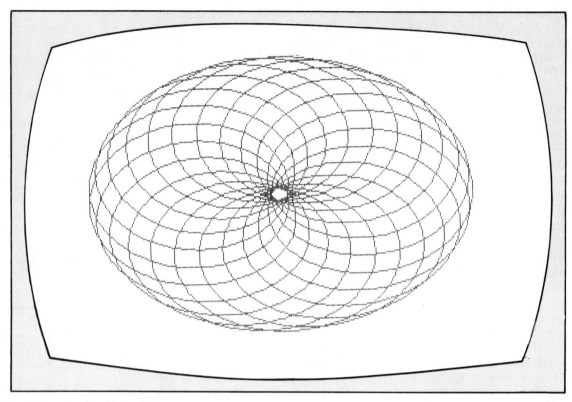

Fig. 2-6. Output of the SPIRAL program.

Listing 2-6. MANDELBR.TRU generates and plots complex numbers belonging to the Mandelbrot set (continued to page 39).

```
!  **********************************
!  **   File:      MANDELBR.TRU    **
!  **   Date:      8/5/85          **
!  **   Author:    John Craig      **
!  **   Language:  True BASIC      **
!  **********************************
!
!  This program creates Mandelbrot set plots as described in
!  the August, 1985 issue of Scientific American.

!  Declare external functions
   DECLARE FUNCTION Mandelbrot

!  Build the pixel array
   DIM Pixel(160,100)

!  Build the array of graphics "pixels"
   DIM Pixel$(6)

!  Start with a clean slate
   CLEAR

!  Display program name
```

```
      PRINT "* MANDELBR *"
      PRINT

   ! Where are we going to explore today?
      INPUT PROMPT "Enter lower left coordinate, real part ? ": Acorner
      INPUT PROMPT "Enter lower left coordinate, imag part ? ": Bcorner
      PRINT
      INPUT PROMPT "Enter length of side (bottom edge of screen) ? ": Side

   ! Create 2 by 2 "pixels" for IBM color graphics
      SET WINDOW 0,319,0,199
      FOR I = 1 TO 6
          FOR X = 0 TO 1
              FOR Y = 0 TO 1
                  READ C
                  SET COLOR C
                  PLOT POINTS: X,Y
              NEXT Y
          NEXT X
          BOX KEEP 0,1,0,1 IN Pixel$(I)
      NEXT I

      DATA 1,0,0,1,1,1,1,1
      DATA 2,1,1,2,2,2,2,2
      DATA 3,2,2,3,3,3,3,3

   ! Set a limit on our count size
      LET Limit = 121

   ! Pixel range for IBM PC in 1/2 medium resolution mode
      LET Px = 160
      LET Py = 100
      SET WINDOW 0,Px,0,Py
      CLEAR

   ! Determine The "Gap" Amount
      LET Gap = Side / Px

   ! Loop through each pixel and make the calculations
      FOR X = 1 TO Px
          SET CURSOR 10,10
          SET COLOR 1
          PRINT USING "## percent completed": 100 * X / Px
          FOR Y = 1 TO Py STEP 1
              LET Ac = X * Gap + Acorner
              LET Bc = Y * Gap + Bcorner
              LET Pixel(X,Y) = Mandelbrot(Ac,Bc,Limit)
          NEXT Y
      NEXT X

   ! Determine range of counts
      CLEAR
      SET CURSOR 10,11
      PRINT "Determining range"
      LET Minimum = Limit
      LET Maximum = 0
      FOR X = 1 TO Px
          FOR Y = 1 TO Py
              IF Pixel(X,Y) < Minimum THEN LET Minimum = Pixel(X,Y)
              IF Pixel(X,Y) < Limit THEN
```

```
                    IF Pixel(X,Y) > Maximum THEN LET Maximum = Pixel(X,Y)
              END IF
          NEXT Y
    NEXT X

  ! Set color ranges
    DIM Range(6)
    FOR I = 1 TO 6
        LET Range(I) = Round((Maximum - Minimum) * I / 6 + Minimum)
    NEXT I

  ! Plot the pixels
    CLEAR
    FOR X = 1 TO Px
        FOR Y = 1 TO Py
            IF Pixel(X,Y) <> Limit THEN
                FOR I = 1 TO 6
                    IF Pixel(X,Y) < Range(I) THEN
                        BOX SHOW Pixel$(I) AT X,Y
                        EXIT FOR
                    END IF
                NEXT I
            END IF
        NEXT Y
    NEXT X

  ! Store copy of screen to disk file
    CALL Store_screen

  ! Wait for a key stroke
    GET KEY Before_continuing

  ! All done
    END

  ! Mandelbrot function of a complex number
    FUNCTION Mandelbrot(Ac,Bc,Limit)

        FOR Count = 1 TO Limit
            LET Az2 = Az * Az
            LET Bz2 = Bz * Bz
            LET Bz = 2 * Az * Bz + Bc
            LET Az = Az2 - Bz2 + Ac
            IF Az2 + Bz2 > 4 THEN EXIT FOR
        NEXT Count

        LET Mandelbrot = Count
    END FUNCTION

  ! Subroutine to store copy of IBM PC medium resolution screen image
    SUB Store_screen

      ! Find first unused image type file
        DO
            WHEN EXCEPTION IN
                LET File$ = USING$("IMG%%%%",Fnumber)
                OPEN #1: NAME File$,CREATE New,ORGANIZATION Byte
                CLOSE #1
                EXIT DO
            USE
```

```
                    LET Fnumber = Fnumber + 1
                    IF Fnumber > 9999 THEN STOP
               END WHEN
         LOOP

      ! Call the routine that stores the image
      CALL Save_screen(File$)

   END SUB

! Subroutine to save copy of IBM PC medium resolution screen image
   SUB Save_screen(File$)

      ! Copy screen bytes into a string
      FOR Location = 1 TO 8000
           LET Img$ = Img$ & Chr$(Peek(753663+Location))
           LET Img$ = Img$ & Chr$(Peek(761855+Location))
      NEXT Location

      ! Open the file
      OPEN #1: NAME File$, CREATE Newold, ORGANIZATION Byte

      ! Store string in file
      WRITE #1: Img$

      ! Close the file
      CLOSE #1

   END SUB
```

the location in the complex plane being plotted, the calculations can take anywhere from about 20 minutes to 3 or 4 hours. Each point on the plot can require up to 121 iterations of a set of numerical calculations, as shown in the Mandelbrot function. True BASIC will complete these calculations several times faster than other brands of BASIC. In fact, this program would probably take an unrealistic amount of time to complete if it were written in the "other" BASIC. As the calculations progress you are informed of the progress by a message on the screen.

It's fun to explore various locations in the complex number plane. Every area of the plane is unique; there is theoretically an infinite variety of complex images in the Mandelbrot set. The program **NEXTPLOT** helps you zoom in on a small area of a plot. Figures 2-9 through 2-14 show the results of an exploration into one tiny part of Mandelbrot land. Notice how each plot magnifies by 10 a small portion of the previous plot. The *Scientific American* article covers the subject well and is recommended reading if you find this program interesting.

GETMANDL

This program (Listing 2-7) was written specifically for loading screen image files created by the **MANDELBR** program. Much of the program is the same as **LOADPIC**, but the file names created by **MANDELBR** follow a unique pattern, allowing this program to make it easier to specify which image file is to be loaded.

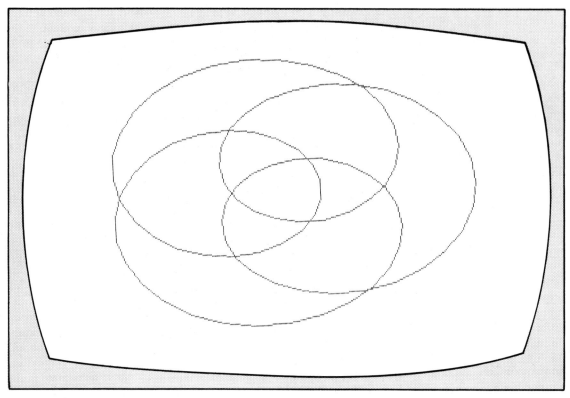

Fig. 2-7. Output of the SPIRAL program.

Listing 2-7. GETMANDL.TRU program.

```
!   *********************************
!   **   File:       GETMANDL.TRU   **
!   **   Date:       8/12/85        **
!   **   Author:     John Craig     **
!   **   Language:   True BASIC     **
!   *********************************
!
! This program loads in image files created by the MANDELBR program.

! Start with a clean slate
CLEAR

! Display program name
PRINT "* GETMANDL *"
PRINT

! Explain the operation to the user
PRINT "This program loads onto the screen an image stored in"
PRINT "a file by the MANDLEBR program."
PRINT
PRINT "The image file names are of the form IMG0000, where"
PRINT "the zeros are replace with a number from 1 to 9999."
PRINT "You must enter that number for the image file you"
```

```
      PRINT "want to view on the screen."
      PRINT

   ! Ask for the number
      INPUT PROMPT "What number for the file name ? ": N

   ! Create the file name using the number
      LET File$ = USING$("IMG%%%%",N)

   ! Set graphics window
      SET WINDOW 0,1,0,1

   ! Load in the image
      CALL Load_screen(File$)

   ! Wait for any key press
      GET KEY Before_quitting

   ! All done
      END

   ! Subroutine to load copy of IBM PC medium resolution screen image
      SUB Load_screen(File$)

         ! Open the file
            OPEN #1: NAME File$, ORGANIZATION Byte

         ! Load string from file
            READ #1, Bytes 16000: Img$

         ! Close the file
            CLOSE #1

         ! Copy string bytes onto screen
            FOR Location = 1 TO 8000
                LET Ptr = Ptr + 1
                CALL Poke(753663+Location,Ord(Img$(Ptr:Ptr)))
                LET Ptr = Ptr + 1
                CALL Poke(761855+Location,Ord(Img$(Ptr:Ptr)))
            NEXT Location

      END SUB
```

Screen image files created by **MANDELBR** are automatically named **IMG0000.TRU**, **IMG0001.TRU**, **IMG0002.TRU**, and so on. You can use the DOS directory command (**DIR**) with the "?" wild card character to list all of the image files currently on a disk. Type

DIR IMG????.TRU

to generate a list of all these files. To reload a given file into the screen, run the **GET-MANDL** program and respond with the number representing the file you want to load.

The **USING$** function is used in this program to format the file names. Notice how this function is similar in concept to the **USING** modifier of the **PRINT** statement, yet it is much more powerful because a string is created that may be processed further by BASIC.

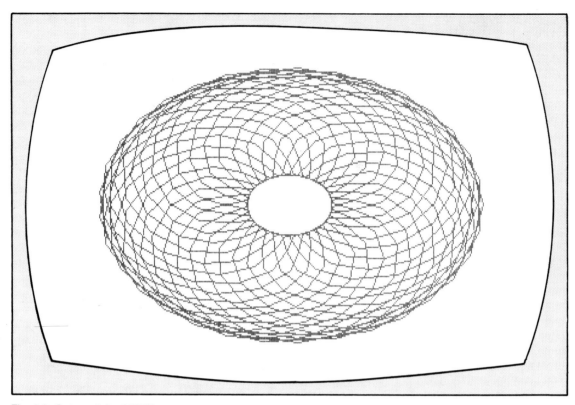

Fig. 2-8. Output of the SPIRAL program.

Listing 2-8. NEXTPLOT.TRU helps you zoom in on specific areas of Mandelbrot plots.

```
! **********************************
! ** File:      NEXTPLOT.TRU    **
! ** Date:      8/14/85         **
! ** Author:    John Craig      **
! ** Language:  True BASIC      **
! **********************************
!
! This program helps you calculate the coordinates and side
! length of the next area in a MANDELBR plot to zoom in on.
! Measure the number of millimeters from the left side of the
! plot and from the bottom edge to the point of interest.
! The corner coordinates and side length for the next plot will
! be calculated.  This next plot will magnify the area by a
! factor of 10.

! Start with a clean slate
  CLEAR

! Display program name
  PRINT "* NEXTPLOT *"
  PRINT

! Ask user for the details
```

```
        INPUT PROMPT "Distance from left to center (mm) ?    ": Xmm
        INPUT PROMPT "Distance from bottom to center (mm) ? ": Ymm
        INPUT PROMPT "X corner of present plot ?            ": Xcorner
        INPUT PROMPT "Y corner of present plot ?            ": Ycorner
        INPUT PROMPT "Side length of present plot ?         ": Side

    ! Figure the accuracy we need to use
      LET Side$ = Str$(Side)
      LET Places = Len(Side$) - Pos(Side$,".") + 2

    ! Tell user what can be deduced
      PRINT
      PRINT "New plot values for Xcorner, Ycorner, Side ...."
      PRINT
      PRINT Round((Xmm-10)*Side/200+Xcorner,Places),
      PRINT Round((Ymm-7)*Side/224+Ycorner,Places),
      PRINT Side / 10
      PRINT

    ! Wait for user
      PRINT "Press any key to continue..."
      GET KEY Before_continuing

    ! All done
      END
```

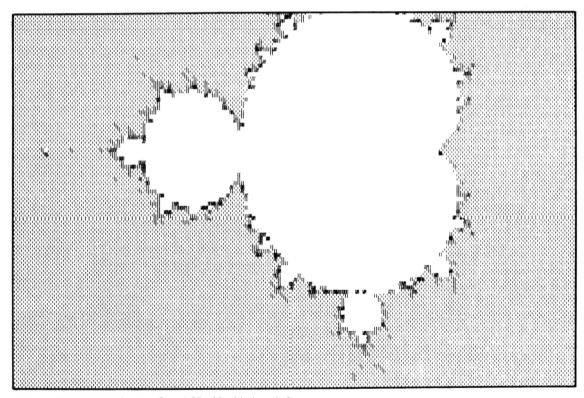

Fig. 2-9. Mandelbrot plot at −2, −1.25 with side length 3.

Fig. 2-10. Mandelbrot plot at − .65, − .68 with side length 0.3.

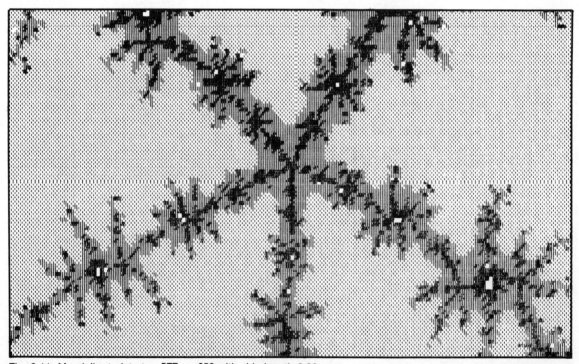

Fig. 2-11. Mandelbrot plot at − .577, − .653 with side length 0.03.

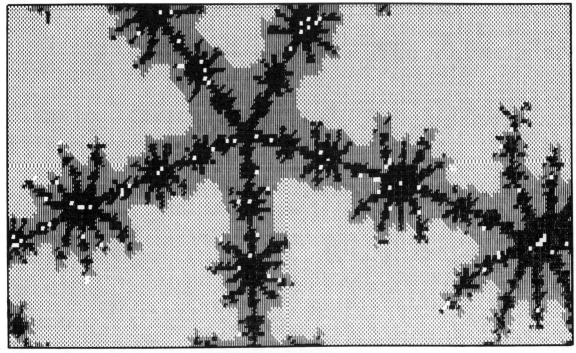

Fig. 2-12. Mandelbrot plot at − .5635, − .6439 with side length 0.003.

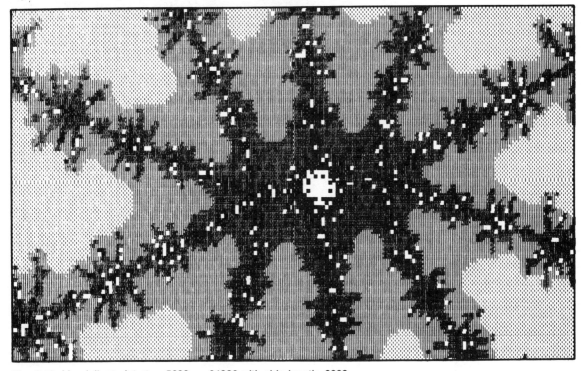

Fig. 2-13. Mandelbrot plot at − .5632, − .64326 with side length .0003.

Fig. 2-14. Mandelbrot plot at − .563083, − .643181 with side length .00003.

NEXTPLOT

This program (Listing 2-8) helps you decide where next to explore in the complex number plane using the **MANDELBR** program. If you see an interesting point in a plot and wish to magnify the area by 10 times, this program will calculate the new corner coordinates and side length for the next plot. Figures 2-11 through 2-14 show just such an excursion, with each plot zooming in on an interesting area of the preceding plot.

To use this program, dump the Mandelbrot plot of interest to your printer by pressing < Shift + PrtSc > . On the paper copy, measure the number of millimeters from the left edge of the image to the center of the area you wish to zoom in on. Also measure from the bottom edge of the image to this same point. Run the **NEXTPLOT** program and answer the questions as you are prompted (Fig. 2-15). The program will provide numbers to be used in input when you next run the **MANDELBR** program.

This program demonstrates one use for the **ROUND** statement. Here it is used to round the answers off to just the number of digits necessary for defining the coordinates of plots. Extra digits are unnecessary and just get in the way.

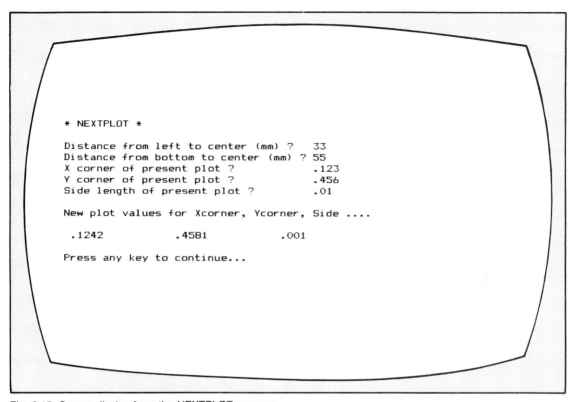

```
* NEXTPLOT *

Distance from left to center (mm) ?    33
Distance from bottom to center (mm) ? 55
X corner of present plot ?             .123
Y corner of present plot ?             .456
Side length of present plot ?          .01

New plot values for Xcorner, Ycorner, Side ....

 .1242          .4581          .001

Press any key to continue...
```

Fig. 2-15. Screen display from the NEXTPLOT program.

Chapter 3

The Passing of Time

These programs create calendars, unique clock displays, and even show you what the moon will look like tonight!

CALENDAR

This program demonstrates several calendar-related functions and subroutines, and provides quick answers to questions about dates from March 1, 1900, to February 28, 2100.

The calendar calculation you wish to perform is selected from a menu of choices by pressing a single key from A to H. It doesn't matter if you hold the shift key while pressing a key, because the program automatically converts your keypress to uppercase. Typing "A" or "a" will in both cases correctly select the first menu choice.

Figure 3-1 shows the display that appears while the program waits for your choice.

The first three menu choices calculate the day of the week, the day of the year, and the day of the century, respectively. The entered date in each case is first converted to its Astronomical Julian day number. The day of the week is calculated by use of the **MOD** function, which finds the remainder of dividing the Astronomical Julian day number by 7, and the year day and century day are calculated by subtracting the day number for the day just before the start of the year or the century.

Menu selection D calculates the above mentioned Astronomical Julian day number for the day you enter.

Selections E, F, and G, perform the opposite calculations from the first three. For example, if you wish to know on what date the 200th day of 1987 falls, select option E.

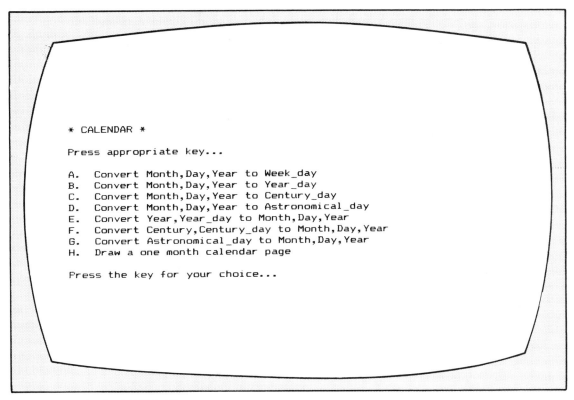

```
 * CALENDAR *

Press appropriate key...

A.   Convert Month,Day,Year to Week_day
B.   Convert Month,Day,Year to Year_day
C.   Convert Month,Day,Year to Century_day
D.   Convert Month,Day,Year to Astronomical_day
E.   Convert Year,Year_day to Month,Day,Year
F.   Convert Century,Century_day to Month,Day,Year
G.   Convert Astronomical_day to Month,Day,Year
H.   Draw a one month calendar page

Press the key for your choice...
```

Fig. 3-1. Menu for the CALENDAR program.

Choice H sketches a one-month calendar page for any month in the range of valid dates. For example, December of 1986 looks like the page shown in Fig. 3-2.

Eight functions and subroutines are presented in this program that you may be able to use in other programs you develop. Take a look at the group of calendar calculation routines, beginning with Mdy_to_w, in Listing 3-1.

CLOCK_1

This program (Listing 3-2) demonstrates the use of the PICTURE statement for creating graphics images.

Notice that all three clock hands in Fig. 3-3 are drawn by calling the same PICTURE statement, named Hand. Each is scaled differently to change its length from the center of the clock face, and each is rotated according to the current calculations for time.

The roman numeral digits are also drawn with PICTURE statements. In this case, each digit is relocated with a shift transformation to place it at the correct location around the face of the clock. This kind of structure and organization is impossible with other versions of BASIC.

CLOCK_2

This program (Listing 3-3) displays the current system time in a digital format.

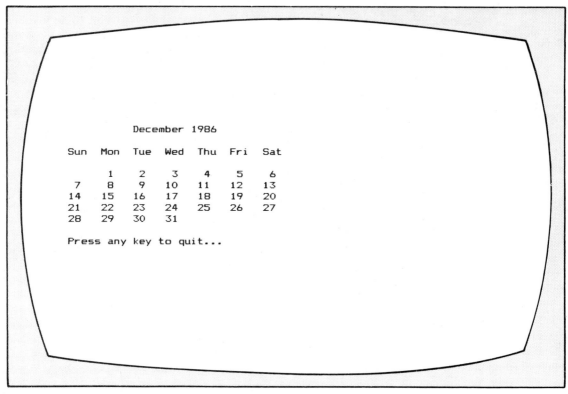

```
                December 1986

     Sun   Mon   Tue   Wed   Thu   Fri   Sat

            1     2     3     4     5     6
     7      8     9     10    11    12    13
     14     15    16    17    18    19    20
     21     22    23    24    25    26    27
     28     29    30    31

     Press any key to quit...
```

Fig. 3-2. Typical calendar generated by the CALENDAR program.

Listing 3-1. CALENDAR.TRU (continued to page 56).

```
! *********************************
! **   File:      CALENDAR.TRU    **
! **   Date:      7/17/85         **
! **   Author:    John Craig      **
! **   Language:  True BASIC      **
! *********************************
!
! This program demonstrates several useful calendar
! functions and subroutines.

! Declare external functions
  DECLARE FUNCTION Mdy_to_a
  DECLARE FUNCTION Mdy_to_c
  DECLARE FUNCTION Mdy_to_y
  DECLARE FUNCTION Mdy_to_w

! Start with a clean slate
  CLEAR

! Display program name
  PRINT "* CALENDAR *"
  PRINT
```

```
! Ask user for the desired calendar calculation
  PRINT "Press appropriate key..."
  PRINT
  PRINT "A. Convert Month,Day,Year to Week_day"
  PRINT "B. Convert Month,Day,Year to Year_day"
  PRINT "C. Convert Month,Day,Year to Century_day"
  PRINT "D. Convert Month,Day,Year to Astronomical_day"
  PRINT "E. Convert Year,Year_day to Month,Day,Year"
  PRINT "F. Convert Century,Century_day to Month,Day,Year"
  PRINT "G. Convert Astronomical_day to Month,Day,Year"
  PRINT "H. Draw a one month calendar page"
  PRINT
  PRINT "Press the key for your choice..."
  PRINT

! Wait until one of the keys is pressed
  DO

     ! Wait for any key press
       DO
       LOOP UNTIL KEY INPUT

     ! Grab the key and check for appropriate choice
       GET KEY Keycode
       LET Choice = Pos("ABCDEFGH",Ucase$(Chr$(Keycode)))

     ! Keep trying for an appropriate key press
  LOOP UNTIL Choice > 0

! Ask user for required parameters and do the calculations
  SELECT CASE Choice
  CASE 1
      PRINT "Month,Day,Year to Week_day"
      PRINT
      INPUT PROMPT "Enter month,day,year ? ": Month,Day,Year
      IF Year < 100 THEN LET Year = Year + 1900
      CALL Check_date(Month,Day,Year)
      PRINT "The day of the week is ";
      SELECT CASE Mdy_to_w(Month,Day,Year)
      CASE 0
          PRINT "Sunday"
      CASE 1
          PRINT "Monday"
      CASE 2
          PRINT "Tuesday"
      CASE 3
          PRINT "Wednesday"
      CASE 4
          PRINT "Thursday"
      CASE 5
          PRINT "Friday"
      CASE 6
          PRINT "Saturday"
      END SELECT
      PRINT
  CASE 2
      PRINT "Month,Day,Year to Year_day"
      PRINT
      INPUT PROMPT "Enter month,day,year ? ": Month,Day,Year
```

```
            IF Year < 100 THEN LET Year = Year + 1900
            CALL Check_date(Month,Day,Year)
            PRINT "The day of the year is ";Mdy_to_y(Month,Day,Year)
            PRINT
      CASE 3
            PRINT "Month,Day,Year to Century_day"
            PRINT
            INPUT PROMPT "Enter month,day,year ? ": Month,Day,Year
            IF Year < 100 THEN LET Year = Year + 1900
            CALL Check_date(Month,Day,Year)
            PRINT "The day of the century is ";Mdy_to_c(Month,Day,Year)
            PRINT
      CASE 4
            PRINT "Month,Day,Year to Astronomical_day"
            PRINT
            INPUT PROMPT "Enter month,day,year ? ": Month,Day,Year
            IF Year < 100 THEN LET Year = Year + 1900
            CALL Check_date(Month,Day,Year)
            PRINT "The astronomical Julian day number is ";
            PRINT Mdy_to_a(Month,Day,Year)
            PRINT
      CASE 5
            PRINT "Year,Year_day to Month,Day,Year"
            PRINT
            INPUT PROMPT "Enter Year,Year_day ? ": Year,Year_day
            IF Year < 100 THEN LET Year = Year + 1900
            CALL Yy_to_mdy(Year,Year_day,Month,Day,Year)
            PRINT USING "The date is ##/##/####": Month,Day,Year
            PRINT
      CASE 6
            PRINT "Century,Century_day to Month,Day,Year"
            PRINT
            INPUT PROMPT "Enter Century (ex. 1900) ? ": Century
            INPUT PROMPT "Enter Century day number ? ": Century_day
            CALL Cc_to_mdy(Century,Century_day,Month,Day,Year)
            PRINT USING "The date is ##/##/####": Month,Day,Year
            PRINT
      CASE 7
            PRINT "Astronomical_day to Month,Day,Year"
            PRINT
            INPUT PROMPT "Astronomical day number ? ": Astronomical_day
            CALL Ast_to_mdy(Astronomical_day,Month,Day,Year)
            PRINT USING "The date is ##/##/####": Month,Day,Year
            PRINT
      CASE 8
            PRINT "Draw a one month calendar page"
            PRINT
            INPUT PROMPT "Enter month,year ? ": Month,Year
            IF Year < 100 THEN LET Year = Year + 1900
            CALL Month_page(Month,Year)
      END SELECT

   ! Wait for key press
      PRINT
      PRINT "Press any key to quit..."
      GET KEY Before_continuing

   ! All done
      END
```

```
! The following group of calendar functions
! are accurate for dates from March 1, 1900
! to February 28, 2100.

! This function calculates the day of the week
! given the month, day, and year.
!
  FUNCTION Mdy_to_w(Month,Day,Year)
      DECLARE FUNCTION Mdy_to_a
      LET Mdy_to_w = Mod(Mdy_to_a(Month,Day,Year)+1,7)
  END FUNCTION

! This function calculates the day of the year
! given the month, day, and year.
!
  FUNCTION Mdy_to_y(Month,Day,Year)
      DECLARE FUNCTION Mdy_to_a
      LET Mdy_to_y = Mdy_to_a(Month,Day,Year)-Mdy_to_a(12,31,Year-1)
  END FUNCTION

! This function calculates the day of the century
! given the Month, Day, and Year.
!
  FUNCTION Mdy_to_c(Month,Day,Year)
      DECLARE FUNCTION Mdy_to_a
      IF Year < 2000 THEN
          LET Mdy_to_c = Mdy_to_a(Month,Day,Year) - 2415020
      ELSE
          LET Mdy_to_c = Mdy_to_a(Month,Day,Year) - 2451544
      END IF
  END FUNCTION

! This function calculates the astronomical Julian
! day number given the Month, Day, and Year.
!
  FUNCTION Mdy_to_a(Month,Day,Year)
      IF Month < 3 THEN
          LET Year = Year - 1
          LET Month = Month + 13
      ELSE
          LET Month = Month + 1
      END IF
      LET Tmp = Int(Year*365.25)+Int(Month*30.6001)+Day+1720982
      IF Tmp < 2415080 OR Tmp > 2488127 THEN
          CAUSE ERROR 1,"ERROR - Date out of range"
      END IF
      LET Mdy_to_a = Tmp
  END FUNCTION

! This subroutine calculates the date given the
! year and the day of the year
!
  SUB Yy_to_mdy(Year,Year_day,Month,Day,Year)
      DECLARE FUNCTION Mdy_to_a
      CALL Ast_to_mdy(Mdy_to_a(12,31,Year-1)+Year_day,Month,Day,Year)
  END SUB

! This subroutine calculates the date given the
! Century and the day of the century
```

```
!
   SUB Cc_to_mdy(Century,Century_day,Month,Day,Year)
       DECLARE FUNCTION Mdy_to_a
       IF Century = 1900 THEN
           LET Tmp = 2415020 + Century_day
       ELSEIF Century = 2000 THEN
           LET Tmp = 2451544 + Century_day
       ELSE
           CAUSE ERROR 1,"ERROR - Century must be 1900 or 2000"
       END IF
       CALL Ast_to_mdy(Tmp,Month,Day,Year)
   END SUB

! This function calculates the date given the
! astronomical Julian day number
!
   SUB Ast_to_mdy(Astronomical_day,Month,Day,Year)
       IF Astronomical_day < 2415080 OR Astronomical_day > 2488127 THEN
           CAUSE ERROR 1,"ERROR - Date out of range"
       END IF
       LET Day = Astronomical_day - 1720982
       LET Year = Int((Day - 122.1)/365.25)
       LET Tmp = Int(365.25 * Year)
       LET Month = Int((Day-Tmp)/30.6001)
       LET Day = Day - Tmp - Int(30.6001 * Month)
       LET Month = Month - 1
       IF Month > 12 THEN LET Month = Month - 12
       IF Month < 3 THEN LET Year = Year + 1
   END SUB

! This function checks a date to make sure it
! represents a valid date
!
   SUB Check_date(Month,Day,Year)
       DECLARE FUNCTION Mdy_to_a
       LET T1 = Month
       LET T2 = Day
       LET T3 = Year
       CALL Ast_to_mdy(Mdy_to_a(Month,Day,Year),Month,Day,Year)
       IF T1 <> Month OR T2 <> Day OR T3 <> Year THEN
           CAUSE ERROR 1,"ERROR - Date is not valid"
       END IF
   END SUB

! This subroutine sketches a one month calendar sheet
!
   SUB Month_page(Month,Year)

     ! Declare external functions
       DECLARE FUNCTION Mdy_to_a
       DECLARE FUNCTION Mdy_to_w

     ! Find first day numbers
       LET D1 = Mdy_to_a(Month,1,Year)
       LET Wday = Mdy_to_w(Month,1,Year)

     ! Find second day numbers
       IF Month < 12 THEN
           LET D2 = Mdy_to_a(Month+1,1,Year) - 1
```

```
      ELSE
          LET D2 = Mdy_to_a(1,1,Year+1) - 1
      END IF

! Clear the screen and title it
      CLEAR
      PRINT
      SELECT CASE Month
      CASE 1
          LET Title$ = "January"
      CASE 2
          LET Title$ = "February"
      CASE 3
          LET Title$ = "March"
      CASE 4
          LET Title$ = "April"
      CASE 5
          LET Title$ = "May"
      CASE 6
          LET Title$ = "June"
      CASE 7
          LET Title$ = "July"
      CASE 8
          LET Title$ = "August"
      CASE 9
          LET Title$ = "September"
      CASE 10
          LET Title$ = "October"
      CASE 11
          LET Title$ = "November"
      CASE 12
          LET Title$ = "December"
      END SELECT
      LET Title$ = USING$(Repeat$("#",37),Title$ & " " & Str$(Year))
      PRINT Title$

! Label the days of the week
      PRINT
      PRINT "  Sun  Mon  Tue  Wed  Thu  Fri  Sat"

! Space over to day one
      PRINT
      FOR I = 1 TO Wday
          PRINT "     ";
      NEXT I

! Print the day numbers
      FOR I = D1 TO D2
          PRINT USING "#####": I - D1 + 1;
          IF Wday < 6 THEN
              LET Wday = Wday + 1
          ELSE
              LET Wday = 0
              PRINT
          END IF
      NEXT I

! Space down a little
      PRINT
      PRINT
```

```
    ! Done sketching calendar sheet
    END SUB
```

Listing 3-2. Analog clock program CLOCK__1.TRU (continued to page 59).

```
! **********************************
! **   File:       CLOCK_1.TRU    **
! **   Date:       3/1/85         **
! **   Author:     John Craig     **
! **   Language:   True BASIC     **
! **********************************
!
! Creates a round clock face with roman numerals and fat hands

! Draws a roman numeral digit "I"
  PICTURE One
      LET Size3 = Size * 3
      PLOT LINES: -Size,Size3; Size,Size3
      PLOT LINES: -Size,-Size3; Size,-Size3
      PLOT LINES: 0,Size3; 0,-Size3
  END PICTURE

! Draws a roman numeral digit "V"
  PICTURE Five
      LET Size3 = Size * 3
      PLOT LINES: -Size,Size3; 0,-Size3; Size,Size3
  END PICTURE

! Draws a roman numeral digit "X"
  PICTURE Ten
      LET Size3 = Size * 3
      PLOT LINES: -Size,Size3; Size,-Size3
      PLOT LINES: Size,Size3; -Size,-Size3
  END PICTURE

! Draws the hands of the clock, variable thickness
  PICTURE Hand(Thickness)
      PLOT LINES: 0,Thickness/4;
      PLOT LINES: .8,Thickness;
      PLOT LINES: 1,0;
      PLOT LINES: .8,-Thickness;
      PLOT LINES: 0,-Thickness/4;
      PLOT LINES: 0,Thickness/4
  END PICTURE

! Creates the clock image, minus the hands.
  SUB Build_clock_face
      OPTION ANGLE DEGREES

    ! Scale the screen so clock will be fairly round
      SET WINDOW -4.4,4.4,-3.3,3.3

    ! A brown background looks nice
      SET BACKGROUND COLOR "brown"

    ! Draw the magenta ring around clock face
      SET COLOR "magenta"
```

56

```
        BOX ELLIPSE -3,3,-3,3
        BOX ELLIPSE -3.3,3.3,-3.3,3.3
        FLOOD -3.1,0

    ! Fill in face with white
        SET COLOR "white"
        FLOOD 0,0
    ! Draw the roman numeral digits using brown
        SET COLOR "background"

    ! The size of the digits is determined here
        LET Size = .07

    ! Draw the roman numerals, centered around clock face
        FOR I = 1 TO 12
            LET X = 2.5 * Cos(90 - I * 30)
            LET Y = 2.5 * Sin(90 - I * 30)
            CALL Roman_numerals(I,X,Y)
        NEXT I
    END SUB

! Draws the hour hand, scaled, rotated, and with given thickness.
    SUB Draw_hour_hand
        OPTION ANGLE DEGREES
        SET COLOR 4
        DRAW Hand(.1) WITH Scale(1) * Rotate(90-(Hour+Minute/60)*30)
    END SUB

! Draws the minute hand, scaled, rotated, and with given thickness.
    SUB Draw_minute_hand
        OPTION ANGLE DEGREES
        SET COLOR 4
        DRAW Hand(.07) WITH Scale(1.7) * Rotate(90-Minute*6)
    END SUB

! Draws the second hand, scaled, rotated, and with given thickness.
    SUB Draw_second_hand
        OPTION ANGLE DEGREES
        SET COLOR 5
        DRAW Hand(.04) WITH Scale(1.9) * Rotate(90 - Second * 6)
    END SUB

! Erases the old hour hand just before it's drawn at new location
    SUB Erase_old_hour_hand
        OPTION ANGLE DEGREES
        SET COLOR "white"
        DRAW Hand(.1) WITH Scale(1) * Rotate(90-(Old_hour+Old_minute/60)*30)
    END SUB

! Erases the old minute hand just before it's drawn at new location
    SUB Erase_old_minute_hand
        OPTION ANGLE DEGREES
        SET COLOR "white"
        DRAW Hand(.07) WITH Scale(1.7) * Rotate(90-Old_minute*6)
    END SUB

! Erases the old second hand just before it's drawn at new location
    SUB Erase_old_second_hand
        OPTION ANGLE DEGREES
```

```
          SET COLOR "white"
          DRAW Hand(.Ø4) WITH Scale(1.9) * Rotate(9Ø-Old_second*6)
   END SUB

! Watches the time until a new second arrives
  SUB Get_time

     ! Record current time for erasing old hands
       LET Old_hour = Hour
       LET Old_minute = Minute
       LET Old_second = Second
       LET T$ = Time$
       LET Hour = Val(T$(1:2))
       LET Minute = Val(T$(4:5))
       LET Second = Val(T$(7:8))
   END SUB

! Creates roman numerals centered at X,Y location.
  SUB Roman_numerals(Number,X,Y)
       SELECT CASE Number
       CASE 1
           DRAW One WITH Shift(X,Y)
       CASE 2
           DRAW One WITH Shift(X-Size*1.5,Y)
           DRAW One WITH Shift(X+Size*1.5,Y)
       CASE 3
           DRAW One WITH Shift(X-Size*3,Y)
           DRAW One WITH Shift(X,Y)
           DRAW One WITH Shift(X+Size*3,Y)
       CASE 4
           DRAW One WITH Shift(X-Size*1.5,Y)
           DRAW Five WITH Shift(X+Size*1.5,Y)
       CASE 5
           DRAW Five WITH Shift(X,Y)
       CASE 6
           DRAW One WITH Shift(X+Size*1.5,Y)
           DRAW Five WITH Shift(X-Size*1.5,Y)
       CASE 7
           DRAW Five WITH Shift(X-Size*3,Y)
           DRAW One WITH Shift(X,Y)
           DRAW One WITH Shift(X+Size*3,Y)
       CASE 8
           DRAW Five WITH Shift(X-Size*4.5,Y)
           DRAW One WITH Shift(X-Size*1.5,Y)
           DRAW One WITH Shift(X+Size*1.5,Y)
           DRAW One WITH Shift(X+Size*4.5,Y)
       CASE 9
           DRAW One WITH Shift(X-Size*1.5,Y)
           DRAW Ten WITH Shift(X+Size*1.5,Y)
       CASE 1Ø
           DRAW Ten WITH Shift(X,Y)
       CASE 11
           DRAW Ten WITH Shift(X-Size*1.5,Y)
           DRAW One WITH Shift(X+Size*1.5,Y)
       CASE 12
           DRAW Ten WITH Shift(X-Size*3,Y)
           DRAW One WITH Shift(X,Y)
           DRAW One WITH Shift(X+Size*3,Y)
       END SELECT
```

```
    END SUB

! Main program unit begins here
  CALL Build_clock_face

! Main loop, where most of the time is spent
  DO UNTIL KEY INPUT
      CALL Get_time
      IF Second < Old_second THEN
          CALL Erase_old_hour_hand
          CALL Erase_old_minute_hand
      END IF
      CALL Erase_old_second_hand
      CALL Draw_second_hand
      CALL Draw_hour_hand
      CALL Draw_minute_hand
  LOOP

! All done after a key is pressed
  END
```

The main purpose of the program is to demonstrate several of the powerful graphics commands of True BASIC.

Each digit of the time is displayed as a seven-segment display, popular back in the "good old days" when people used to wear those bright red LED display watches. (What-

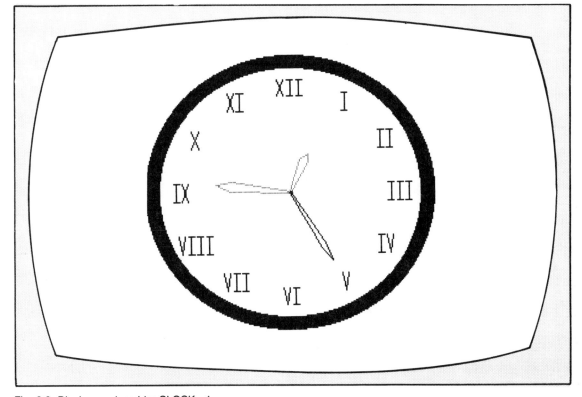

Fig. 3-3. Display produced by CLOCK__1.

Listing 3-3. Digital clock program CLOCK__2.TRU.

```
! **********************************
! **  File:       CLOCK_2.TRU    **
! **  Date:       3/4/85         **
! **  Author:     John Craig     **
! **  Language:   True BASIC     **
! **********************************
!
! This program creates a simulated red "LED" display of the time.

! Draws the upper horizontal segment
  PICTURE Seg_u_h
     PLOT LINES: 1,50; 23,50; 19,46; 5,46; 1,50
     FLOOD 9,48
  END PICTURE

! Draws the middle horizontal segment
  PICTURE Seg_m_h
     PLOT LINES: 3,28; 5,30; 19,30; 21,28;
     PLOT LINES: 19,26; 5,26; 3,28
     FLOOD 9,28
  END PICTURE

! Draws the lower horizontal segment
  PICTURE Seg_l_h
     PLOT LINES: 1,6; 5,10; 19,10; 23,6; 1,6
     FLOOD 9,9
  END PICTURE

! Draws the upper left segment
  PICTURE Seg_u_l
     PLOT LINES: 0,49; 4,45; 4,31;
     PLOT LINES: 2,29; 0,31; 0,49
     FLOOD 2,40
  END PICTURE

! Draws the upper right segment
  PICTURE Seg_u_r
     PLOT LINES: 20,45; 24,49; 24,31;
     PLOT LINES: 22,29; 20,31; 20,45
     FLOOD 22,40
  END PICTURE

! Draws the lower left segment
  PICTURE Seg_l_l
     PLOT LINES: 0,7; 0,25; 2,27;
     PLOT LINES: 4,25; 4,11; 0,7
     FLOOD 2,20
  END PICTURE

! Draws the lower right segment
  PICTURE Seg_l_r
     PLOT LINES: 20,11; 20,25; 22,27;
     PLOT LINES: 24,25; 24,7; 20,11
     FLOOD 22,20
  END PICTURE

! Create the digits "0" through "9"
```

```
      OPTION ANGLE DEGREES
      OPTION BASE 0
      DIM Digit$(10)
      SET WINDOW 0,159,5,104
      SET COLOR "red/green"

   ! Create "1"
      DRAW Seg_u_r
      DRAW Seg_l_r
      BOX KEEP 0,24,5,50 IN Digit$(1)

   ! Create "7"
      DRAW Seg_u_h
      BOX KEEP 0,24,5,50 IN Digit$(7)

   ! Create "3"
      DRAW Seg_m_h
      DRAW Seg_l_h
      BOX KEEP 0,24,5,50 IN Digit$(3)

   ! Create "9"
      DRAW Seg_u_l
      BOX KEEP 0,24,5,50 IN Digit$(9)

   ! Create "8"
      DRAW Seg_l_l
      BOX KEEP 0,24,5,50 IN Digit$(8)

   ! Create "0"
      SET COLOR "background"
      DRAW Seg_m_h
      BOX KEEP 0,24,5,50 IN Digit$(0)

   ! Create "6"
      DRAW Seg_u_r
      SET COLOR "red"
      DRAW Seg_m_h
      BOX KEEP 0,24,5,50 IN Digit$(6)

   ! Create "5"
      SET COLOR "background"
      DRAW Seg_l_l
      BOX KEEP 0,24,5,50 IN Digit$(5)

   ! Create "4"
      DRAW Seg_l_h
      DRAW Seg_u_h
      SET COLOR "red"
      DRAW Seg_u_r
      BOX KEEP 0,24,5,50 IN Digit$(4)

   ! Create "2"
      DRAW Seg_u_h
      DRAW Seg_l_h
      DRAW Seg_l_l
      SET COLOR "background"
      DRAW Seg_u_l
      DRAW Seg_l_r
      BOX KEEP 0,24,5,50 IN Digit$(2)
```

61

```
! Create ":"
  DRAW Seg_u_h
  DRAW Seg_m_h
  DRAW Seg_l_h
  DRAW Seg_u_l
  DRAW Seg_u_r
  DRAW Seg_l_l
  SET COLOR "red"
  BOX AREA 10,15,15,20
  BOX AREA 10,15,35,40
  BOX KEEP 0,24,5,50 IN Digit$(10)

! Erase what's left
  SET COLOR "background"
  BOX AREA 0,24,5,50

! Scale the screen
  SET WINDOW 1,6,1,4

! Display time until any key is pressed
  DO UNTIL KEY INPUT

      ! Record current time for erasing old hands
        LET Old_t$ = T$

      ! Hang around until next second arrives
        DO
            LET T$ = Time$
        LOOP UNTIL T$ <> Old_t$

      ! Display the digits
        FOR I = 1 TO 8
            IF I <> 6 THEN
                IF I < 6 THEN
                    LET X = I
                    LET Y = 2.5
                ELSE
                    LET X = I - 4.5
                    LET Y = 1
                END IF
                IF I = 3 THEN
                    LET N = 10
                ELSE
                    LET N = Val(T$(I:I))
                END IF
                BOX SHOW Digit$(N) AT X,Y
            END IF
        NEXT I
  LOOP

! All done after a key is pressed
  END
```

ever happened to all those watches?) Each of the seven segments is drawn using **PIC-TURE** statements, and each of the decimal digits is peeled off the screen and saved in a string by means of the **BOX KEEP** statement. The advantage of storing each digit in this way is the speed with which each digit can be placed back on the screen with

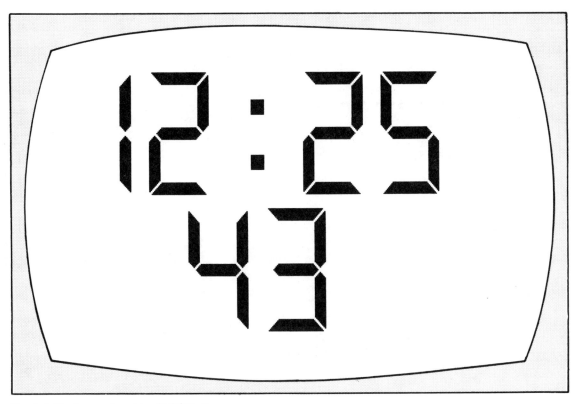

Fig. 3-4. Display produced by CLOCK__2.

the **BOX SHOW** statement. All six digits and a colon are placed on the screen each second, with plenty of time to spare. Figure 3-4 represents the output display.

CLOCK__3

This program displays the current time in a rather eccentric but fun manner. Its main purpose is to demonstrate the remarkable graphics animation capabilities that True BASIC provides, rather than just to tell you want time it is. With that in mind, let's take a look at this strange program (Listing 3-4).

The first group of **PICTURE** statements draw various parts of a helicopter such as the body, the rotor blades in three positions, the tail rotor, and the landing skids. Following these **PICTURE** definitions, several complete helicopter images in various orientations are created by drawing the pictures with various transformations and storing them in strings using the **BOX KEEP** statement. The images are drawn fairly fast originally, but not as fast as they will be displayed with the **BOX SHOW** statements once the action starts.

A round yellow ball, a green grassy yard, and a "clock building" are also created (Fig. 3-5) and stored in strings. Then the action begins. Each section of the program listing has comments describing the various actions; follow these comments and recall the events on the screen to see how the action is created. The helicopter picks the ball up, carries it over to the building, and drops it into the building. The whole earth bounces

```
!  **********************************
!  **   File:       CLOCK_3.TRU     **
!  **   Date:       3/5/85          **
!  **   Author:     John Craig      **
!  **   Language:   True BASIC      **
!  **********************************
!
!  Animated graphics clock, just for fun.

!  Creates the helicopter body, minus the blades
   PICTURE Body

      !  Edges of the canopy
         SET COLOR "green"
         PLOT LINES: 37,40;30,40;25,39;20,36;17,33;16,30;16,26;
         PLOT LINES: 17,22;25,22;30,24;35,27;37,30;37,40

      !  Main body
         SET COLOR "red"
         PLOT LINES: 17,22;20,19;25,18;45,18;50,22;54,30;
         PLOT LINES: 85,36;91,49;90,50;80,39;50,40;37,40
         FLOOD 40,25

      !  Landing rails
         SET COLOR "green"
         PLOT LINES: 13,15;15,13;55,13;57,15
         PLOT LINES: 30,18;30,13;40,13;40,18
   END PICTURE

!  Creates the tail rotor
   PICTURE Tail_rotor
         SET COLOR "yellow"
         PLOT LINES: 85,50;86+Rnd,53+Rnd;90,55;93+Rnd,53+Rnd;
         PLOT LINES: 95,50;93+Rnd,46+Rnd;90,45;86+Rnd,46+Rnd;85,50
   END PICTURE

!  Creates the main blades in the first position
   PICTURE Blades_a
         SET COLOR "green"
         PLOT LINES: 42,40;42,47
         PLOT LINES: 48,40;48,47
         SET COLOR "yellow"
         PLOT LINES: 10,47;10,49;80,49;80,47;10,47
         FLOOD 48,48
         DRAW Tail_rotor
   END PICTURE

!  Creates the main blades in the second position
   PICTURE Blades_b
         SET COLOR "green"
         PLOT LINES: 44,40;44,47
         PLOT LINES: 46,40;46,47
         SET COLOR "yellow"
         PLOT LINES: 30,49;30,51;60,47;60,45;30,49
         FLOOD 45,48
         DRAW Tail_rotor
   END PICTURE
```

```
! Creates the main blades in the third position
  PICTURE Blades_c
       SET COLOR "green"
       PLOT LINES: 44,40;44,47
       PLOT LINES: 46,40;46,47
       SET COLOR "yellow"
       PLOT LINES: 30,45;30,47;60,51;60,49;30,45
       FLOOD 45,48
       DRAW Tail_rotor
  END PICTURE

! Build the various helicopter images
  OPTION ANGLE DEGREES
  DIM Chopper$(3,3)
  SET MODE "graphics"
  SET BACKGROUND COLOR "blue"
  SET WINDOW -200,200,-150,150
  FOR I = 1 TO 3
       FOR J = 1 TO 3
            SELECT CASE I
            CASE 1
                 LET R = 0
            CASE 2
                 LET R = 20
            CASE 3
                 LET R = -20
            END SELECT
            IF J = 1 THEN
                 DRAW Body WITH Shift(-50,-30) * Rotate(R)
                 BOX KEEP -50,50,-30,40 IN Body$
            ELSE
                 BOX SHOW Body$ AT -50,-30
            END IF
            SELECT CASE J
            CASE 1
                 DRAW Blades_a WITH Shift(-50,-30) * Rotate(R)
            CASE 2
                 DRAW Blades_b WITH Shift(-50,-30) * Rotate(R)
            CASE 3
                 DRAW Blades_c WITH Shift(-50,-30) * Rotate(R)
            END SELECT
            BOX KEEP -50,50,-30,40 IN Chopper$(I,J)
            IF J = 3 THEN BOX CLEAR -50,50,-30,40
       NEXT J
  NEXT I

! Build the ball image
  SET COLOR "yellow"
  BOX ELLIPSE -10,10,-10,10
  FLOOD 0,0
  BOX KEEP -14,14,-14,14 IN Ball$
  BOX CLEAR -10,10,-10,10

! Scale the screen for the main action
  SET WINDOW 0,400,0,300

! Build the ground
  SET COLOR "green"
  FOR X = 0 TO 440 STEP 5
```

```
            PLOT LINES: X,19; X-40,0
      NEXT X

  ! Build the clock building
    SET COLOR "red"
    BOX AREA 40,180,20,90
    SET COLOR "yellow"
    PLOT TEXT, AT 67,60: Repeat$(Chr$(8),8)
    BOX KEEP 0,400,15,105 IN Bump$

  ! Do this sequence over and over
    DO

       ! First hover at ground level
         FOR I = 1 TO 25
             BOX SHOW Chopper$(1,Mod(I,3)+1) AT 300,50
         NEXT I
  ! Next have it move up the screen
    FOR I = 50 TO 210 STEP 2
        LET View = Mod(View,3) + 1
        BOX SHOW Chopper$(1,View) AT 300,I
        BOX SHOW Ball$ AT 330,I-30
    NEXT I

  ! Then fly to the left
    FOR I = 300 TO 70 STEP -3
        LET View = Mod(View,3) + 1
        BOX SHOW Chopper$(2,View) AT I,210
        BOX SHOW Ball$ AT I+30,180
    NEXT I

  ! Hover and drop the ball towards the building
    LET Velocity,Count,Last_i = 0
    FOR I = 180 TO 92 STEP -1
        LET Count = Count + 1
        IF Count > Velocity THEN
            LET Count = 0
            LET Velocity = Velocity + 1
            LET View = Mod(View,3) + 1
            BOX SHOW Chopper$(1,View) AT 70,210

          ! Erase the last ball image
          IF Last_i > 0 THEN
              BOX SHOW Ball$ AT 100,Last_i USING "xor"
          END IF
          BOX SHOW Ball$ AT 100,I
          LET Last_i = I
        END IF
    NEXT I

  ! Erase the last ball image before it goes in building
    BOX SHOW Ball$ AT 100,Last_i USING "xor"

  ! Hover while the ball hits and things bounce
    FOR I = 7 TO 1 STEP -1
        LET View = Mod(View,3) + 1
        BOX SHOW Chopper$(1,View) AT 70,210
        IF I = 2 THEN
            BOX SHOW Bump$ AT 0,20
```

```
                FOR Freq = 30 TO 300 STEP 50
                     SOUND Freq,.02
                NEXT Freq
            END IF
            IF I = 1 THEN
                BOX SHOW Bump$ AT 0,15
                FOR Freq = 400 TO 70 STEP -70
                     SOUND Freq,.02
                NEXT Freq
                PLOT TEXT, AT 67,60: Time$
            END IF
        NEXT I

   ! Hover while watching the clock carefully
     DO
                LET View = Mod(View,3) + 1
                BOX SHOW Chopper$(1,View) AT 70,210
                LET T$ = Time$(7:8)
                IF T$ = "06" OR T$ = "36" THEN
                    LET Time_to_go = 1
                ELSE
                    LET Time_to_go = 0
                END IF
        LOOP UNTIL Time_to_go = 1

        ! Hover while the ball rolls back out of the building
        FOR I = 180 TO 330 STEP 2
            LET View = Mod(View,3) + 1
            BOX SHOW Chopper$(1,View) AT 70,210
            IF I > 180 THEN
                BOX SHOW Ball$ AT I-2,17 USING "xor"
            END IF
            BOX SHOW Ball$ AT I,17 USING "or"
        NEXT I

        ! Then fly back to the right
        FOR I = 70 TO 300 STEP 3
            LET View = Mod(View,3) + 1
            BOX SHOW Chopper$(3,View) AT I,210
        NEXT I

        ! Back down the screen
        FOR I = 210 TO 50 STEP -3
            LET View = Mod(View,3) + 1
            BOX SHOW Chopper$(1,View) AT 300,I
        NEXT I

      ! And do it all again, until user spoils all the fun
   LOOP UNTIL KEY INPUT

 ! All done after user presses a key
   END
```

when the ball hits (a little sound effect was added at this point to demonstrate the
SOUND statement) and after a short delay the ball rolls out of the building, ready for
the helicopter to go pick it up once again.

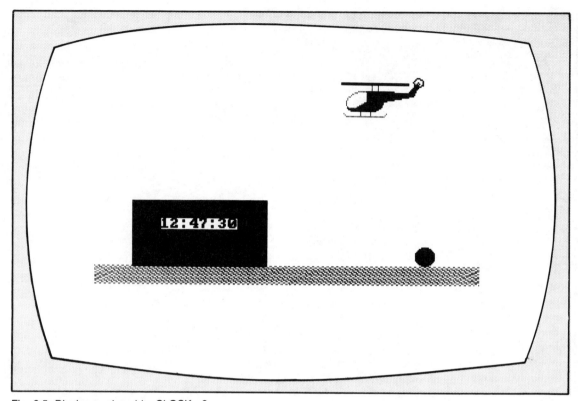

Fig. 3-5. Display produced by CLOCK_3.

The action is timed such that the ball should hit and the building should bounce every half minute, displaying seconds of either "00" or "30" each time. This timing was set up for an IBM PC but may need to be changed if your computer has different timing characteristics. Find the **DO LOOP** labeled "Hover while watching the clock carefully" and notice the IF test that begins with

IF T$ = "06" OR T$ = "36" THEN.

Alter the "06" and "36" characters to start the helicopter round trip at some other time each minute. These two numbers are the seconds in each minute to start rolling the ball out of the building so that the time will be displayed exactly on the whole or half minute.

The program quits when any keypress is detected during one of the helicopter's round trips. Of course, you can always stop a True BASIC program by pressing the "stop" key, which in the case of the IBM PC is the <Ctrl-Break> key combination.

MOON

Going fishing this weekend? Wondering if you should plant your potatoes? Or would you just like to know how much moonlight there will be tonight? This program (List-

Listing 3-5. MOON.TRU.

```
! **********************************
! **   File:      MOON.TRU      **
! **   Date:      7/25/85       **
! **   Author:    John Craig    **
! **   Language:  True BASIC    **
! **********************************
!
! This program calculates the phase of the moon for any
! given date from March 1, 1900 to February 28, 2100.

    OPTION ANGLE DEGREES

! Declare external function
    DECLARE FUNCTION Mdy_to_w
    DECLARE FUNCTION Mdy_to_a

! Start with a clean slate
    CLEAR

! Display program name
    PRINT "* MOON *"
    PRINT
! Ask user for the date of concern
    PRINT "Enter the date... month,day,year... ";
    INPUT Month,Day,Year
    PRINT

! Check that date is valid
    IF Year < 100 THEN LET Year = Year + 1900
    CALL Check_date(Month,Day,Year)

! Calculate the day of the week
    LET Wday = Mdy_to_w(Month,Day,Year)

! Calculate the astronomical julian day number
    LET Aday = Mdy_to_a(Month,Day,Year)

! Calculate the approximate phase of the moon
    LET Phase = 360 * Mod((Aday + 4.867) / 29.53059, 1)

! Prepare the graphics area
    OPEN #1: SCREEN .2,.8,.25,1
    SET WINDOW -1,1,-1,1
    SET COLOR "yellow"

! Draw the round edge of the moon
    BOX ELLIPSE -1,1,-1,1

! Draw the elliptical edge where the sunlight ends
    FOR A = -90 TO 90 STEP 2
        LET X = Cos(A)
        LET Y = Sin(A)
        LET Z = 0
        IF Phase < 180 THEN
            CALL Yrotate(X,Y,Z,Phase)
        ELSE
            CALL Yrotate(X,Y,Z,Phase + 180)
```

```
            END IF
            PLOT LINES: X,Y;
            IF A = Ø THEN LET Light_edge = X
        NEXT A

    ! Let there be light, where the sun do shine
        IF Phase < 18Ø THEN
            FLOOD (Light_edge - 1) / 2, Ø
        ELSE
            FLOOD (Light_edge + 1) / 2, Ø
        END IF

    ! Prepare the text part of the screen
        OPEN #2: SCREEN Ø,1,Ø,.2
        SET COLOR "green"

    ! Label the graphics
        LET Moon$ = USING$("The waxing moon on ##/##/####",Month,Day,Year)
        IF Phase < 18Ø THEN LET Moon$(7:7) = "n"
        SET CURSOR 1,7
        PRINT Moon$

    ! Wait for any key press
        GET KEY Before_quitting
    ! All done
        END

    ! This function calculates the day of the week
    ! given the month, day, and year.
    !
        FUNCTION Mdy_to_w(Month,Day,Year)
            DECLARE FUNCTION Mdy_to_a
            LET Mdy_to_w = Mod(Mdy_to_a(Month,Day,Year)+1,7)
        END FUNCTION

    ! This function calculates the astronomical Julian
    ! day number given the Month, Day, and Year.
    !
        FUNCTION Mdy_to_a(Month,Day,Year)
            IF Month < 3 THEN
                LET Year = Year - 1
                LET Month = Month + 13
            ELSE
                LET Month = Month + 1
            END IF
            LET Tmp = Int(Year*365.25)+Int(Month*3Ø.6001)+Day+172Ø982
            IF Tmp < 2415Ø8Ø OR Tmp > 2488127 THEN
                CAUSE ERROR 1,"ERROR - Date out of range"
            END IF
            LET Mdy_to_a = Tmp
        END FUNCTION

    ! This function calculates the date given the
    ! astronomical Julian day number
    !
        SUB Ast_to_mdy(Astronomical_day,Month,Day,Year)
            IF Astronomical_day < 2415Ø8Ø OR Astronomical_day > 2488127 THEN
                CAUSE ERROR 1,"ERROR - Date out of range"
            END IF
```

```
        LET Day = Astronomical_day - 1720982
        LET Year = Int((Day - 122.1)/365.25)
        LET Tmp = Int(365.25 * Year)
        LET Month = Int((Day-Tmp)/30.6001)
        LET Day = Day - Tmp - Int(30.6001 * Month)
        LET Month = Month - 1
        IF Month > 12 THEN LET Month = Month - 12
        IF Month < 3 THEN LET Year = Year + 1
    END SUB

! This subroutine checks a date to make
! sure it represents a valid date
!
  SUB Check_date(Month,Day,Year)
      DECLARE FUNCTION Mdy_to_a
      LET T1 = Month
      LET T2 = Day
      LET T3 = Year
      CALL Ast_to_mdy(Mdy_to_a(Month,Day,Year),Month,Day,Year)
      IF T1 <> Month OR T2 <> Day OR T3 <> Year THEN
          CAUSE ERROR 1,"ERROR - Date is not valid"
      END IF
  END SUB
! This subroutine rotates a point in space around
! the Y axis, using the right hand rule.
!
  SUB Yrotate(X,Y,Z,Ang)
      OPTION ANGLE DEGREES
      LET Cos_ang = Cos(Ang)
      LET Sin_ang = Sin(Ang)
      LET T = X * Cos_ang + Z * Sin_ang
      LET Z = Z * Cos_ang - X * Sin_ang
      LET X = T
  END SUB
```

ing 3-5) will tell you graphically what the moon looks like—for tonight or any night from March 1, 1900, to February 28, 2100, accurate to approximately one day.

The outer edge of the moon is drawn using the **BOX ELLIPSE** statement, which is very fast. The curved edge of light on the moon's surface (where sunlight and darkness meet) is drawn as a circle rotated in space about the Y axis and then projected back onto the X,Y plane. A three-dimensional coordinate transformation subroutine, named **Yrotate**, was borrowed from the program named **THREE__D** for this purpose. Take a look at the **THREE__D** program for more information about three-dimensional graphics transformations.

The lit portion of the moon's face is flooded with sunlight (using the **FLOOD** statement, of course) and a message is displayed indicating whether the moon is waxing or waning. (The moon is *waxing* when each night brings it closer to a full moon, *waning* when the lit portion is shrinking.)

Figure 3-6 shows the moon on a December evening. Notice that this illustration is somewhat misleading; the lit portion of the moon is drawn in on the screen yellow—which prints as black when the graphics screen is dumped to a printer.

SIDEREAL

Astronomers use *sidereal time* to calculate the exact location in the heavens of stars,

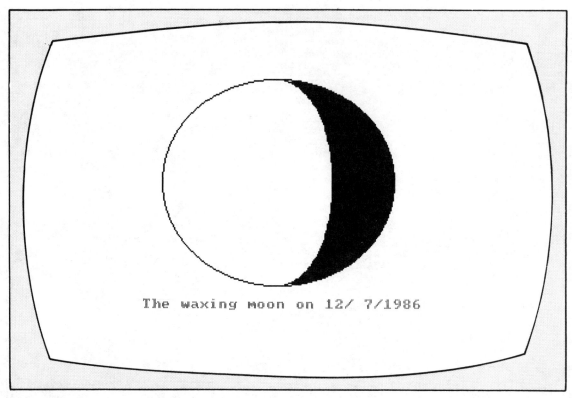

Fig. 3-6. The moon's appearance on December 7, 1986.

Listing 3-6. Program to calculate local sidereal time (continued to page 76).

```
!  ********************************
!  **   File:       SIDEREAL.TRU   **
!  **   Date:       7/27/85        **
!  **   Author:     John Craig     **
!  **   Language:   True BASIC     **
!  ********************************
!
!  This program displays local sidereal time

!  Declare external functions
   DECLARE FUNCTION Sidereal$
   DECLARE FUNCTION Mdy$

!  Title
   CLEAR
   PRINT "* SIDEREAL *"

!  Ask user for longitude
   PRINT
   INPUT PROMPT "Enter your longitude ? ": Longitude
   PRINT
```

```
! Ask user for time zone information
  PRINT "Hours difference from Coordinated Universal Time:"
  PRINT
  PRINT "Eastern       5"
  PRINT "Central       6"
  PRINT "Mountain      7"
  PRINT "Pacific       8"
  PRINT "(For daylight savings time add one more hour)"
  PRINT
  INPUT PROMPT "Enter your time difference ? ": Zone
  CLEAR

! Draws the upper horizontal segment
  PICTURE Seg_u_h
      PLOT LINES: 1,50; 23,50; 19,46; 5,46; 1,50
      FLOOD 9,48
  END PICTURE

! Draws the middle horizontal segment
  PICTURE Seg_m_h
      PLOT LINES: 3,28; 5,30; 19,30; 21,28;
      PLOT LINES: 19,26; 5,26; 3,28
      FLOOD 9,28
  END PICTURE

! Draws the lower horizontal segment
  PICTURE Seg_l_h
      PLOT LINES: 1,6; 5,10; 19,10; 23,6; 1,6
      FLOOD 9,9
  END PICTURE

! Draws the upper left segment
  PICTURE Seg_u_l
      PLOT LINES: 0,49; 4,45; 4,31;
      PLOT LINES: 2,29; 0,31; 0,49
      FLOOD 2,40
  END PICTURE

! Draws the upper right segment
  PICTURE Seg_u_r
      PLOT LINES: 20,45; 24,49; 24,31;
      PLOT LINES: 22,29; 20,31; 20,45
      FLOOD 22,40
  END PICTURE

! Draws the lower left segment
  PICTURE Seg_l_l
      PLOT LINES: 0,7; 0,25; 2,27;
      PLOT LINES: 4,25; 4,11; 0,7
      FLOOD 2,20
  END PICTURE

! Draws the lower right segment
  PICTURE Seg_l_r
      PLOT LINES: 20,11; 20,25; 22,27;
      PLOT LINES: 24,25; 24,7; 20,11
      FLOOD 22,20
  END PICTURE
```

```
! Create the digits "0" through "9"
  OPTION ANGLE DEGREES
  OPTION BASE 0
  DIM Digit$(10)
  OPEN #1: SCREEN 0,.5,0,.5
  SET WINDOW 0,159,5,104
  LET Fgd$ = "yellow"
  SET COLOR Fgd$ & "/blue"

! Create "1"
  DRAW Seg_u_r
  DRAW Seg_l_r
  BOX KEEP 0,24,5,50 IN Digit$(1)

! Create "7"
  DRAW Seg_u_h
  BOX KEEP 0,24,5,50 IN Digit$(7)

! Create "3"
  DRAW Seg_m_h
  DRAW Seg_l_h
  BOX KEEP 0,24,5,50 IN Digit$(3)

! Create "9"
  DRAW Seg_u_l
  BOX KEEP 0,24,5,50 IN Digit$(9)

! Create "8"
  DRAW Seg_l_l
  BOX KEEP 0,24,5,50 IN Digit$(8)

! Create "0"
  SET COLOR "background"
  DRAW Seg_m_h
  BOX KEEP 0,24,5,50 IN Digit$(0)

! Create "6"
  DRAW Seg_u_r
  SET COLOR Fgd$
  DRAW Seg_m_h
  BOX KEEP 0,24,5,50 IN Digit$(6)

! Create "5"
  SET COLOR "background"
  DRAW Seg_l_l
  BOX KEEP 0,24,5,50 IN Digit$(5)

! Create "4"
  DRAW Seg_l_h
  DRAW Seg_u_h
  SET COLOR Fgd$
  DRAW Seg_u_r
  BOX KEEP 0,24,5,50 IN Digit$(4)

! Create "2"
  DRAW Seg_u_h
  DRAW Seg_l_h
  DRAW Seg_l_l
  SET COLOR "background"
```

```
      DRAW Seg_u_l
      DRAW Seg_l_r
      BOX KEEP 0,24,5,50 IN Digit$(2)

! Create ":"
      DRAW Seg_u_h
      DRAW Seg_m_h
      DRAW Seg_l_h
      DRAW Seg_u_l
      DRAW Seg_u_r
      DRAW Seg_l_l
      SET COLOR Fgd$
      BOX AREA 10,15,15,20
      BOX AREA 10,15,35,40
      BOX KEEP 0,24,5,50 IN Digit$(10)

! Erase what's left
      SET COLOR "background"
      BOX AREA 0,24,5,50

! Scale the screen
      CLOSE #1
      SET WINDOW .5,9.5,2,4

! Display unchanging information
      SET COLOR "red"
      SET CURSOR 1,13
      PRINT "SIDEREAL CLOCK"
      SET COLOR "green"
      SET CURSOR 3,1
      PRINT "Longitude";Longitude
      PRINT "Time zone";Zone

! Display time until any key is pressed
      DO UNTIL KEY INPUT

         ! Record current time for erasing old hands
         LET Old_t$ = Time$

         ! Hang around until next second arrives
         DO
         LOOP UNTIL Time$ <> Old_t$

         ! Calculate sidereal time
         CALL Mdy(Date$,Month,Day,Year)
         LET T$ = Sidereal$(Longitude,Zone,Month,Day,Year,Time/3600)

         ! Display clock time
         SET CURSOR 3,32
         PRINT Mdy$(Date$)
         SET CURSOR 4,32
         PRINT Time$

         ! Display the digits
         FOR I = 1 TO 8
             IF T$(I:I) = ":" THEN
                 LET N = 10
             ELSE
                 LET N = Val(T$(I:I))
```

```
            END IF
            BOX SHOW Digit$(N) AT I,3
        NEXT I
    LOOP

! All done after a key is pressed
    END

! Function to calculate sidereal time.  Sidereal time
! is returned in a 24 hour notation string...   HH:MM:SS
!
    FUNCTION Sidereal$(Longitude,Zone,Month,Day,Year,Hours)
        LET Year = Mod(Year,100)
        LET T1 = Int(Day - 30 + 275 * Month / 9)
        IF Month > 2 THEN
            LET T1 = T1 - 1
            IF Mod(Year,4) > 0 THEN LET T1 = T1 - 1
        END IF
        LET T2 = Zone + Hours
        LET T3 = (Int(T1 + 365.25 * Year - .25) - .5) / 36525
        LET T4 = 23925.836 + 8640184.542 * T3 + .0929 * T3^2
        LET T5 = 360 * T4 / 86400 + 15.04106864 * T2 - Longitude
        CALL Divide(Mod(T5,360)/15,1,S_hour,S_minute)
        CALL Divide(60 * S_minute,1,S_minute,S_second)
        LET S_second = Round(S_second * 60, 0)
        LET Sidereal$ = USING$("%%:%%:%%",S_hour,S_minute,S_second)
    END FUNCTION

! Function to convert DATE$ format from "YYYYMMDD" to "MM/DD/YY"
    FUNCTION Mdy$(D$) = D$(5:6) & "/" & D$(7:8) & "/" & D$(3:4)

! Subroutine to extract Month,Day,Year from DATE$ format
    SUB Mdy(D$,Month,Day,Year)
        LET Month = Val(D$(5:6))
        LET Day = Val(D$(7:8))
        LET Year = Val(D$(1:4))
    END SUB

! Subroutine to extract Hour,Minute,Second from TIME$ format
    SUB Hms(T$,Hour,Minute,Second)
        LET Hour = Val(T$(1:2))
        LET Minute = Val(T$(4:5))
        LET Second = Val(T$(7:8))
    END SUB
```

planets, and other heavenly bodies. This program (Listing 3-6) generates a real-time display of local sidereal time, suitable for amateur astronomy calculations. The program will prompt you for your longitude and the number of hours difference from Coordinated Universal Time (Fig. 3-7). From then on, your screen is turned into a digital clock, displaying normal system time and local sidereal time (Fig. 3-8).

Sidereal time is measured relative to the stars in the sky as the earth spins. At sidereal midnight, the stars will be in the same location in the sky each day. Because the earth orbits around the sun once per year, a sidereal clock and a normal clock will disagree by one complete day at the end of a year. Sidereal time changes with any east-west motion of the observer on the earth's surface. This is why the longitude must

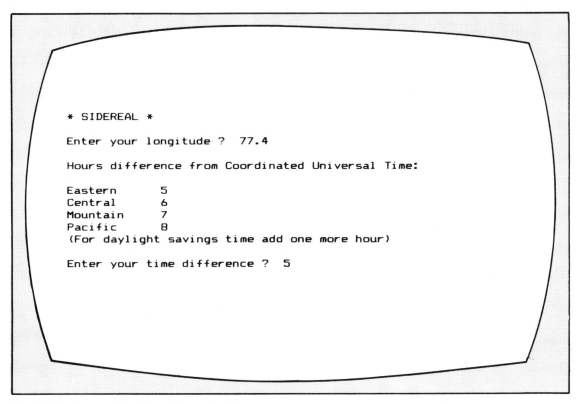

```
* SIDEREAL *

Enter your longitude ?  77.4

Hours difference from Coordinated Universal Time:

Eastern        5
Central        6
Mountain       7
Pacific        8
(For daylight savings time add one more hour)

Enter your time difference ?  5
```

Fig. 3-7. Input screen for sidereal time calculation program.

be known, and why it's called *local* sidereal time.

This program uses graphics techniques developed more fully in the **CLOCK_2** program. Several functions are presented that you may find useful. The subroutines **Hms** and **Mdy** extract time and date information from strings in the format returned by the **Time$** and **Date$** functions. The **Mdy$** function returns a data in MM/DD/YY format when given a string in the YYYYMMDD format as returned by the standard **DATE$** function.

TIMING

This program (Listing 3-7) demonstrates several functions for converting time (as returned by True BASIC's time function) to hours, minutes, and seconds. Recall that the time function returns the number of seconds since midnight.

Also shown is an example of formatting hours, minutes, and seconds with the **PRINT USING** statement.

An alternative method of calculating the hours, minutes, and seconds provided by the system clock would be to extract this information from the string returned by the function **Date$**. For example:

```
LET Hour = Val (Time$(1:2))
```

Fig. 3-8. Display produced by the SIDEREAL program.

Listing 3-7. TIMING.TRU makes your computer to an elapsed time counter.

```
! **********************************
! **   File:        TIMING.TRU    **
! **   Date:        5/29/85       **
! **   Author:      John Craig    **
! **   Language:    True BASIC    **
! **********************************
!
! Displays time elapsed since start of program in HH:MM:SS format

! Extracts the elapsed hours using the time function
  FUNCTION Hour
      LET Hour = Int((Time-T0)/3600)
  END FUNCTION

! Extracts the elapsed minutes using the time function
  FUNCTION Minute
      LET Minute = Int((Time-T0)/60)-Hour*60
  END FUNCTION

! Extracts the elapsed seconds using the time function
  FUNCTION Second
      LET Second = Int(Time-T0)-Minute*60-Hour*3600
  END FUNCTION
```

```
! Record the starting time
  LET TØ = Time

! The main loop
  DO

     ! Put the time at the same location
       SET CURSOR 10,17

     ! Formatted output using numbers returned by functions
       PRINT "Time since start of program:      ";
       PRINT USING "%%:%%:%%": Hour,Minute,Second

     ! If key is pressed, display elapsed time
       IF KEY INPUT THEN
          LET Now = Time
          GET KEY But_ignore_it
          SET CURSOR 12,17
          PRINT "Elapsed seconds at key stroke:   ";
          PRINT USING "#######.#": Now - TØ
       END IF

     ! Hang around until STOP key is pressed
  LOOP

! All done after a key is pressed
  END
```

```
        LET Minute = Val (Time$(4:5))
        LET Second = Val (Time$(7:8))
```

When the program is running, the elapsed time since the start of the program and the elapsed time whenever a key is pressed are displayed:

```
Time since start of program:        00:03:17
Elapsed seconds at keystroke:          179.7
```

Chapter 4

Electronics

The programs in this chapter perform many of the most common computations used in the analysis of electronic circuits. Many subroutines are provided that allow you to expand these capabilities easily.

ANGLES

One of the powerful features of True BASIC is the ability to break programming tasks into manageable pieces. We find this true not only in the use of subroutines and functions in a given program file, but also in the ability to create collections of these program units in separate files, called *libraries*. We can prevent a lot of duplication of effort by keeping our most frequently used routines in a separate file, ready to patch into any program we develop.

This short library (Listing 4-1) contains two subroutines and one function, and demonstrates the powerful concept of creating external libraries. Take a look at the programs for electronic impedance calculations for examples of how this **ANGLES** library can be used in a program. The impedance programs have filenames that begin with "Z__."

The **Hypot** function performs the common calculation of finding the hypotenuse of a right triangle given the lengths of the other two sides. This function is used by one of the subroutines in this library and is not called by any of the main programs that load this library. However, it's perfectly legal to use this function in your own programs even though its main purpose is to provide some of the calculations in the **Rect__polar** subroutine.

Listing 4-1. ANGLES.TRU library listing.

```
!  *********************************
!  **   File:       ANGLES.TRU    **
!  **   Date:       6/11/85       **
!  **   Author:     John Craig    **
!  **   Language:   True BASIC    **
!  *********************************
!
!  This library contains some commonly used subroutines and
!  functions involving angles and sides in right triangles.

   EXTERNAL

!  Calculates hypotenuse, given sides X and Y
   FUNCTION Hypot(X,Y) = Sqr(X * X + Y * Y)

!  Converts rectangular to polar
   SUB Rect_polar(X,Y,Rho,Theta)
       DECLARE FUNCTION Hypot
       LET Rho = Hypot(X,Y)
       LET Theta = ANGLE(X,Y)
   END SUB

!  Converts polar to rectangular
   SUB Polar_rect(Rho,Theta,X,Y)
       LET X = Rho * Cos(Theta)
       LET Y = Rho * Sin(Theta)
   END SUB
```

The **Rect_polar** subroutine converts a point (X,Y) expressed in cartesian or rectangular coordinates to a magnitude and angle (**Rho, Theta**) expressed in polar form. This is a common calculation in electronics, as evidenced by the impedance programs that use this library.

The **Polar_rect** subroutine converts polar coordinates back to rectangular.

The True BASIC function **ANGLE(X,Y)** is used here and deserves special mention. In nonstandard BASICs the **ATN** function would have to be used to calculate the angle from the X axis for a point in the X,Y plane. This works fine for points in the first quadrant, where X and Y are both positive, but falls apart when the point is in the other quadrants or on one of the axes. Several lines of complicated code can be used to calculate the **ATN** function correctly for all cartesian coordinates, but the **ANGLE** function presented here solves the whole problem. For any point except 0,0 the **ANGLE** function will tell you the angle from the positive X axis. At the point 0,0 an error will be generated, as the angle at this point is undefined.

MORSE

This program (Listing 4-2) converts a string to equivalent Morse code. This program provides a good example of the use of a **SELECT CASE** structure. A typical sample run is shown in Fig. 4-1.

Listing 4-2. MORSE.TRU.

```
! *********************************
! **   File:       MORSE.TRU      **
! **   Date:       7/15/85        **
! **   Author:     John Craig     **
! **   Language:   True BASIC     **
! *********************************
!
! This program converts input words
! to Morse code.

! Start with a clean slate
  CLEAR

! Title of program
  PRINT "* Morse Code *"
  PRINT

! Ask for the word to convert
  INPUT PROMPT "Message to encode ? ": A$
  PRINT

! Process each character
  FOR I = 1 TO Len(A$)
      LET B$ = Ucase$(A$(I:I))

    ! Display the Morse code equivalent
      PRINT B$;" = ";
      SELECT CASE B$
      CASE "A"
          PRINT "dit dah"
      CASE "B"
          PRINT "dah dit dit dit"
      CASE "C"
          PRINT "dah dit dah dit"
      CASE "D"
          PRINT "dah dit dit"
      CASE "E"
          PRINT "dit"
      CASE "F"
          PRINT "dit dit dah dit"
      CASE "G"
          PRINT "dah dah dit"
      CASE "H"
          PRINT "dit dit dit dit"
      CASE "I"
          PRINT "dit dit"
      CASE "J"
          PRINT "dit dah dah dah"
      CASE "K"
          PRINT "dah dit dah"
      CASE "L"
          PRINT "dit dah dit dit"
      CASE "M"
          PRINT "dah dah"
      CASE "N"
          PRINT "dah dit"
      CASE "O"
```

```
                    PRINT "dah dah dah"
            CASE "P"
                    PRINT "dit dah dah dit"
            CASE "Q"
                    PRINT "dah dah dit dah"
            CASE "R"
                    PRINT "dit dah dit"
            CASE "S"
                    PRINT "dit dit dit"
            CASE "T"
                    PRINT "dah"
            CASE "U"
                    PRINT "dat dat dah"
            CASE "V"
                    PRINT "dit dit dit dah"
            CASE "W"
                    PRINT "dit dah dah"
            CASE "X"
                    PRINT "dah dit dit dah"
            CASE "Y"
                    PRINT "dah dit dah dah"
            CASE "Z"
                    PRINT "dah dah dit dit"
            CASE "Ø"
                    PRINT "dah dah dah dah dah"
            CASE "1"
                    PRINT "dit dah dah dah dah"
            CASE "2"
                    PRINT "dit dit dah dah dah"
            CASE "3"
                    PRINT "dit dit dit dah dah"
            CASE "4"
                    PRINT "dit dit dit dit dah"
            CASE "5"
                    PRINT "dit dit dit dit dit"
            CASE "6"
                    PRINT "dah dit dit dit dit"
            CASE "7"
                    PRINT "dah dah dit dit dit"
            CASE "8"
                    PRINT "dah dah dah dit dit"
            CASE "9"
                    PRINT "dah dah dah dah dit"
            CASE ELSE
                    PRINT
            END SELECT
    NEXT I

! Wait for user to press any key
    PRINT
    PRINT "Press any key..."
    GET KEY Before_quitting

    END
```

OHMS__LAW

This program (Listing 4-3) solves common circuit analysis problems of determining

```
                  * Morse Code *

        Message to encode ?  BASIC MORSE CODE

        B = dah dit dit dit
        A = dit dah
        S = dit dit dit
        I = dit dit
        C = dah dit dah dit
            =
        M = dah dah
        O = dah dah dah
        R = dit dah dit
        S = dit dit dit
        E = dit
            =
        C = dah dit dah dit
        O = dah dah dah
        D = dah dit dit
        E = dit

        Press any key...
```

Fig. 4-1. Typical screen display for the Morse code program.

Listing 4-3. Ohm's Law calculation program.

```
!  ********************************
!  **  File:      OHMS_LAW.TRU   **
!  **  Date:      5/30/85        **
!  **  Author:    John Craig     **
!  **  Language:  True BASIC     **
!  ********************************
!
!  This program solves for voltage, current, resistance
!  and power, given known values for any two.

!  External functions
   DECLARE FUNCTION Answer

!  Start with a clean slate
   CLEAR

!  Heading
   PRINT "* Ohm's Laws *"
   PRINT
   PRINT "Enter the known values..."
   PRINT

!  answer' for the variables
```

```
   LET E = Answer("Voltage    (volts)")
   LET I = Answer("Current    (amps)")
   LET R = Answer("Resistance (ohms)")
   LET P = Answer("Power      (watts)")
   PRINT

! Calculate the unknowns
   IF E <> Ø AND I <> Ø THEN
       LET R = E / I
       LET P = E * I
   ELSEIF E <> Ø AND R <> Ø THEN
       LET I = E / R
       LET P = E * E / R
   ELSEIF E <> Ø AND P <> Ø THEN
       LET I = P / E
       LET R = E * E / P
   ELSEIF I <> Ø AND R <> Ø THEN
       LET E = I * R
       LET P = I * I * R
   ELSEIF I <> Ø AND P <> Ø THEN
       LET E = P / I
       LET R = P / I / I
   ELSEIF R <> Ø AND P <> Ø THEN
       LET E = Sqr(P * R)
       LET I = Sqr(P / R)
   ELSE
       PRINT "Not enough information"
   END IF

! Output the results
   PRINT "Voltage    (E) = ";E
   PRINT "Current    (I) = ";I
   PRINT "Resistance (R) = ";R
   PRINT "Power      (P) = ";P
   PRINT

! Wait for any key press
   PRINT "Press any key to continue..."
   DO
   LOOP UNTIL KEY INPUT

! All done
   END

! Prompts for number, returns zero if none entered
   FUNCTION Answer(Question$)
       PRINT Question$;
       LINE INPUT X$
       WHEN EXCEPTION IN
           LET Answer = Val(X$)
       USE
           LET Answer = Ø
       END WHEN
   END FUNCTION
```

voltage, current, resistance, or power from any two known values.

True BASIC demands that a number be entered whenever an **INPUT** statement prompts for one. If you just press the Return key, without having typed in a numerical

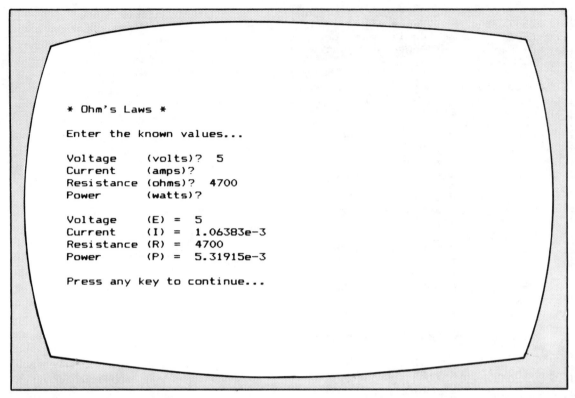

```
* Ohm's Laws *

Enter the known values...

Voltage    (volts)?  5
Current    (amps)?
Resistance (ohms)?   4700
Power      (watts)?

Voltage    (E) =  5
Current    (I) =  1.06383e-3
Resistance (R) =  4700
Power      (P) =  5.31915e-3

Press any key to continue...
```

Fig. 4-2. Input screen for Ohm's law calculations.

response, True BASIC will display a message and reprompt for a numerical input. In most cases this is a desirable way for the language to behave; it prevents a host of other problems that could occur if the user responds inappropriately, whether accidental or not.

However, there are cases where entering no value is beneficial. This program demonstrates a function that returns 0 (or any number you wish to set it up to return) if a number was not entered; if one was, the number entered is returned. The function is named **Answer**, and can be found at the end of the program listing.

To use this program, type in numbers for any two quantities you are prompted for. For unknowns, just press the Return key. All unknowns will be solved and a table of all the values will be displayed.

Example: What current flows through a 4700-ohm resistor when 5 volts are applied across it? Figure 4-2 shows the results.

RCTIMING

This program solves electronic analysis problems involving resistance-capacitance charging. Six parameters are involved; any five may be given and the sixth will be calculated.

The RCTIMING program (Listing 4-4) uses a subroutine named **Request** to prompt you for input values. If no number is input, a flag is returned to the calling routine to indicate that no value was entered. This effectively overrides True BASIC's **INPUT** statement, which insists that a numerical value be entered.

Listing 4-4. RCTIMING.TRU.

```
! **********************************
! ** File:      RCTIMING.TRU   **
! ** Date:      6/7/85         **
! ** Author:    John Craig     **
! ** Language:  True BASIC     **
! **********************************
!
! This program solves problems involving an RC timing
! circuit involving a resistance (R) in series with a
! capacitance (C), the instantaneous voltage across the
! capacitance (Vi), the voltage applied across the circuit
! before a step (V1), the voltage applied after the step
! (V2), and the time since the step (T).  This program
! calculates one of these variables given the other five.
!
! Start with a clean slate
  CLEAR

! Heading
  PRINT "* RC Timing *"
  PRINT
  PRINT "Enter values for all but one variable..."
  PRINT

! Ask for the variables
  CALL Request("Resistance in ohms                 (R) ",R,Flag_r)
  CALL Request("Capacitance in farads              (C) ",C,Flag_c)
  CALL Request("Time since voltage step, seconds (T) ",T,Flag_t)
  CALL Request("Voltage before step              (V1) ",V1,Flag_v1)
  CALL Request("Voltage after step               (V2) ",V2,Flag_v2)
  CALL Request("Instantaneous Voltage            (Vi) ",Vi,Flag_vi)
  PRINT

! Calculate the unknown
  IF Flag_r = 1   THEN
      LET R = T/C/(-Log((Vi-V2)/(V1-V2)))
  ELSEIF Flag_c = 1 THEN
      LET C = T/R/(-Log((Vi-V2)/(V1-V2)))
  ELSEIF Flag_t = 1 THEN
      LET T = -Log((Vi-V2)/(V1-V2))*R*C
  ELSEIF Flag_v1 = 1 THEN
      LET V1 = (Vi-V2)/Exp(-T/R/C)+V2
  ELSEIF Flag_v2 = 1 THEN
      LET V2 = (Vi-V1*Exp(-T/R/C))/(1-Exp(-T/R/C))
  ELSEIF Flag_vi = 1 THEN
      LET Vi = (V1 - V2) * Exp(-T/R/C) + V2
  ELSE
      PRINT "Don't enter a number for the unknown"
  END IF
```

```
! Output the results
PRINT "Resistance        (R)  ";R;" ohms"
PRINT "Capacitance       (C)  ";C;" farads"
PRINT "Time since step   (T)  ";T;" seconds"
PRINT "Voltage before    (V1) ";V1;" volts"
PRINT "Voltage after     (V2) ";V2;" volts"
PRINT "Voltage on C now  (Vi) ";Vi;" volts"
PRINT

! Wait for any key press
PRINT "Press any key to continue..."
DO
LOOP UNTIL KEY INPUT

! All done
END

! Prompts for number, sets a flag if none given
SUB Request(Req$,X,Flag)
    PRINT Req$;
    LINE INPUT X$
    WHEN EXCEPTION IN
        LET X = Val(X$)
        LET Flag = 0
    USE
        LET Flag = 1
    END WHEN
END SUB
```

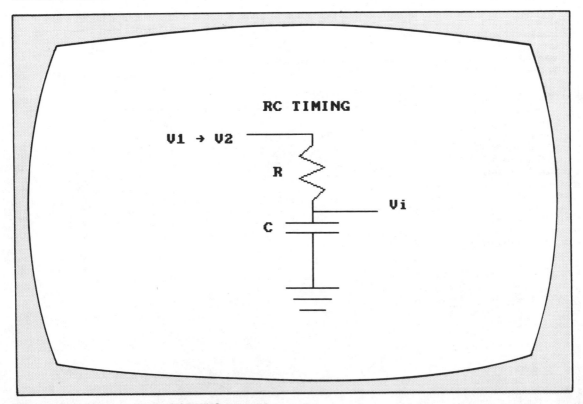

Fig. 4-3. Circuit diagram for the RCTIMING program.

Example: The voltage applied across an RC network such as the one shown in Fig. 4-3, comprised of a 4700-ohm resistor in series with a 1-microfarad capacitor, suddenly changes from 0 to 5 volts. What voltage will exist across the capacitor after 1 millisecond of charging time? Figure 4-4 is the sample run:

R__BRIDGE

This program finds the unknown resistance in a common resistive bridge that balances the bridge (this circuit is shown in Fig. 4-5).

Example: What resistance will balance a bridge comprised of a 4700-ohm resistance opposite the unknown resistance, with 2000-ohm and 5000-ohm resistances next to it? A sample run is shown below, and the code appears as Listing 4-5.

```
* Resistive Bridge Balancing *

Resistance opposite unknown ?        4700
First resistance next to unknown ?   2000
Second resistance next to unknown ?  5000

Balancing resistance = 2127.66

Press any key to continue . . .
```

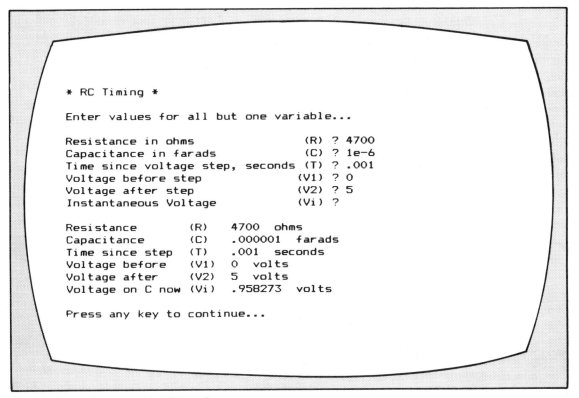

```
* RC Timing *

Enter values for all but one variable...

Resistance in ohms                (R) ? 4700
Capacitance in farads             (C) ? 1e-6
Time since voltage step, seconds  (T) ? .001
Voltage before step               (V1) ? 0
Voltage after  step               (V2) ? 5
Instantaneous Voltage             (Vi) ?

Resistance       (R)    4700   ohms
Capacitance      (C)    .000001   farads
Time since step  (T)    .001   seconds
Voltage before   (V1)   0   volts
Voltage after    (V2)   5   volts
Voltage on C now (Vi)   .958273   volts

Press any key to continue...
```

Fig. 4-4. Data entry screen for RCTIMING program.

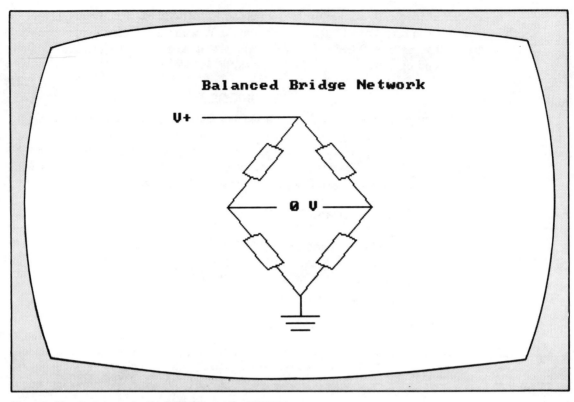

Fig. 4-5. Circuit diagram for R__BRIDGE and Z__BRIDGE.

Listing 4-5. Program for resistive bridge calculations.

```
! ***********************************
! **   File:      R_BRIDGE.TRU    **
! **   Date:      6/11/85         **
! **   Author:    John Craig      **
! **   Language:  True BASIC      **
! ***********************************
!
! This program calculates the resistance necessary to
! balance a resistive bridge network given the other
! three resistances.

! Start with a clean slate
  CLEAR

! Heading
  PRINT "* Resistive Bridge Balancing *"
  PRINT

  INPUT PROMPT "Resistance opposite unknown ?        ":R1
  INPUT PROMPT "First resistance next to unknown ?   ":R2
  INPUT PROMPT "Second resistance next to unknown ? ":R3
```

90

```
   LET R = R2 * R3 / R1
   PRINT
   PRINT "Balancing resistance = ";R
   PRINT

 ! Wait for user to press any key
   PRINT "Press any key to continue..."
   DO
   LOOP UNTIL KEY INPUT

 ! All done
   END
```

R_CLRCOD

This program calculates the resistance and tolerance indicated by the color bands on a standard resistor. Two examples of the use of the **SELECT CASE** statement are presented in this program (Listing 4-6).

Listing 4-6. Program to determine the value of a resistor from its color code. (continued to page 93).

```
 ! ********************************
 ! **   File:      R_CLRCOD.TRU   **
 ! **   Date:      7/15/85        **
 ! **   Author:    John Craig     **
 ! **   Language:  True BASIC     **
 ! ********************************
 !
 ! This program helps you decipher the color code
 ! bands on resistors.

 ! Function to convert a color stripe to its value
   FUNCTION Stripe_value
       SELECT CASE Lcase$(A$)
       CASE "black"
           LET Stripe_value = 0
       CASE "brown"
           LET Stripe_value = 1
       CASE "red"
           LET Stripe_value = 2
       CASE "orange"
           LET Stripe_value = 3
       CASE "yellow"
           LET Stripe_value = 4
       CASE "green"
           LET Stripe_value = 5
       CASE "blue"        .
           LET Stripe_value = 6
       CASE "violet"
           LET Stripe_value = 7
       CASE "gray"
           LET Stripe_value = 8
       CASE "white"
```

```
            LET Stripe_value = 9
        CASE ELSE
            LET Stripe_value = 99
        END SELECT
    END FUNCTION

! Multiplier code
    FUNCTION Multiplier
        LET N = Stripe_value
        IF N <> 99 THEN LET N = 10^N
        IF A$ = "gold" THEN LET N = .1
        IF A$ = "silver" THEN LET N = .01
        LET Multiplier = N
    END FUNCTION

! Tolerance code
    FUNCTION Tolerance
        SELECT CASE Lcase$(A$)
        CASE "brown"
            LET Tolerance = 1
        CASE "red"
            LET Tolerance = 2
        CASE "orange"
            LET Tolerance = 3
        CASE "yellow"
            LET Tolerance = 4
        CASE "gold"
            LET Tolerance = 5
        CASE "silver"
            LET Tolerance = 10
        CASE ELSE
            LET Tolerance = 20
        END SELECT
    END FUNCTION

    SUB Bad_color
        SOUND 500,.5
        PRINT
        PRINT "The color you entered doesn't"
        PRINT "make sense... try again"
        PRINT
    END SUB

! Start with a clean slate
    CLEAR

! Title of program
    PRINT "* Resistor color codes *"
    PRINT

! Tell user the legal color names
    PRINT "Color stripe names:"
    PRINT
    PRINT "   black       brown       red"
    PRINT "   orange      yellow      green"
    PRINT "   blue        violet      gray"
    PRINT "   white       gold        silver"
    PRINT
```

92

```
! Ask for the first color stripe
  DO
        INPUT PROMPT "Color of stripe #1 ": A$
        LET N = Stripe_value
        IF N = 99 THEN CALL Bad_color
  LOOP UNTIL N <> 99
  LET R = N

! Ask for second color stripe
  DO
        INPUT PROMPT "Color of stripe #2 ": A$
        LET N = Stripe_value
        IF N = 99 THEN CALL Bad_color
  LOOP UNTIL N <> 99
  LET R = R * 10 + N

! Ask for the third color stripe
  DO
        INPUT PROMPT "Color of stripe #3 ": A$
        LET N = Multiplier
        IF N = 99 THEN CALL Bad_color
  LOOP UNTIL N <> 99
  LET R = R * N

! Ask for the fourth color stripe
  INPUT PROMPT "Color of stripe #4 ": A$
  LET T = Tolerance

! Print the calculated resistance and tolerance values
  PRINT
  PRINT "Resistance = ";R;" ohms"
  PRINT "Tolerance  = ";T;" percent"

! Wait for any key press
  PRINT
  PRINT "Press any key to continue..."
  GET KEY Before_quitting

! All done
  END
```

Example: What is the resistance and tolerance of a resistor with color stripes of yellow, violet, red, and gold? See Fig. 4-6 for the answer.

R_PARALL

This program (Listing 4-7) calculates the equivalent resistance of two or more resistors connected in parallel. A calculation for two 4700-ohm resistors in parallel with one of 2000 ohms is shown below.

* Resistors in parallel *

How many resistors in parallel ? 3
Resistance of resistor 1 ?   2000

```
  * Resistor color codes *

  Color stripe names:

     black      brown       red
     orange     yellow      green
     blue       violet      gray
     white      gold        silver

  Color of stripe #1 yellow
  Color of stripe #2 violet
  Color of stripe #3 red
  Color of stripe #4 gold

  Resistance  =  4700 ohms
  Tolerance   =  5 percent

  Press any key to continue...
```

Fig. 4-6. Typical run of the resistor color code program.

```
    Resistance of resistor 2 ?   4700
    Resistance of resistor 3 ?   4700

    Total resistance = 1080.46

    Press any key to continue . . .
```

Listing 4-7. Parallel resistance program.

```
 !  **********************************
 !  **   File:       R_PARALL.TRU    **
 !  **   Date:       6/11/85         **
 !  **   Author:     John Craig      **
 !  **   Language:   True BASIC      **
 !  **********************************
 !
 !  This program calculates equivalent resistance for two or
 !  more resistors in parallel.

 !  Start with a clean slate.
    CLEAR
```

```
! Heading
  PRINT "* Resistors in parallel *"
  PRINT

! Ask user how many resistors are involved
  INPUT PROMPT "How many resistors in parallel ? ":N

! Calculate the parallel equivalent resistance
  LET R = Ø .
  FOR I = 1 TO N
      PRINT "Resistance of resistor ";I;
      INPUT X
      IF R > Ø THEN
          LET R = R * X / (R+X)
      ELSE
          LET R = X
      END IF
  NEXT I
  PRINT "Total resistance = ";R
  PRINT

! Wait for user to press any key
  PRINT "Press any key to continue..."
  DO
  LOOP UNTIL KEY INPUT

! All done
  END
```

R_SERIES

This program (Listing 4-8) calculates the equivalent resistance of two or more resistors connected in series. Here's a series calculation using the three resistances from the preceding example.

* Resistors in series *

How many resistors in series ? 3
Resistance of resistor 1 ?   2000
Resistance of resistor 2 ?   4700
Resistance of resistor 3 ?   4700
Total resistance = 11400

Press any key to continue . . .

R_DELWYE

This program (Listing 4-9) calculates the equivalent resistive wye network for a given delta network. (These two types of networks are shown in Fig. 4-7.)

Listing 4-8. Series resistance calculation program.

```
! *********************************
! ** File:       R_SERIES.TRU  **
! ** Date:       6/11/85       **
! ** Author:     John Craig    **
! ** Language:   True BASIC    **
! *********************************
!
! This program calculates equivalent resistance for two or
! more resistors in series.
! Start with a clean slate
  CLEAR

! Heading
  PRINT "* Resistors in series *"
  PRINT

! Ask user how many resistors are involved
  INPUT PROMPT "How many resistors in series ? ":N

! Calculate the series equivalent resistance
  LET R = Ø
  FOR I = 1 TO N
      PRINT "Resistance of resistor ";I;
      INPUT X
      LET R = R + X
  NEXT I
  PRINT "Total resistance = ";R
  PRINT

! Wait for user to press any key
  PRINT "Press any key to continue..."
  DO
  LOOP UNTIL KEY INPUT

! All done
  END
```

Listing 4-9. Resistive delta-wye conversion program.

```
! ************************************
! ** File:       R_DELWYE.TRU   **
! ** Date:       6/11/85        **
! ** Author:     John Craig     **
! ** Language:   True BASIC     **
! ************************************
!
! This program converts a delta resistive network
! to the equivalent wye network.
! Start with a clean slate
  CLEAR

! Heading
  PRINT "* Resistive Delta to Wye Network Conversion *"
  PRINT
```

```
! Ask user for the delta network to convert
  PRINT "Delta network..."
  INPUT PROMPT "First resistance ?   ":R1
  INPUT PROMPT "Second resistance ?  ":R2
  INPUT PROMPT "Third resistance ?   ":R3

! Calculate the equivalent wye network
  LET Ra = R2*R3/(R1+R2+R3)
  LET Rb = R1*R3/(R1+R2+R3)
  LET Rc = R1*R2/(R1+R2+R3)

! Display the results
  PRINT
  PRINT "Wye network equivalent..."
  PRINT "Opposite first resistance  = ";Ra
  PRINT "Opposite second resistance = ";Rb
  PRINT "Opposite third resistance  = ";Rc

! Wait for user to press any key
  PRINT
  PRINT "Press any key to continue..."
  DO
  LOOP UNTIL KEY INPUT

! All done
  END
```

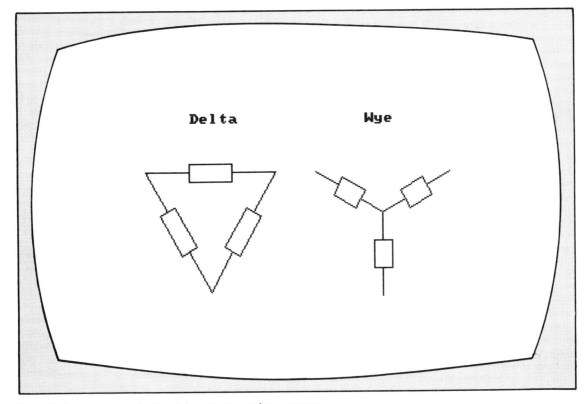

Fig. 4-7. Circuit diagram for the delta-wye conversion programs.

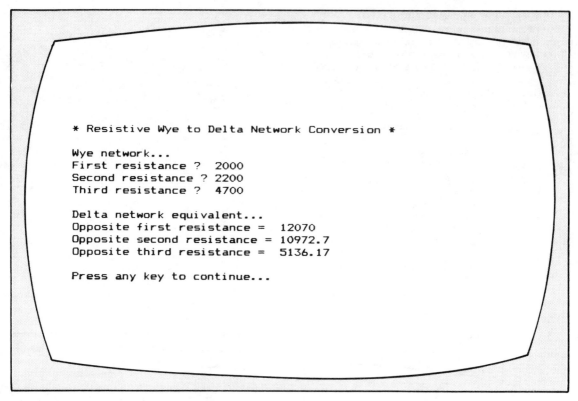

```
* Resistive Wye to Delta Network Conversion *

Wye network...
First resistance ?  2000
Second resistance ? 2200
Third resistance ?  4700

Delta network equivalent...
Opposite first resistance =   12070
Opposite second resistance = 10972.7
Opposite third resistance =  5136.17

Press any key to continue...
```

Fig. 4-8. Input screen for delta-wye resistive network conversion.

Example: What is the equivalent wye network for a delta network comprised of 2000-, 2200-, and 4700-ohm resistors? The calculation is shown in Fig. 4-8.

R_WYEDEL

This program (Listing 4-10) calculates the equivalent resistive delta network for a given wye network.

Example: What is the equivalent delta network for a wye network comprised of 2000-, 2200-, and 4700-ohm resistors? See Fig. 4-9 for the answer.

Listing 4-10. Resistive wye-delta conversion program.

```
! **********************************
! **  File:       R_WYEDEL.TRU   **
! **  Date:       6/11/85        **
! **  Author:     John Craig     **
! **  Language:   True BASIC     **
! **********************************
!
! This program converts a wye resistive network
! to the equivalent delta network.
```

```
! Start with a clean slate
  CLEAR

! Heading
  PRINT "* Resistive Wye to Delta Network Conversion *"
  PRINT

! Ask user for the wye network to convert
  PRINT "Wye network..."
  INPUT PROMPT "First resistance ?   ":Ra
  INPUT PROMPT "Second resistance ? ":Rb
  INPUT PROMPT "Third resistance ?   ":Rc

! Calculate the equivalent delta network
  LET R1 = (Ra*Rb+Rb*Rc+Rc*Ra)/Ra
  LET R2 = (Ra*Rb+Rb*Rc+Rc*Ra)/Rb
  LET R3 = (Ra*Rb+Rb*Rc+Rc*Ra)/Rc

! Display the results
  PRINT
  PRINT "Delta network equivalent..."
  PRINT "Opposite first resistance  = ";R1
  PRINT "Opposite second resistance = ";R2
  PRINT "Opposite third resistance  = ";R3
  PRINT

! Wait for user to press any key
  PRINT "Press any key to continue..."
  DO
  LOOP UNTIL KEY INPUT

! All done
  END
```

R__MENU

This program (Listing 4-11) demonstrates a method of running a group of similar programs from one common menu. Any of five resistance analysis programs may be selected from this menu; when the selected program finishes, you will be returned to this menu to select another program.

To make a menu selection, press the key indicated by the angle brackets. For instance, to select series resistors, press the S key and the program will run the **R__SERIES** program by use of the **CHAIN** statement.

* Resistors *

<S>eries resistors
<P>arallel resistors
<B>ridge balancing
<D>elta to wye conversion
<Q>uit

Press one of the indicated letters . . .

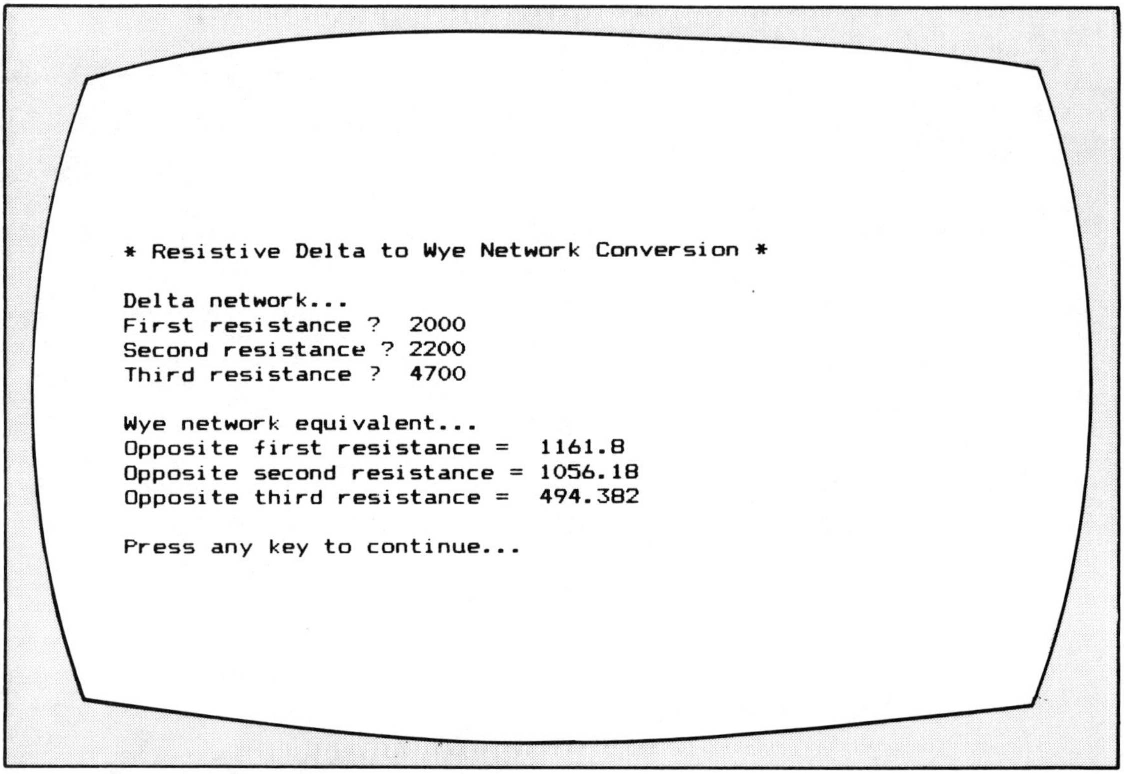

```
     * Resistive Delta to Wye Network Conversion *

     Delta network...
     First resistance ?  2000
     Second resistance ? 2200
     Third resistance ?  4700

     Wye network equivalent...
     Opposite first resistance =  1161.8
     Opposite second resistance = 1056.18
     Opposite third resistance =  494.382

     Press any key to continue...
```

Fig. 4-9. Input screen for wye-delta conversion.

Listing 4-11. Menu program for resistance calculations.

```
!  ********************************
!  **  File:       R_MENU.TRU     **
!  **  Date:       6/7/85         **
!  **  Author:     John Craig     **
!  **  Language:   True BASIC     **
!  ********************************
!
!
! This program calculates equivalent circuits for networks
! of resistors.  Five common resistance calculations may be
! selected...
!
! Resistors in series
! Resistors in parallel
! Resistive bridge balancing
! Delta to wye network conversion
! Wye to delta network conversion

! Wait for user to make a valid selection
DO

   ! Clean slate
   CLEAR
```

```
   ! Heading
     PRINT "* Resistors *"
     PRINT

   ! Print the menu
     PRINT "<S>eries resistors"
     PRINT "<P>arallel resistors"
     PRINT "<B>ridge balancing"
     PRINT "<D>elta to wye conversion"
     PRINT "<W>ye to delta conversion"
     PRINT "<Q>uit"
     PRINT
     PRINT "Press one of the indicated letters..."
     PRINT

   ! Wait for a key press
     DO
     LOOP UNTIL KEY INPUT

   ! Grab the key and convert to a character
     GET KEY Key_code
     LET Key_code$ = Ucase$(Chr$(Key_code))

   ! Check for valid selection
     IF Key_code$ = "S" THEN CHAIN "R_SERIES",RETURN
     IF Key_code$ = "P" THEN CHAIN "R_PARALL",RETURN
     IF Key_code$ = "B" THEN CHAIN "R_BRIDGE",RETURN
     IF Key_code$ = "D" THEN CHAIN "R_DELWYE",RETURN
     IF Key_code$ = "W" THEN CHAIN "R_WYEDEL",RETURN
     IF Key_code$ = "Q" THEN LET Quit_flag = 1

   ! Hang around until a valid key press
  LOOP UNTIL Quit_flag = 1

! End of program
  END
```

Z__POLREC

This program (Listing 4-12) converts impedances expressed in polar notation (magnitude and phase angle) to rectangular notation (resistance and reactance). The library named **ANGLES** is used by this program.

Example: Convert an impedance of 1000 ohms at 37.2 degrees phase angle to rectangular notation. Figure 4-10 shows this example run.

Listing 4-12. Polar to rectangular coordinate conversion program for impedances.

```
! **********************************
! **   File:      Z_POLREC.TRU   **
! **   Date:      6/12/85        **
! **   Author:    John Craig      **
! **   Language:  True BASIC      **
! **********************************
!
! This program converts impedances expressed in
```

```
! magnitude/phase-angle notation to resistance/reactance
! notation.

  LIBRARY "ANGLES"

! Start with a clean slate
  CLEAR

! Heading
  PRINT "* Magnitude/phase-angle to resistance/reactance *"
  PRINT

! Which type of phase angle?
  PRINT "<R>adian or <D>egree angular units ?"
  DO
      IF KEY INPUT THEN
          GET KEY Key_code
          LET Unit$ = Ucase$(Chr$(Key_code))
      END IF
  LOOP UNTIL Unit$ = "R" OR Unit$ = "D"

! Show which units were selected
  PRINT
  IF Unit$ = "D" THEN
      PRINT "Degrees..."
  ELSE
      PRINT "Radians..."
  END IF
  PRINT

! Ask for impedance
  PRINT "Impedance:"
  INPUT PROMPT "Magnitude   ? ":R
  INPUT PROMPT "Phase angle ? ":A
  PRINT

! Convert impedance to rectangular notation
  IF Unit$ = "D" THEN LET A = Rad(A)
  CALL Polar_rect(R,A,X,Y)

! Display the results
  PRINT "Equivalent impedence:"
  PRINT "Resistance = ";X
  PRINT "Reactance  = ";Y
  PRINT

! Wait for user to press any key
  PRINT "Press any key to continue..."
  DO
  LOOP UNTIL KEY INPUT

! All done
  END
```

Z_RECPOL

This program (Listing 4-13) converts impedances expressed in rectangular notation (resistance and reactance) to polar notation (magnitude and phase angle). This pro-

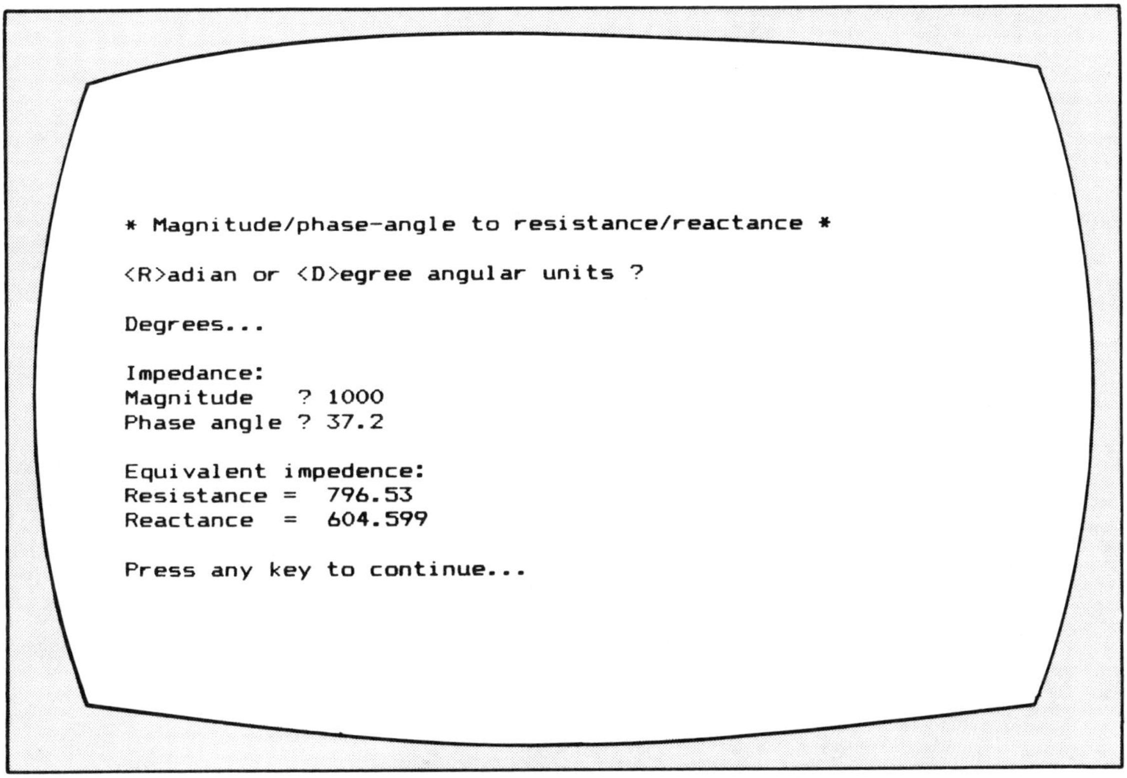

```
    * Magnitude/phase-angle to resistance/reactance *

    <R>adian or <D>egree angular units ?

    Degrees...

    Impedance:
    Magnitude   ? 1000
    Phase angle ? 37.2

    Equivalent impedence:
    Resistance =   796.53
    Reactance  =   604.599

    Press any key to continue...
```

Fig. 4-10. Converting magnitude/phase angle measurements to resistance and reactance.

Listing 4-13. Rectangular to polar coordinate conversion program.

```
  ! ********************************
  ! **  File:      Z_RECPOL.TRU    **
  ! **  Date:      6/12/85         **
  ! **  Author:    John Craig      **
  ! **  Language:  True BASIC      **
  ! ********************************
  !
  ! This program converts impedances expressed in
  ! resistance/reactance notation to magnitude/phase-angle
  ! notation.

    LIBRARY "ANGLES"

  ! Start with a clean slate
    CLEAR

  ! Heading
    PRINT "* Resistance/reactance to magnitude/phase-angle *"
    PRINT

  ! Which type of phase angle?
    PRINT "<R>adian or <D>egree angular units ?"
    DO
```

```
            IF KEY INPUT THEN
                GET KEY Key_code
                LET Unit$ = Ucase$(Chr$(Key_code))
            END IF
       LOOP UNTIL Unit$ = "R" OR Unit$ = "D"

    ! Show which units were selected
       PRINT
       IF Unit$ = "D" THEN
            PRINT "Degrees..."
       ELSE
            PRINT "Radians..."
       END IF
       PRINT

    ! Ask for impedance
       PRINT "Impedance:"
       INPUT PROMPT "Resistance ? ":X
       INPUT PROMPT "Reactance  ? ":Y
       PRINT

    ! Convert impedance rectangular to polar
       CALL Rect_polar(X,Y,R,A)
       IF Unit$ = "D" THEN LET A = Deg(A)

    ! Display the results
       PRINT "Equivalent impedence:"
       PRINT "Magnitude   = ";R
       PRINT "Phase angle = ";A
       PRINT

    ! Wait for user to press any key
       PRINT "Press any key to continue..."
       DO

       LOOP UNTIL KEY INPUT

    ! All done
       END
```

gram uses the library named **ANGLES**.

   Example: Convert an impedance of 2200 ohms resistance and 2817 ohms reactance to polar notation. See Fig. 4-11 for the calculation.

Z_BRIDGE

   This program (Listing 4-14) finds the unknown impedance in a common impedance bridge that balances the bridge. (Refer to Fig. 4-5 for a typical bridge circuit.) This program uses the library named **ANGLES**.

   Example: What impedance will balance a bridge comprised of an impedance of 1000 ohms at 37.2 degrees phase angle opposite the unknown impedance, and impedances of 2000 ohms at 14.9 degrees and 4700 ohms at −73.5 degrees next to the unknown? Figure 4-12 shows the calculation.

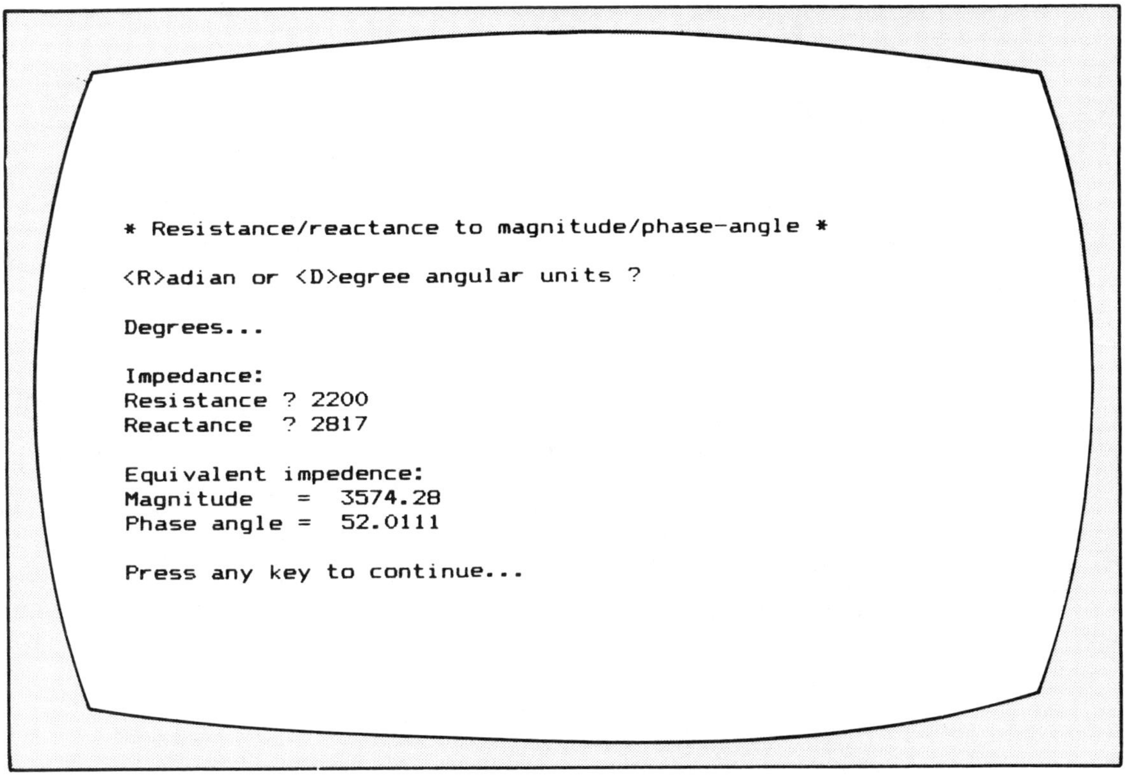

```
    * Resistance/reactance to magnitude/phase-angle *

    <R>adian or <D>egree angular units ?

    Degrees...

    Impedance:
    Resistance ? 2200
    Reactance  ? 2817

    Equivalent impedence:
    Magnitude   =   3574.28
    Phase angle =   52.0111

    Press any key to continue...
```

Fig. 4-11. Converting resistance/reactance measurements to magnitude and phase angle.

Listing 4-14. Program to balance an impedance bridge.

```
!  *********************************
!  **  File:      Z_BRIDGE.TRU    **
!  **  Date:      6/12/85         **
!  **  Author:    John Craig      **
!  **  Language:  True BASIC      **
!  *********************************
!
! This program calculates the impedance necessary to
! balance a bridge given the other three impedances.

   LIBRARY "ANGLES"

! Start with a clean slate
   CLEAR

! Heading
   PRINT "* Impedance bridge balancing *"
   PRINT

! Which type of phase angle units?
   PRINT "<R>adian or <D>egree angular units ?"
   DO
```

```
           IF KEY INPUT THEN
                 GET KEY Key_code
                 LET Unit$ = Ucase$(Chr$(Key_code))
           END IF
    LOOP UNTIL Unit$ = "R" OR Unit$ = "D"

 ! Show which units were selected
   PRINT
   IF Unit$ = "D" THEN
        PRINT "Degrees..."
   ELSE
        PRINT "Radians..."
   END IF
   PRINT

 ! Ask for impedance opposite unknown
   PRINT "Impedance opposite the unknown impedance:"
   INPUT PROMPT "Magnitude    ? ":Mag1
   INPUT PROMPT "Phase angle ? ":Ang1
   PRINT

 ! Ask for first impedance next to unknown
   PRINT "First impedance next to the unknown impedance:"
   INPUT PROMPT "Magnitude    ? ":Mag2
   INPUT PROMPT "Phase angle ? ":Ang2
   PRINT

 ! Ask for other impedance next to unknown
   PRINT "Other impedance next to the unknown impedance:"
   INPUT PROMPT "Magnitude    ? ":Mag3
   INPUT PROMPT "Phase angle ? ":Ang3
   PRINT

 ! Calculate the balancing impedance
   IF Unit$ = "D" THEN
        LET Ang1 = Rad(Ang1)
        LET Ang2 = Rad(Ang2)
        LET Ang3 = Rad(Ang3)
   END IF
   CALL Polar_rect(Mag2 * Mag3 / Mag1,Ang2 + Ang3 - Ang1,X,Y)
   CALL Rect_polar(X,Y,Mag,Ang)
   IF Unit$ = "D" THEN LET Ang = Deg(Ang)

 ! Display the results
   PRINT "Impedance to balance the bridge:"
   PRINT "Magnitude    = ";Mag
   PRINT "Phase angle = ";Ang
   PRINT

 ! Wait for user to press any key
   PRINT "Press any key to continue..."
   DO
   LOOP UNTIL KEY INPUT

 ! All done
   END
```

```
 ! ********************************
 ! **   File:        Impedance bridge balancing *
```

```
 * Impedance bridge balancing *

 <R>adian or <D>egree angular units ?

 Degrees...

 Impedance opposite the unknown impedance:
 Magnitude ?    1000
 Phase angle ? 37.2

 First impedance next to the unknown impedance:
 Magnitude    ? 2000
 Phase angle ? 14.9

 Other impedance next to the unknown impedance:
 Magnitude    ? 4700
 Phase angle ? -73.5

 Impedance to balance the bridge:
 Magnitude   =  9400.
 Phase angle = -95.8

 Press any key to continue...
```

Fig. 4-12. Balancing an impedance bridge.

Z_PARALL

This program (Listing 4-15) calculates the equivalent impedance of two impedances connected in parallel. This program uses the library named **ANGLES**.

Example: Two impedances, of 1000 ohms at 37.2 degrees and 2000 ohms at 14.9 degree are connected in parallel. What is the equivalent impedance? Figure 4-13 provides the answer.

Listing 4-15. Program to evaluate impedances in parallel.

```
 ! ********************************
 ! **   File:        Z_PARALL.TRU   **
 ! **   Date:        6/12/85        **
 ! **   Author:      John Craig     **
 ! **   Language:    True BASIC     **
 ! ********************************
 !
 ! This program calculates equivalent impedance
 ! for two impedances in parallel

 LIBRARY "ANGLES"
```

```
! Start with a clean slate
  CLEAR

! Heading
  PRINT "* Impedances in parallel *"
  PRINT

! Which type of angles?
  PRINT "<R>adian or <D>egree angular units ?"
  DO
       IF KEY INPUT THEN
            GET KEY Key_code
            LET Unit$ = Ucase$(Chr$(Key_code))
       END IF
  LOOP UNTIL Unit$ = "R" OR Unit$ = "D"

! Show which units were selected
  PRINT
  IF Unit$ = "D" THEN
       PRINT "Degrees..."
  ELSE
       PRINT "Radians..."
  END IF
  PRINT

! Ask for first impedance
  PRINT "First impedance:"
  INPUT PROMPT "Magnitude ":R
  INPUT PROMPT "Angle     ":A
  PRINT

! Convert 1 / Z1 to rectangular notation
  IF Unit$ = "D" THEN LET A = Rad(A)
  CALL Polar_rect(1/R,-A,X1,Y1)

! Ask for second impedance
  PRINT "Second impedance:"
  INPUT PROMPT "Magnitude ":R
  INPUT PROMPT "Angle     ":A
  PRINT

! Convert 1 / Z2 to rectangular notation
  IF Unit$ = "D" THEN LET A = Rad(A)
  CALL Polar_rect(1/R,-A,X2,Y2)

! Find sum and calculate 1 / result
  CALL Rect_polar(X1+X2,Y1+Y2,R,A)
  LET R = 1 / R
  LET A = -A
  IF Unit$ = "D" THEN LET A = Deg(A)

! Display the results
  PRINT "Parallel equivalent impedence:"
  PRINT "Magnitude = ";R
  PRINT "Angle     = ";A
  PRINT

! Wait for user to press any key
  PRINT "Press any key to continue..."
```

```
    DO
    LOOP UNTIL KEY INPUT

! All done
    END
```

Z__SERIES

This program (Listing 4-16) calculates the equivalent impedance of two impedances connected in series. This program uses the library named **ANGLES**.

Example: Two impedances, 1000 ohms at 37.2 degrees and 2000 ohms at 14.9 degrees; see Fig. 4-14 for the result.

Z__DELWYE

This program (Listing 4-17) calculates the equivalent wye impedance network for a given delta network; both configurations were introduced in Fig. 4-7. The library named **ANGLES** is used by this program.

Example: The following three impedances are connected in a delta network: 1000 ohms at 37.2 degrees, 2000 ohms at 14.9 degrees, and 4700 ohms at −73.5 degrees. What is the equivalent wye network? Figure 4-15 shows the calculation.

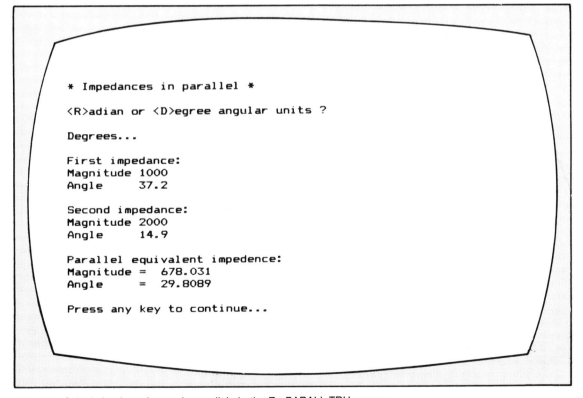

```
    * Impedances in parallel *

    <R>adian or <D>egree angular units ?

    Degrees...

    First impedance:
    Magnitude 1000
    Angle     37.2

    Second impedance:
    Magnitude 2000
    Angle     14.9

    Parallel equivalent impedence:
    Magnitude =  678.031
    Angle     =  29.8089

    Press any key to continue...
```

Fig. 4-13. Calculating impedances in parallel via the Z__PARALL.TRU program.

Listing 4-16. Program to evaluate impedances in series.

```
! *******************************
! **   File:        Z_SERIES.TRU    **
! **   Date:        6/11/85         **
! **   Author:      John Craig      **
! **   Language:    True BASIC      **
! *******************************
!
! This program calculates equivalent impedance
! for two impedances in series.

  LIBRARY "ANGLES"

! Start with a clean slate
  CLEAR

! Heading
  PRINT "* Impedances in series *"
  PRINT

! Which type of angles?
  PRINT "<R>adian or <D>egree angular units ?"
  DO
       IF KEY INPUT THEN
            GET KEY Key_code
            LET Unit$ = Ucase$(Chr$(Key_code))
       END IF
  LOOP UNTIL Unit$ = "R" OR Unit$ = "D"

! Show which units were selected
  PRINT
  IF Unit$ = "D" THEN
       PRINT "Degrees..."
  ELSE
       PRINT "Radians..."
  END IF
  PRINT

! Ask for first impedance
  PRINT "First impedance:"
  INPUT PROMPT "Magnitude ":R
  INPUT PROMPT "Angle     ":A
  PRINT

! Convert first impedance to rectangular notation
  IF Unit$ = "D" THEN LET A = Rad(A)
  CALL Polar_rect(R,A,X1,Y1)

! Ask for second impedance
  PRINT "Second impedance:"
  INPUT PROMPT "Magnitude ":R
  INPUT PROMPT "Angle     ":A
  PRINT

! Convert second impedance to rectangular notation
  IF Unit$ = "D" THEN LET A = Rad(A)
  CALL Polar_rect(R,A,X2,Y2)
```

```
! Sum the two impedances and convert back to polar
  CALL Rect_polar(X1+X2,Y1+Y2,R,A)
  IF Unit$ = "D" THEN LET A = Deg(A)

! Display the results
  PRINT "Series equivalent impedence:"
  PRINT "Magnitude = ";R
  PRINT "Angle     = ";A
  PRINT

! Wait for user to press any key
  PRINT "Press any key to continue..."
  DO
  LOOP UNTIL KEY INPUT

! All done
  END
```

Z__WYEDEL

This program (Listing 4-18) calculates the equivalent delta impedance network for a given wye network, using the library named **ANGLES**.

Example: The following three impedances are connected in a wye network: 1000 ohms at 37.2 degrees, 2000 ohms at 14.9 degrees, and 4700 ohms at −73.5 degrees.

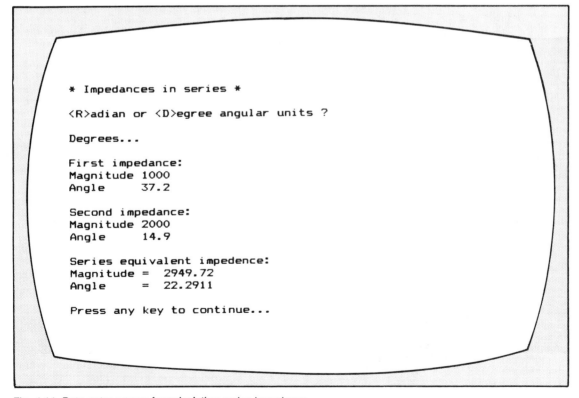

```
* Impedances in series *

<R>adian or <D>egree angular units ?

Degrees...

First impedance:
Magnitude 1000
Angle      37.2

Second impedance:
Magnitude 2000
Angle      14.9

Series equivalent impedence:
Magnitude =  2949.72
Angle      =  22.2911

Press any key to continue...
```

Fig. 4-14. Data entry screen for calculating series impedance.

Listing 4-17. Delta-to-wye conversion for impedances.

```
!  ********************************
!  **  File:       Z_DELWYE.TRU    **
!  **  Date:       6/12/85         **
!  **  Author:     John Craig      **
!  **  Language:   True BASIC      **
!  ********************************
!
!  This program converts a delta network of impedances to
!  the equivalent wye network.

   LIBRARY "ANGLES"

!  Start with a clean slate
   CLEAR

!  Heading
   PRINT "* Delta to wye impedance network conversion *"
   PRINT

!  Which type of phase angle units?
   PRINT "<R>adian or <D>egree angular units ?"
   DO
       IF KEY INPUT THEN
           GET KEY Key_code
           LET Unit$ = Ucase$(Chr$(Key_code))
       END IF
   LOOP UNTIL Unit$ = "R" OR Unit$ = "D"

!  Show which units were selected
   PRINT
   IF Unit$ = "D" THEN
       PRINT "Degrees..."
   ELSE
       PRINT "Radians..."
   END IF
   PRINT

!  Ask for first impedance
   PRINT "First impedance:"
   INPUT PROMPT "Magnitude   ? ":Mag_1
   INPUT PROMPT "Phase angle ? ":Ang_1
   PRINT

!  Ask for second impedance
   PRINT "Second impedance:"
   INPUT PROMPT "Magnitude   ? ":Mag_2
   INPUT PROMPT "Phase angle ? ":Ang_2
   PRINT

!  Ask for third impedance
   PRINT "Third impedance:"
   INPUT PROMPT "Magnitude   ? ":Mag_3
   INPUT PROMPT "Phase angle ? ":Ang_3
   PRINT

!  Convert the angles if degrees were selected
```

```
      IF Unit$ = "D" THEN
          LET Ang_1 = Rad(Ang_1)
          LET Ang_2 = Rad(Ang_2)
          LET Ang_3 = Rad(Ang_3)
      END IF

  ! Calculate the equivalent wye network
    CALL Polar_rect(Mag_1,Ang_1,X1,Y1)
    CALL Polar_rect(Mag_2,Ang_2,X2,Y2)
    CALL Polar_rect(Mag_3,Ang_3,X3,Y3)
    CALL Rect_polar(X1+X2+X3,Y1+Y2+Y3,Mag_4,Ang_4)
    LET Mag_a = Mag_2 * Mag_3 / Mag_4
    LET Mag_b = Mag_1 * Mag_3 / Mag_4
    LET Mag_c = Mag_1 * Mag_2 / Mag_4
    LET Ang_a = Ang_2 + Ang_3 - Ang_4
    LET Ang_b = Ang_1 + Ang_3 - Ang_4
    LET Ang_c = Ang_1 + Ang_2 - Ang_4

  ! Bring the angles into the proper range
    CALL Normalize(Mag_a,Ang_a)
    CALL Normalize(Mag_b,Ang_b)
    CALL Normalize(Mag_c,Ang_c)

  ! Convert the angles if degrees were selected
    IF Unit$ = "D" THEN
        LET Ang_a = Deg(Ang_a)
        LET Ang_b = Deg(Ang_b)
        LET Ang_c = Deg(Ang_c)
    END IF

  ! Display the first resultant impedance
    PRINT "Impedance opposite the first:"
    PRINT "Magnitude   = ";Mag_a
    PRINT "Phase angle = ";Ang_a
    PRINT

  ! Display second resultant impedance
    PRINT "Impedance opposite the second:"
    PRINT "Magnitude   = ";Mag_b
    PRINT "Phase angle = ";Ang_b
    PRINT

  ! Display third resultant impedance
    PRINT "Impedance opposite the third:"
    PRINT "Magnitude   = ";Mag_c
    PRINT "Phase angle = ";Ang_c
    PRINT

  ! Wait for user to press any key
    PRINT "Press any key to continue..."
    DO
    LOOP UNTIL KEY INPUT

  ! All done
    END

  ! Brings the angles into the range +/- 2*PI radians
    SUB Normalize(Mag,Ang)
        CALL Polar_rect(Mag,Ang,X,Y)
        CALL Rect_polar(X,Y,Mag,Ang)
    END SUB
```

```
      * Delta to wye impedance network conversion *

      <R>adian or <D>egree angular units ?

      Degrees...

      First impedance:
      Magnitude   ? 1000
      Phase angle ? 37.2

      Second impedance:
      Magnitude   ? 2000
      Phase angle ? 14.9

      Third impedance:
      Magnitude   ? 4700
      Phase angle ? -73.5

      Impedance opposite the first:
      Magnitude   =  1776.65
      Phase angle = -18.7878

      Impedance opposite the second:
      Magnitude   =  888.326
      Phase angle =  3.51217

      Impedance opposite the third:
      Magnitude   =  378.011
      Phase angle =  91.9122

      Press any key to continue...
```

Fig. 4-15. Delta-to-wye impedance network calculation.

Listing 4-18. Wye-to-delta impedance conversion.

```
   ! *********************************
   ! **  File:      Z_WYEDEL.TRU    **
   ! **  Date:      6/12/85         **
   ! **  Author:    John Craig      **
   ! **  Language:  True BASIC      **
   ! *********************************
   !
   ! This program converts a wye network of impedances to
   ! the equivalent delta network.
   !

     LIBRARY "ANGLES"

   ! Start with a clean slate
     CLEAR

   ! Heading
     PRINT "* Wye to delta impedance network conversion *"
     PRINT

   ! Which type of phase angle units?
     PRINT "<R>adian or <D>egree angular units ?"
```

```
         DO
             IF KEY INPUT THEN
                 GET KEY Key_code
                 LET Unit$ = Ucase$(Chr$(Key_code))
             END IF
         LOOP UNTIL Unit$ = "R" OR Unit$ = "D"

      ! Show which units were selected
         PRINT
         IF Unit$ = "D" THEN
             PRINT "Degrees..."
         ELSE
             PRINT "Radians..."
         END IF
         PRINT

      ! Ask for first impedance
         PRINT "First impedance:"
         INPUT PROMPT "Magnitude    ? ":Mag_a
         INPUT PROMPT "Phase angle ? ":Ang_a
         PRINT

      ! Ask for second impedance
         PRINT "Second impedance:"
         INPUT PROMPT "Magnitude    ? ":Mag_b
         INPUT PROMPT "Phase angle ? ":Ang_b
         PRINT

      ! Ask for third impedance
         PRINT "Third impedance:"
         INPUT PROMPT "Magnitude    ? ":Mag_c
         INPUT PROMPT "Phase angle ? ":Ang_c
         PRINT

      ! Convert the angles if degrees were selected
         IF Unit$ = "D" THEN
             LET Ang_a = Rad(Ang_a)
             LET Ang_b = Rad(Ang_b)
             LET Ang_c = Rad(Ang_c)
         END IF

      ! Calculate the equivalent delta impedances
         CALL Polar_rect(Mag_a * Mag_b,Ang_a + Ang_b,X1,Y1)
         CALL Polar_rect(Mag_b * Mag_c,Ang_b + Ang_c,X2,Y2)
         CALL Polar_rect(Mag_c * Mag_a,Ang_c + Ang_a,X3,Y3)
         CALL Rect_polar(X1+X2+X3,Y1+Y2+Y3,Mag_d,Ang_d)
         LET Mag_1 = Mag_d / Mag_a
         LET Mag_2 = Mag_d / Mag_b
         LET Mag_3 = Mag_d / Mag_c
         LET Ang_1 = Ang_d - Ang_a
         LET Ang_2 = Ang_d - Ang_b
         LET Ang_3 = Ang_d - Ang_c

      ! Bring the angles into the proper range
         CALL Normalize(Mag_1,Ang_1)
         CALL Normalize(Mag_2,Ang_2)
         CALL Normalize(Mag_3,Ang_3)

      ! Convert the angles if degrees were selected
```

```
     IF Unit$ = "D" THEN
          LET Ang_1 = Deg(Ang_1)
          LET Ang_2 = Deg(Ang_2)
          LET Ang_3 = Deg(Ang_3)
     END IF

   ! Display the first resultant impedance
     PRINT "Impedance opposite the first:"
     PRINT "Magnitude   = ";Mag_1
     PRINT "Phase angle = ";Ang_1
     PRINT

   ! Display second resultant impedance
     PRINT "Impedance opposite the second:"
     PRINT "Magnitude   = ";Mag_2
     PRINT "Phase angle = ";Ang_2
     PRINT

   ! Display third resultant impedance
     PRINT "Impedance opposite the third:"
     PRINT "Magnitude   = ";Mag_3
     PRINT "Phase angle = ";Ang_3
     PRINT

   ! Wait for user to press any key
     DO
     LOOP UNTIL KEY INPUT

   ! All done
     END

   ! Brings the angles into the range +/- 2*PI radians
     SUB Normalize(Mag,Ang)
          CALL Polar_rect(Mag,Ang,X,Y)
          CALL Rect_polar(X,Y,Mag,Ang)
     END SUB
```

What is the equivalent delta network? See Fig. 4-16 for the results.

Z__MENU

This program (Listing 4-19) demonstrates a method of running a group of similar programs from one common menu. Any of five impedance analysis programs may be selected from the menu shown in Fig. 4-17; when the selected program finishes, you will be returned to this menu to select another program.

To make a menu selection, press the key indicated by the angle brackets. For instance, to select series impedances, press the S key and the program will run the **Z__SERIES** program by the use of the **CHAIN** statement.

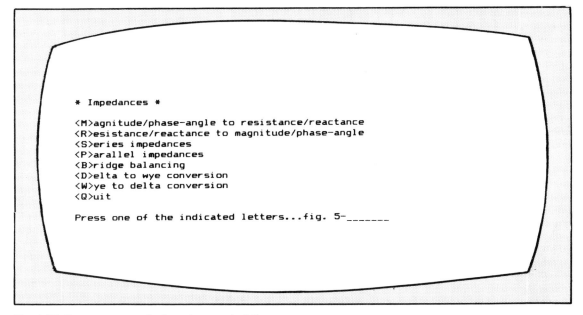

```
* Wye to delta impedance network conversion *

<R>adian or <D>egree angular units ?

Degrees...

First impedance:
Magnitude   ? 1000
Phase angle ? 37.2

Second impedance:
Magnitude   ? 2000
Phase angle ? 14.9

Third impedance:
Magnitude   ? 4700
Phase angle ? -73.5

Impedance opposite the first:
Magnitude   =  13543.8
Phase angle = -80.1467

Impedance opposite the second:
Magnitude   =  6771.92
Phase angle = -57.8467

Impedance opposite the third:
Magnitude   =  2881.67
Phase angle =  30.5533
```

Fig. 4-16. Wye-to-delta impedance network calculation.

```
* Impedances *

<M>agnitude/phase-angle to resistance/reactance
<R>esistance/reactance to magnitude/phase-angle
<S>eries impedances
<P>arallel impedances
<B>ridge balancing
<D>elta to wye conversion
<W>ye to delta conversion
<Q>uit

Press one of the indicated letters...fig. 5-_____
```

Fig. 4-17. On-screen menu for impedance calculations.

Listing 4-19. Menu program for impedance calculations.

```
! **********************************
! **  File:       Z_MENU.TRU    **
! **  Date:       6/7/85        **
! **  Author:     John Craig    **
! **  Language:   True BASIC    **
! **********************************
!
! This program calculates equivalent circuits for networks
! of impedances.  Seven common impedance calculations may
! be selected...
!
! Convert magnitude/phase-angle to resistance/reactance
! Convert resistance/reactance to magnitude/phase-angle
! Impedances in series
! Impedances in parallel
! Impedance bridge balancing
! Delta to wye network conversion
! Wye to delta network conversion

! Wait for user to make a valid selection
  DO

      ! Clean slate
      CLEAR

      ! Heading
      PRINT "* Impedances *"
      PRINT

      ! Print the menu
      PRINT "<M>agnitude/phase-angle to resistance/reactance"
      PRINT "<R>esistance/reactance to magnitude/phase-angle"
      PRINT "<S>eries impedances"
      PRINT "<P>arallel impedances"
      PRINT "<B>ridge balancing"
      PRINT "<D>elta to wye conversion"
      PRINT "<W>ye to delta conversion"
      PRINT "<Q>uit"
      PRINT
      PRINT "Press one of the indicated letters..."
      PRINT

      ! Wait for a key press
      DO
      LOOP UNTIL KEY INPUT

      ! Grab the key and convert to a character
      GET KEY Key_code
      LET Key_code$ = Ucase$(Chr$(Key_code))

      ! Check for valid selection
      IF Key_code$ = "M" THEN CHAIN "Z_POLREC",RETURN
      IF Key_code$ = "R" THEN CHAIN "Z_RECPOL",RETURN
      IF Key_code$ = "S" THEN CHAIN "Z_SERIES",RETURN
      IF Key_code$ = "P" THEN CHAIN "Z_PARALL",RETURN
      IF Key_code$ = "B" THEN CHAIN "Z_BRIDGE",RETURN
```

```
            IF Key_code$ = "D" THEN CHAIN "Z_DELWYE",RETURN
            IF Key_code$ = "W" THEN CHAIN "Z_WYEDEL",RETURN
            IF Key_code$ = "Q" THEN LET Quit_flag = 1

        ! Hang around until a valid key press
      LOOP UNTIL Quit_flag = 1

   ! End of program
      END
```

Chapter 5

Analytical

Geometry and Math

The programs in this chapter demonstrate the very powerful, fast, and easy-to-use mathematical capabilities of True BASIC.

CIRCLE3P

This program demonstrates a subroutine for finding the center coordinates and radius of a circle that passes through any three given points. If the points fall on a straight line, the subroutine returns the value of **MAXNUM** for the radius.

The short subroutine named **Swap** is useful for the common task of switching the contents of two numerical variables. As an exercise, you might try writing a similar subroutine for switching the contents of two string variables.

The one-line function named **Hypot** also solves a common problem: finding the length of the hypotenuse of a right triangle, given the lengths of the two sides. This function is used several places throughout this book.

Example: What circle just touches the points (1,1), (7,8) and (5,12)? Shown below is the sample run; Fig. 5-1 is the plotted output and Listing 5-1 is the program code.

```
* CIRCLE3P *

Enter three X,Y points . . .

X1,Y1 1,1
X2,Y2 7,8
```

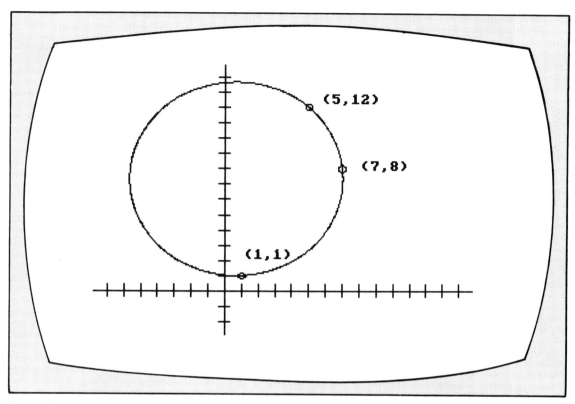

Fig. 5-1. Circle determined by CIRCLE3P program.

Listing 5-1. CIRCLE3P.TRU program.

```
!  ************************************
!  **   File:      CIRCLE3P.TRU    **
!  **   Date:      7/19/85         **
!  **   Author:    John Craig      **
!  **   Language:  True BASIC      **
!  ************************************
!
! This program finds the center and radius of the
! circle that passes through three given X,Y points.

! Start with a clean slate
  CLEAR

! Display program name
  PRINT "* CIRCLE3P *"
  PRINT

! Ask user for three points
  PRINT "Enter three X,Y points..."
  PRINT
  INPUT PROMPT "X1,Y1 ": X1,Y1
  INPUT PROMPT "X2,Y2 ": X2,Y2
  INPUT PROMPT "X3,Y3 ": X3,Y3
```

```
 ! Calculate circle
   CALL Circle_3(X1,Y1,X2,Y2,X3,Y3,Xcenter,Ycenter,Radius)

 ! Display the results
   PRINT
   IF Radius = Maxnum THEN
       PRINT "They fall on a straight line"
   ELSE
       PRINT "Radius = ";Radius
       PRINT "Center... X = ";Xcenter;"   Y = ";Ycenter
       PRINT
   END IF

 ! Wait for a key press
   PRINT
   PRINT "Press any key..."
   GET KEY Before_continuing

 ! All done
   END

 ! Subroutine to find the center and radius of
 ! a circle given three X,Y points.  If the points
 ! fall on a straight line, then the radius is
 ! returned equal to MAXNUM
   SUB Circle_3(X1,Y1,X2,Y2,X3,Y3,Xcenter,Ycenter,Radius)

     ! Declare the Hypotenuse function
       DECLARE FUNCTION Hypot

     ! Make sure that point 1 is off to the side of point 2
       IF X1 = X2 THEN
           CALL Swap(X1,X3)
           CALL Swap(Y1,Y3)
       END IF

     ! Make sure that point 1 is off to the side of point 3
       IF X1 = X3 THEN
           CALL Swap(X1,X2)
           CALL Swap(Y1,Y2)
       END IF

     ! If two slopes are the same, then we have a straight line
       IF (Y3-Y1) * (X2-X1) = (Y2-Y1) * (X3-X1) THEN
           LET Radius = Maxnum
           LET Xcenter = 0
           LET Ycenter = 0

         ! Otherwise, we have a circle
       ELSE
           LET Calc_2 = ((X2-X1)*(X1+X2) + (Y2-Y1)*(Y1+Y2)) / (X2-X1) / 2
           LET Calc_3 = ((X3-X1)*(X1+X3) + (Y3-Y1)*(Y1+Y3)) / (X3-X1) / 2
           LET Slope_2 = (Y2-Y1) / (X2-X1)
           LET Slope_3 = (Y3-Y1) / (X3-X1)
           LET Ycenter = (Calc_3 - Calc_2) / (Slope_3 - Slope_2)
           LET Xcenter = Calc_3 - Slope_3 * Ycenter
           LET Radius = Hypot(X1 - Xcenter, Y1 - Ycenter)
       END IF
```

```
        ! End of the Circle_3 subroutine
    END SUB

! Subroutine to switch contents of two variables
    SUB Swap(A,B)
        LET Temporary = A
        LET A = B
        LET B = Temporary
    END SUB

! Calculates hypotenuse, given sides X and Y
    FUNCTION Hypot(X,Y) = Sqr(X * X + Y * Y)
```

X3,Y3 5,12

Radius = 6.34996
Center . . . X = .684211 Y = 7.34211

Press any key . . .

COORD3D

This program converts three-dimensional coordinates between the three common spatial coordinate systems: cartesian, spherical, and cylindrical.

This program (Listing 5-2) also presents a menu-building technique that you may find useful for other programming tasks. The function named **Choose** is passed a string array of menu selections and a string containing the prompt to be displayed at the head of the menu. Returned from the function is the number of the menu selection chosen. The **Choose** function is called twice, once to ask which of the three coordinate systems in which the original coordinates are expressed, and once to ask which type of angle measurements are assumed. This function is also used in the **MUSIC** program, if you wish to see a second example of its use.

Listing 5-2. Three-dimensional coordinate program COORD3D.TRU (continued through page 126).

```
! *********************************
! ** File:      COORD3D.TRU    **
! ** Date:      8/16/85        **
! ** Author:    John Craig     **
! ** Language:  True BASIC     **
! *********************************
!
! This program converts three dimensional coordinates
! between the cartesian, spherical, and cylindrical systems.

! Declare external functions
    DECLARE FUNCTION Choose

! Start with a clean slate
    CLEAR

! Set up first menu
```

```
    DIM Menu$(10)
    READ Question$
    FOR I = 1 TO 4
        READ Menu$(I)
    NEXT I
    DATA "Starting coordinate system ?"
    DATA Cartesian,Spherical,Cylindrical,""

! Ask user for starting coordinate system
    LET Start_system = Choose(Question$,Menu$)

! Set up menu for type of angle measurements
    READ Question$
    FOR I = 1 TO 3
        READ Menu$(I)
    NEXT I
    DATA "Which system for all angular measurements ?"
    DATA "Degrees","Radians",""

! Ask user for type of angle measurements
    LET Angle_units = Choose(Question$,Menu$)

! Ask user for required parameters
    SELECT CASE Start_system
    CASE 1     ! Cartesian
        INPUT PROMPT "X ? ": X
        INPUT PROMPT "Y ? ": Y
        INPUT PROMPT "Z ? ": Z
    CASE 2     ! Spherical
        INPUT PROMPT "Rho ? ": Rho
        INPUT PROMPT "Theta ? ": Theta
        INPUT PROMPT "Phi ? ": Phi
        IF Angle_units = 1 THEN
            LET Theta = Rad(Theta)
            LET Phi = Rad(Phi)
        END IF
        CALL Sph_car(Rho,Theta,Phi,X,Y,Z)
    CASE 3     ! Cylindrical
        INPUT PROMPT "R ? ": R
        INPUT PROMPT "Theta ? ": Theta
        INPUT PROMPT "Z ? ": Z
        IF Angle_units = 1 THEN
            LET Theta = Rad(Theta)
        END IF
        CALL Cyl_car(R,Theta,Z,X,Y,Z)
    END SELECT

! Calculate the rest given cartesian coordinates
    CALL Car_sph(X,Y,Z,Rho,Theta,Phi)
    CALL Car_cyl(X,Y,Z,R,Theta,Z)
    IF Angle_units = 1 THEN
        LET Theta = Deg(Theta)
        LET Phi = Deg(Phi)
    END IF

! Display all three systems
    PRINT
    PRINT "Cartesian (X,Y,Z) =",X,Y,Z
    PRINT "Spherical (Rho,Theta,Phi) =",Rho,Theta,Phi
    PRINT "Cylindrical (R,Theta,Z) =",R,Theta,Z
```

```
! Wait for key press
  PRINT
  PRINT "Press any key..."
  GET KEY Before_continuing

! All done
  END

! Function to help user make a menu selection
  FUNCTION Choose(Question$,Menu$())

    ! Display the question
      PRINT Question$
      PRINT

    ! Show the choices
      FOR I = 1 TO 10
          IF Menu$(I) = "" THEN
              LET Count = I - 1
              EXIT FOR
          ELSE
              PRINT USING "#. ": I;
              PRINT Menu$(I)
          END IF
      NEXT I
      PRINT

    ! Tell 'em what to do
      PRINT "Press the key for your choice...";

    ! Build the test string
      LET Test$ = "123456789"(1:Count)

    ! Wait until one of the keys is pressed
      DO

        ! Wait for any key press
          DO
          LOOP UNTIL KEY INPUT

        ! Grab the key and check for appropriate choice
          GET KEY Keycode
          LET Choice = Pos(Test$,Chr$(Keycode))
          IF Choice = 0 THEN SOUND 55,.2

        ! Keep trying for an appropriate key press
      LOOP UNTIL Choice > 0

    ! Send the choice back to the caller
      PRINT Choice
      PRINT
      PRINT
      LET Choose = Choice

  END FUNCTION

! Subroutine to convert Spherical coordinates to Cartesian
  SUB Sph_car(Rho,Theta,Phi,X,Y,Z)
      LET X = Rho * Cos(Theta) * Sin(Phi)
```

```
      LET Y = Rho * Sin(Theta) * Sin(Phi)
      LET Z = Rho * Cos(Phi)
   END SUB

! Subroutine to convert Spherical coordinates to Cylindrical
   SUB Sph_cyl(Rho,Theta1,Phi,R,Theta2,Z)
      LET R = Rho * Sin(Phi)
      LET Theta2 = Theta1
      LET Z = Rho * Cos(Phi)
   END SUB

! Subroutine to convert Cylindrical coordinates to Cartesian
   SUB Cyl_car(R,Theta,Z1,X,Y,Z2)
      LET X = R * Cos(Theta)
      LET Y = R * Sin(Theta)
      LET Z2 = Z1
   END SUB

! Subroutine to convert Cylindrical coordinates to Spherical
   SUB Cyl_sph(R,Theta1,Z,Rho,Theta2,Phi)
      LET Rho = Sqr(R^2 + Z^2)
      IF Rho <> 0 THEN
          LET Theta2 = Theta1
          IF Z <> 0 THEN
              LET Phi = Atn(Sqr(1-(Z/Rho)^2)/(Z/Rho))
          ELSE
              LET Phi = 2 * Atn(1)
          END IF
      ELSE
          LET Theta2 = 0
          LET Phi = 0
      END IF
   END SUB

! Subroutine to convert Cartesian coordinates to Spherical
   SUB Car_sph(X,Y,Z,Rho,Theta,Phi)
      LET Rho = Sqr(X^2 + Y^2 + Z^2)
      IF Rho <> 0 THEN
          LET Theta. = ANGLE(X,Y)
          IF Z <> 0 THEN
              LET Phi = Atn(Sqr(1-(Z/Rho)^2)/(Z/Rho))
          ELSE
              LET Phi = 2 * Atn(1)
          END IF
      ELSE
          LET Theta = 0
          LET Phi = 0
      END IF
   END SUB

! Subroutine to convert Cartesian coordinates to Cylindrical
   SUB Car_cyl(X,Y,Z1,R,Theta,Z2)
      LET R = Sqr(X^2 + Y^2)
      LET Theta = ANGLE(X,Y)
      LET Z2 = Z1
   END SUB
```

```
 Starting coordinate system ?

    1.  Cartesian
    2.  Spherical
    3.  Cylindrical

 Press the key for your choice... 1


 Which system for all angular measurements ?

    1.  Degrees
    2.  Radians

 Press the key for your choice...  1

 X ?  3
 Y ?  4
 Z ?  5

 Cartesian  (X,Y,Z) =            3        4         5
 Spherical  (Rho,Theta,Phi) =  7.07107  53.1301   45.
 Cylindrical (R,Theta,Z) =       5       53.1301    5

 Press any key...
```

Fig. 5-2. Data entry form for three-dimensional coordinate calculation.

Example: Convert the cartesian coordinates (3,4,5) to spherical and cylindrical equivalents, assuming all angles are measured in degrees. Figure 5-2 shows the session.

COMPLEX

In electrical or mechanical engineering, complex numbers are often used for much of the mathematical analysis involved. This program provides quick calculations for the four main functions of complex number math, as well as subroutines and functions that allow you to develop more complicated routines if necessary.

The program (Listing 5-3) displays a menu of the four calculation choices: addi-

Listing 5-3. COMPLEX.TRU program (continued to page 130).

```
! ***********************************
! ** File:       COMPLEX.TRU    **
! ** Date:       8/11/85        **
! ** Author:     John Craig     **
! ** Language:   True BASIC     **
! ***********************************
!
! This program demonstrates several useful subroutines
! and functions for complex number math
```

```
! Declare external functions
  DECLARE FUNCTION Complex$

! Start with a clean slate
  CLEAR

! Display program name
  PRINT "* COMPLEX *"
  PRINT

! Declare all complex number variables as small arrays
  DIM X(2),Y(2),Z(2)

! Ask user for the computation choice
  PRINT "Which complex math operation ?"
  PRINT
  PRINT "<+> Addition"
  PRINT "<-> Subtraction"
  PRINT "<*> Multiplication"
  PRINT "</> Division"
  PRINT
  PRINT "Press the key for your choice..."
  PRINT

! Wait until one of the keys is pressed
  DO

     ! Wait for any key press
     DO
     LOOP UNTIL KEY INPUT

     ! Grab the key and check for appropriate choice
     GET KEY Keycode
     LET Choice = Pos("+-*/",Chr$(Keycode))

     ! Keep trying for an appropriate key press
  LOOP UNTIL Choice > 0

! Ask user for required parameters and do the calculations
  SELECT CASE Choice
  CASE 1     ! Complex number addition
      PRINT "Complex addition"
      CALL ASK(X,Y)
      CALL Complex_add(X,Y,Z)
      PRINT Complex$(X);"plus";Complex$(Y);"is";Complex$(Z)
  CASE 2     ! Complex number subtraction
      PRINT "Complex subtraction"
      CALL ASK(X,Y)
      CALL Complex_sub(X,Y,Z)
      PRINT Complex$(X);"minus";Complex$(Y);"is";Complex$(Z)
  CASE 3     ! Complex number multiplication
      PRINT "Complex multiplication"
      CALL ASK(X,Y)
      CALL Complex_mul(X,Y,Z)
      PRINT Complex$(X);"times";Complex$(Y);"is";Complex$(Z)
  CASE 4     ! Complex number division
      PRINT "Complex division"
      CALL ASK(X,Y)
      CALL Complex_div(X,Y,Z)
```

```
            PRINT Complex$(X);"divided by";Complex$(Y);"is";Complex$(Z)
      END SELECT

! Wait for key press
   PRINT
   PRINT "Press any key..."
   GET KEY Before_continuing

! All done
   END

! Converts a complex number to string for output
   FUNCTION Complex$(C())
      LET A$ = Str$(C(1))
      LET B$ = Str$(Abs(C(2)))
      IF C(2) < Ø THEN
         LET Complex$ = " (" & A$ & "-i" & B$ & ") "
      ELSE
         LET Complex$ = " (" & A$ & "+i" & B$ & ") "
      END IF
   END FUNCTION

! Subroutine to ask user for two complex numbers
   SUB ASK(X(),Y())
      PRINT
      INPUT PROMPT "Enter first complex number (real,imag)...   ": X(1),X(2)
      INPUT PROMPT "Enter other complex number (real,imag)...   ": Y(1),Y(2)
      PRINT
   END SUB

! Subroutine to add two complex numbers
   SUB Complex_add(X(),Y(),Z())
      LET Z(1) = X(1) + Y(1)
      LET Z(2) = X(2) + Y(2)
   END SUB

! Subroutine to subtract two complex numbers
   SUB Complex_sub(X(),Y(),Z())
      LET Z(1) = X(1) - Y(1)
      LET Z(2) = X(2) - Y(2)
   END SUB

! Subroutine to multiply two complex numbers
   SUB Complex_mul(X(),Y(),Z())
      CALL Rect_polar(X(1),X(2),Rho1,Theta1)
      CALL Rect_polar(Y(1),Y(2),Rho2,Theta2)
      CALL Polar_rect(Rho1 * Rho2,Theta1 + Theta2,Z(1),Z(2))
   END SUB

! Subroutine to divide two complex numbers
   SUB Complex_div(X(),Y(),Z())
      CALL Rect_polar(X(1),X(2),Rho1,Theta1)
      CALL Rect_polar(Y(1),Y(2),Rho2,Theta2)
      CALL Polar_rect(Rho1 / Rho2,Theta1 - Theta2,Z(1),Z(2))
   END SUB

! Function to calculate hypotenuse, given sides X and Y
   FUNCTION Hypot(X,Y) = Sqr(X * X + Y * Y)

! Subroutine to convert rectangular to polar
```

```
SUB Rect_polar(X,Y,Rho,Theta)
    DECLARE FUNCTION Hypot
    LET Rho = Hypot(X,Y)
    LET Theta = ANGLE(X,Y)
END SUB

! Subroutine to convert polar to rectangular
SUB Polar_rect(Rho,Theta,X,Y)
    LET X = Rho * Cos(Theta)
    LET Y = Rho * Sin(Theta)
END SUB
```

tion, subtraction, multiplication, or division. A single keypress (detected in the program with the **KEY INPUT** statement) determines your choice. Each complex number is asked for, the math is performed, and the results are displayed in an easy-to-read format.

The four obvious functions for complex addition, subtraction, multiplication, and division are presented, as well as several other useful functions that are called by these routines. The **Hypot** function calculates the hypotenuse of a right triangle, given the other two sides, and is used by the rectangular-polar conversion routines; these are, in turn, used by the complex math routines.

Example: What is the result of multiplying the two complex numbers $(27 - i34)$ and $(-5 + i29.7)$? The completed run is shown in Fig. 5-3.

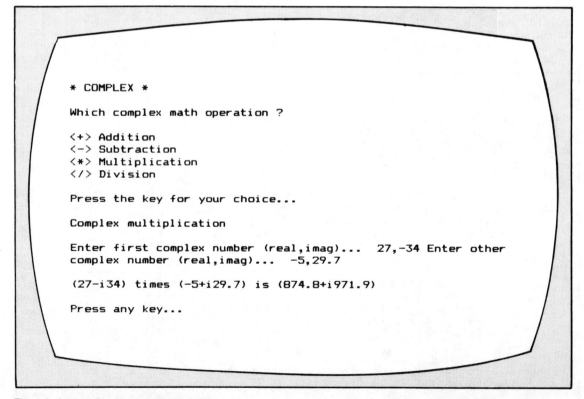

```
* COMPLEX *

Which complex math operation ?

<+> Addition
<-> Subtraction
<*> Multiplication
</> Division

Press the key for your choice...

Complex multiplication

Enter first complex number (real,imag)...  27,-34 Enter other
complex number (real,imag)...  -5,29.7

(27-i34) times (-5+i29.7) is (874.8+i971.9)

Press any key...
```

Fig. 5-3. Arithmetic with complex numbers.

DEC2FRAC

This program (Listing 5-4) calculates increasingly accurate fractional approximations to any given decimal number. A function to calculate the greatest common denominator of two numbers is also presented.

Listing 5-4. Decimal to fraction conversion program.

```
! ********************************
! ** File:      DEC2FRAC.TRU    **
! ** Date:      7/27/85         **
! ** Author:    John Craig      **
! ** Language:  True BASIC      **
! ********************************
!
! This program calculates fraction approximations
! for a given decimal number

! Start with a clean slate
  CLEAR

! Display program name
  PRINT "* DEC2FRAC *"
  PRINT

! Get the decimal number from the user
  INPUT PROMPT "Enter the decimal number... ? ": X
  PRINT

! Title the columns
  PRINT "Numerator","Denominator","Error"

! Do it to it
  LET T1 = 1
  LET T2 = 1
  LET T3 = 1
  CALL Divide(X,1,T4,T5)
  DO
      LET Num = T3 * T4 + T7
      LET Den = T4 * T8 + T2
      LET Err = Num / Den - X
      IF T5 <> 0 THEN
          LET T4 = Int(T1 / T5)
          LET T6 = T5
          LET T5 = T1 - T4 * T5
          LET T1 = T6
          LET T7 = T3
          LET T3 = Num
          LET T2 = T8
          LET T8 = Den
      END IF
      PRINT Num,Den,Err
  LOOP UNTIL Abs(Err) <= Eps(Num) OR Abs(Err) <= Eps(Den)

! Wait for key press
  PRINT
  PRINT "Press any key to continue..."
  GET KEY Before_continuing
```

```
! All done
  END

! Function to calculate the greatest common
! denominator of two numbers
!
  FUNCTION Greatest_common_denominator(A,B)
      DO
            LET C = Mod(A,B)
            LET A = B
            LET B = C
      LOOP WHILE C > Ø
      LET Greatest_common_denominator = A
  END FUNCTION
```

Example: Is it possible to design two meshing gears, each with less than 400 teeth, such that the ratio of their revolutions is the same as PI, accurate to at least one part in a million? The answer is yes; gears with 355 and 113 teeth each will satisfy the requirements, as shown by the sample calculation in Fig. 5-4.

FRACTION

This program (Listing 5-5) reduces a fraction to its lowest terms, using a function for finding the greatest common denominator. Here is a typical run:

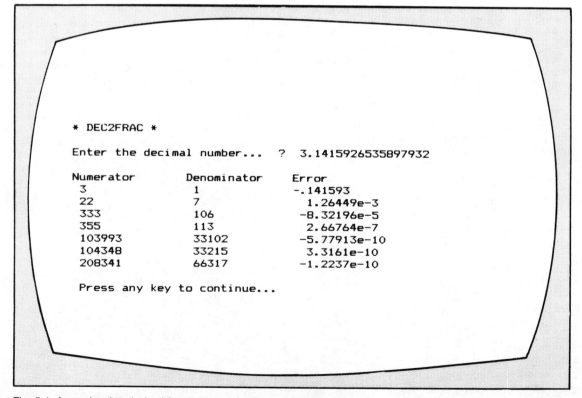

```
* DEC2FRAC *

Enter the decimal number...  ?  3.1415926535897932

Numerator           Denominator          Error
3                   1                    -.141593
22                  7                     1.26449e-3
333                 106                  -8.32196e-5
355                 113                   2.66764e-7
103993              33102                -5.77913e-10
104348              33215                 3.3161e-10
208341              66317                -1.2237e-10

Press any key to continue...
```

Fig. 5-4. Approximating decimal fractions as quotients of integers.

```
* FRACTION *

Enter the fraction . . . numerator,denominator ? 684,969

Greatest common denominator is 57

Reduced to lowest terms is 12 / 17

Press any key to continue . . .
```

Listing 5-5. FRACTION.TRU reduces a fraction to its lowest terms.

```
!  *********************************
!  **   File:       FRACTION.TRU    **
!  **   Date:       7/27/85         **
!  **   Author:     John Craig      **
!  **   Language:   True BASIC      **
!  *********************************
!
!  This program reduces a fraction to it's lowest terms.

!  Declare external function
   DECLARE FUNCTION Greatest_common_denominator

!  Start with a clean slate
   CLEAR

!  Display program name
   PRINT "* FRACTION *"
   PRINT

!  Get the fraction from the user
   PRINT "Enter the fraction... numerator,denominator ";
   INPUT Numerator,Denominator
   PRINT

!  Reduce it to lowest terms
   LET Gcd = Greatest_common_denominator(Numerator,Denominator)
   LET Numerator = Numerator / Gcd
   LET Denominator = Denominator / Gcd
   IF Gcd < 0 THEN
       LET Numerator = -Numerator
       LET Denominator = -Denominator
   END IF

!  Display the results
   PRINT "Greatest common denominator is";Gcd
   PRINT
   PRINT "Reduced to lowest terms is";Numerator;"/";Denominator
   PRINT

!  Wait for key press
   PRINT
   PRINT "Press any key to continue..."
   GET KEY Before_continuing
```

```
! All done
  END

! Function to calculate the greatest common
! denominator of two numbers
!
  FUNCTION Greatest_common_denominator(A,B)
      DO
            LET C = Mod(A,B)
            LET A = B
            LET B = C
      LOOP WHILE C > Ø
      LET Greatest_common_denominator = A
  END FUNCTION
```

LOGS

True BASIC provides three types of logarithm functions— **LOG2(X)**, **LOG10(X)**, and **LOG(X)**—which return logarithms in base 2 and base 10, as well as natural logarithms. This program (Listing 5-6) extends these capabilities by demonstrating a function that finds logarithms to any base.

Listing 5-6. LOGS.TRU calculates logarithms to any base.

```
! *********************************
! **   File:      LOGS.TRU       **
! **   Date:      8/11/85        **
! **   Author:    John Craig     **
! **   Language:  True BASIC     **
! *********************************
!
!
! This program demonstrates a function that
! can find logarithms to any desired base

! Declare external functions
  DECLARE FUNCTION Logarithm

! Start with a clean slate
  CLEAR

! Display program name
  PRINT "* LOGS *"
  PRINT

! Ask user stuff
  INPUT PROMPT "Enter a number X ? ": X
  INPUT PROMPT "Enter the base B ? ": B

! Show the results
  PRINT
  PRINT "The logarithm of";X;"to the base";B;"is ";Logarithm(B,X)

! Wait for key press
  PRINT
  PRINT "Press any key..."
  GET KEY Before_continuing
```

```
! All done
  END

! Function to find logarithms to any base
  FUNCTION Logarithm(BASE,Number)
      LET Logarithm = Log(Number) / Log(BASE)
  END FUNCTION
```

Example: What is the logarithm base-2 of 65536? Shown below is the sample run.

* LOGS *

Enter a number X ? 65536
Enter the base B ? 2

The logarithm of 65536 to the base 2 is 16

Press any key . . .

PI

This program (Listing 5-7) demonstrates subroutines for performing multidigit math on numbers in the form of strings of digits. These routines could be modified and used for other math involving very large, high-accuracy numbers.

Listing 5-7. Program to calculate the value of pi.

```
! *********************************
! **   File:       PI.TRU        **
! **   Date:       2/28/85       **
! **   Author:     John Craig     **
! **   Language:   True BASIC     **
! *********************************

! Start with a clean slate
  CLEAR

! Display program name
  PRINT "* PI *"
  PRINT

! Initialization
  OPTION BASE 0
  DIM A(1),B(1)

! Ask user for number of digits to do
  DO
      INPUT PROMPT "How many digits ? ": Digits
  LOOP UNTIL Digits > 0 AND Digits = Int(Digits)

! Redimension the arrays
  MAT A = Zer(Digits)
  MAT B = Zer(Digits)
```

```
! This is the main calculation routine
  LET S = 2
  CALL Arc_tangent
  LET S = 3
  CALL Arc_tangent
  CALL Array_mult(A,4,Digits)

! Output the numerical results
  PRINT
  FOR I = 0 TO Digits-1
      PRINT Chr$(A(I)+48);
      IF I=0 THEN PRINT ".";
  NEXT I
  PRINT

! Subroutine, computes arc tangent
  SUB Arc_tangent
      LET B(0) = 1
      LET M = S
      CALL Array_divide(B,M,Digits)
      CALL Array_add(A,B,Digits)
      LET N = 1
      DO
          CALL Array_mult(B,N,Digits)
          LET M = S * S
          CALL Array_divide(B,M,Digits)
          LET N = N + 2
          LET M = N
          CALL Array_divide(B,M,Digits)
          CALL Divide(Int((N-1)/2),2,Quot,Rmdr)
          IF Rmdr=1 THEN
              CALL Array_sub(A,B,Digits)
          ELSE
              CALL Array_add(A,B,Digits)
          END IF
          CALL Array_zero(B,Digits,Z)
      LOOP WHILE Z<>0
  END SUB

! Wait for any key
  PRINT
  PRINT "Press any key to continue..."
  GET KEY Before_quitting

! All done
  END

! Multiply array of N digits using carry
  SUB Array_mult(A(),Mult,N)
      LET Carry = 0
      FOR I = N TO Lbound(A) STEP -1
          CALL Divide(A(I)*Mult+Carry,10,Carry,A(I))
      NEXT I
  END SUB

! Divide array of N digits using borrow
  SUB Array_divide(A(),Div,N)
      LET Borrow = 0
      FOR I = Lbound(A) TO N
```

```
             CALL Divide(Borrow*10+A(I),Div,A(I),Borrow)
        NEXT I
  END SUB

! Adds N digits of arrays using carry
  SUB Array_add(A(),B(),N)
        LET Carry = 0
        FOR I = N TO Lbound(A) STEP -1
             CALL Divide(A(I)+B(I)+Carry,10,Carry,A(I))
        NEXT I
  END SUB

! Subtracts N digits of arrays using borrow
  SUB Array_sub(A(),B(),N)
        FOR I = N TO Lbound(A) STEP -1
             CALL Divide(A(I)-B(I)+10,10,Quot,A(I))
             IF Quot = 0 THEN LET A(I-1) = A(I-1) - 1
        NEXT I
  END SUB

! Are N digits all zero?
  SUB Array_zero(A(),N,Zero_flag)
        LET Zero_flag = 0
        FOR I = 0 TO N
             IF A(I) <> 0 THEN
                  LET Zero_flag = 1
                  EXIT FOR
             END IF
        NEXT I
  END SUB
```

Be warned that calculating π to many places can take time. Finding π to 50 digits, as in the example below, takes just a few seconds—but the time required increases nonlinearly with the number of digits to be calculated.

Example: What is π calculated to 50 digits of accuracy?

* PI *

How many digits ? 50

3.14159265358979323846264338327950288419716939937511

Press any key to continue . . .

SIMULTAN

This program solves sets of simultaneous equations using some of the powerful **MAT** statements of True BASIC. The number of equations/unknowns is limited only by the amount of memory in your computer, because the arrays are redimensioned as required.

Two short **MAT** statements perform all the mathematics required for the solution of a variably sized set of simultaneous equations. The **Inv** function is used to invert a square array, a task requiring many lines of code in the "other" BASIC.

137

```
* SIMULTAN *

How many equations/unknowns ?  3

Equation 1  Coefficient 1  ... ? 3
Equation 1  Coefficient 2  ... ? 4
Equation 1  Coefficient 3  ... ? -2
Equation 1  ........ Constant ? 2

Equation 2  Coefficient 1  ... ? 2
Equation 2  Coefficient 2  ... ? -3
Equation 2  Coefficient 3  ... ? 5
Equation 2  ........ Constant ? 19

Equation 3  Coefficient 1  ... ? 1
Equation 3  Coefficient 2  ... ? 5
Equation 3  Coefficient 3  ... ? -1
Equation 3  ........ Constant ? -7

Unknown 1 =    4.
Unknown 2 =   -2.
Unknown 3 =    1.

Press any key...
```

Fig. 5-5. Solving simultaneous equations with the SIMULTAN.TRU program.

A typical run of the program appears in Fig. 5-5, and the code is shown in Listing 5-8.

VECTORS

This program solves several of the most common vector calculations for

Listing 5-8. Program to solve simultaneous equations.

```
! **********************************
! **   File:        SIMULTAN.TRU   **
! **   Date:        2/26/85        **
! **   Author:      John Craig     **
! **   Language:    True BASIC     **
! **********************************
!
! This program solves a set of N simultaneous equations for N unknowns.

! Start with a clean slate
CLEAR

! Display the program name
PRINT "* SIMULTAN *"
PRINT
```

```
! Create the arrays
  DIM A(1,1),B(1)

! Ask user for the size of the problem
  PRINT
  INPUT PROMPT "How many equations/unknowns ? ":N

! Redimension the arrays
  MAT A = Zer(N,N)
  MAT B = Zer(N)

! Input data from the user for all the equations
  FOR Equation = 1 TO N

     ! Space between each equation's input prompts
       PRINT

     ! Get all coefficients for each equation
       FOR Coefficient = 1 TO N
           PRINT "Equation";Equation;
           PRINT " Coefficient";Coefficient;" ... ";
           INPUT A(Equation,Coefficient)
       NEXT Coefficient

     ! Get the constant for each equation
       PRINT "Equation";Equation;
       PRINT " ......... Constant ";
       INPUT B(Equation)

  NEXT Equation

! Do the computations
  MAT A = Inv(A)
  MAT B = A * B

! Output the results
  PRINT
  FOR Unknown = 1 TO N
      PRINT "Unknown";Unknown;"=   ";B(Unknown)
  NEXT Unknown

! Wait for key press
  PRINT
  PRINT "Press any key..."
  GET KEY Before_continuing

! All done
  END
```

three-dimensional vectors. (For two-dimensional vectors, simply enter zero for the third component.) The program is menu-driven: a single keypress selects the desired computation.

The vectors are manipulated as three-element linear arrays A, B, and C. Depending on the calculation involved, you will be asked to input values for one, two, or three vectors. The scalar or vector result of the calculation will be displayed for your review.

The various vector calculations are presented as functions and subroutines, suitable

Listing 5-9. Vector analysis program VECTORS.TRU (continued to page 143).

```
! ***********************************
! ** File:       VECTORS.TRU    **
! ** Date:       8/11/85        **
! ** Author:     John Craig     **
! ** Language:   True BASIC     **
! ***********************************
!
! This program demonstrates several useful subroutines
! and functions for vector analysis

! Declare external functions
  DECLARE FUNCTION Vector$,Stp,Magnitude,Vangle

! Start with a clean slate
  CLEAR

! Display program name
  PRINT "* VECTORS *"
  PRINT

! Declare all vector variables as small arrays
  DIM A(3),B(3),C(3)

! Ask user for the computation choice
  PRINT "Which vector operation ?"
  PRINT
  PRINT "<+> Addition"
  PRINT "<-> Subtraction"
  PRINT "<D> Dot product"
  PRINT "<C> Cross product"
  PRINT "<S> Scalar triple product"
  PRINT "<M> Magnitude of a vector"
  PRINT "<U> Unit vector parallel to vector"
  PRINT "<A> Angle between two vectors"
  PRINT
  PRINT "Press the key for your choice..."
  PRINT

! Wait until one of the keys is pressed
  DO

     ! Wait for any key press
       DO
       LOOP UNTIL KEY INPUT

     ! Grab the key and check for appropriate choice
       GET KEY Keycode
       LET Choice = Pos("+-DCSMUA",Ucase$(Chr$(Keycode)))

     ! Keep trying for an appropriate key press
  LOOP UNTIL Choice > Ø

! Ask user for required parameters and do the calculations
  SELECT CASE Choice
  CASE 1
      PRINT "Vector addition"
      CALL ASK(A)
```

```
            CALL ASK(B)
            CALL Vector_add(A,B,C)
            PRINT Vector$(A);"plus";Vector$(B);"is";Vector$(C)
        CASE 2
            PRINT "Vector subtraction"
            CALL ASK(A)
            CALL ASK(B)
            CALL Vector_sub(A,B,C)
            PRINT Vector$(A);"minus";Vector$(B);"is";Vector$(C)
        CASE 3
            PRINT "Dot product"
            CALL ASK(A)
            CALL ASK(B)
            PRINT "Dot product of";Vector$(A);"and";Vector$(B);"is ";Dot(A,B)
        CASE 4
            PRINT "Cross product"
            CALL ASK(A)
            CALL ASK(B)
            CALL Cross(A,B,C)
            PRINT "Cross product of";Vector$(A)
            PRINT "and";Vector$(B);"is";Vector$(C)
        CASE 5
            PRINT "Scalar triple product"
            CALL ASK(A)
            CALL ASK(B)
            CALL ASK(C)
            PRINT "Scalar triple product of"
            PRINT Vector$(A)
            PRINT Vector$(B)
            PRINT Vector$(C)
            PRINT "is"
            PRINT Stp(A,B,C)
        CASE 6
            PRINT "Magnitude of a vector"
            CALL ASK(A)
            PRINT "Magnitude of";Vector$(A);"is";Magnitude(A)
        CASE 7
            PRINT "Unit vector parallel to a vector"
            CALL ASK(A)
            CALL Unit(A,B)
            PRINT "Unit vector parallel to";Vector$(A)
            PRINT "is";Vector$(B)
        CASE 8
            PRINT "Angle between two vectors"
            CALL ASK(A)
            CALL ASK(B)
            PRINT "Angle between";Vector$(A)
            PRINT "and";Vector$(B);"is";Vangle(A,B);"degrees"
    END SELECT

! Wait for key press
    GET KEY Before_continuing

! All done
    END

! Converts a vector to string for output
    FUNCTION Vector$(V())
        LET V$ = " ("
```

```
        FOR I = 1 TO 3
             IF V(I) >= Ø THEN LET V$ = V$ & "+"
             LET V$ = V$ & Str$(V(I)) & Chr$(104+I)
        NEXT I
        LET Vector$ = V$ & ") "
    END FUNCTION

! Subroutine to ask user for a vector
  SUB ASK(V())
      PRINT "Enter three vector components (i,j,k)...  "
      INPUT V(1),V(2),V(3)
      PRINT
  END SUB

! Subroutine to add two vectors
  SUB Vector_add(A(),B(),C())
      LET C(1) = A(1) + B(1)
      LET C(2) = A(2) + B(2)
      LET C(3) = A(3) + B(3)
  END SUB

! Subroutine to subtract two vectors
  SUB Vector_sub(A(),B(),C())
      LET C(1) = A(1) - B(1)
      LET C(2) = A(2) - B(2)
      LET C(3) = A(3) - B(3)
  END SUB

! Subroutine to compute the cross product of two vectors
  SUB Cross(A(),B(),C())
      LET C(1) = A(2) * B(3) - A(3) * B(2)
      LET C(2) = A(3) * B(1) - A(1) * B(3)
      LET C(3) = A(1) * B(2) - A(2) * B(1)
  END SUB

! Function to compute the scalar triple product of three vectors
  FUNCTION Stp(A(),B(),C())
      LET T1 = A(1) * B(2) * C(3)
      LET T2 = A(2) * B(3) * C(1)
      LET T3 = A(3) * B(1) * C(2)
      LET T4 = A(3) * B(2) * C(1)
      LET T5 = A(2) * B(1) * C(3)
      LET T6 = A(1) * B(3) * C(2)
      LET Stp = T1 + T2 + T3 - T4 - T5 - T6
  END FUNCTION

! Function to compute the magnitude of a vector (also called the norm)
  FUNCTION Magnitude(A()) = Sqr(A(1)^2 + A(2)^2 + A(3)^2)

! Subroutine to compute the unit vector parallel to a given vector
  SUB Unit(A(),B())
      DECLARE FUNCTION Magnitude
      LET M = Magnitude(A)
      FOR I = 1 TO 3
          LET B(I) = A(I) / M
      NEXT I
  END SUB
```

142

```
! Function to compute the angle in degrees between two vectors
  FUNCTION Vangle(A(),B())
      DECLARE FUNCTION Magnitude,Acs
      LET Tmp = A(1) * B(1) + A(2) * B(2) + A(3) * B(3)
      LET Vangle = Deg(Acs(Tmp / Magnitude(A) / Magnitude(B)))
  END FUNCTION

! Function to compute the inverse cosine
  FUNCTION Acs(X)
      WHEN EXCEPTION IN
          LET Acs = Pi/2 - Atn(X/Sqr(1-X^2))
      USE
          CAUSE ERROR 1,"Illegal argument for Acs()"
      END WHEN
  END FUNCTION
```

for inclusion in other programs or placing in a library of routines. The program code is presented in Listing 5-9.

Example: What is the cross product of these two vectors?

3i + 4j + 5k
5i + 4j + 3k ?

The results are shown in Fig. 5-6.

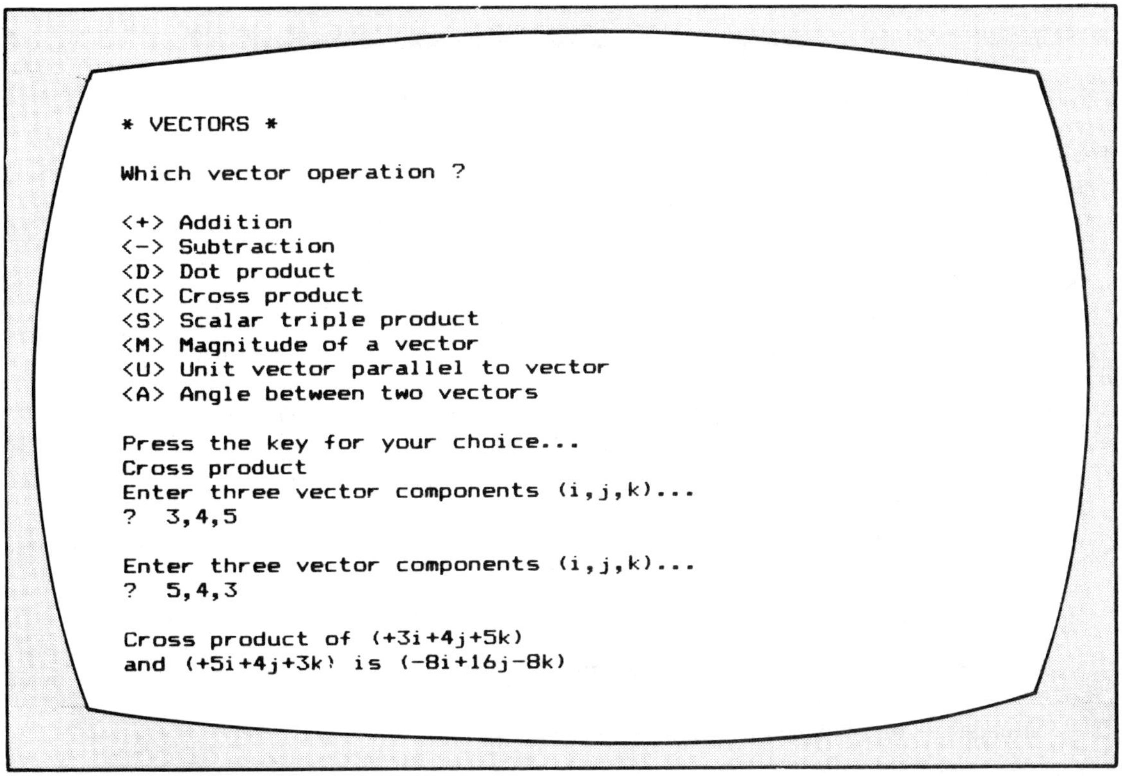

```
* VECTORS *

Which vector operation ?

<+> Addition
<-> Subtraction
<D> Dot product
<C> Cross product
<S> Scalar triple product
<M> Magnitude of a vector
<U> Unit vector parallel to vector
<A> Angle between two vectors

Press the key for your choice...
Cross product
Enter three vector components (i,j,k)...
?  3,4,5

Enter three vector components (i,j,k)...
?  5,4,3

Cross product of (+3i+4j+5k)
and (+5i+4j+3k) is (-8i+16j-8k)
```

Fig 5-6. On-screen menu and data entry for vector calculations.

Chapter 6

Probability
and Statistics

This collection of programs provides many of the common calculations for the studies of probabilities and statistics. Many subroutines are presented, making it easy to use them in other programs you create.

COMBPERM

This program demonstrates functions for calculating combinations and permutations of N objects taken R at a time.

A third function used by the **Combination** and **Permutation** functions is the **Fact** function, which finds the factorial of a number recursively. This function is described in more detail later in this chapter.

For example, what are the possible combinations and permutations of 17 objects taken 3 at a time? Shown below is a simple run.

```
* COMBPERM *

Number of items N? 17
Taken how many at a time ? 3

Combinations of 17 items taken 3 at a time is 680

Permutations of 17 items taken 3 at a time is 4080

Press any key . . .
```

For the program code of **COMBPERM.TRU**, refer to Listing 6-1.

DISTRIBU

This program calculates four types of distributions for probability analysis. Each distribution is presented as a separate function, suitable for use in other programs you create.

The **Fact** function, which calculates the factorial of a number, and a function named **Poly** are also used in this program. The **Fact** function is described elsewhere, but the **Poly** function deserves special recognition, as this function can be very useful in a wide variety of other programs. Its purpose is to efficiently calculate the value of a polynomial of the form

$$AX + BX^2 + CX^3 \ldots$$

for a given value of X and a given set of coefficients, as passed in an array. Notice that the terms have effectively been reordered to eliminate the need to evaluate any powers of X.

Listing 6-1. Program to calculate combinations and permutations.

```
! **********************************
! **   File:      COMBPERM.TRU   **
! **   Date:      7/21/85        **
! **   Author:    John Craig     **
! **   Language:  True BASIC     **
! **********************************
!
! This program calculates both the combinations
! and permutations of N items taken R at a time.

! Declare external functions
  DECLARE FUNCTION Combination
  DECLARE FUNCTION Permutation

! Start with a clean slate
  CLEAR

! Display program name
  PRINT "* COMBPERM *"
  PRINT

! Ask user for N and R
  INPUT PROMPT "Number of items N ?        ": N
  INPUT PROMPT "Taken how many at a time ? ": R

! Show the results
  PRINT
  PRINT "Combinations of";N;"items taken";R;"at a time is";
  PRINT Combination(N,R)
  PRINT
  PRINT "Permutations of";N;"items taken";R;"at a time is";
  PRINT Permutation(N,R)
```

```
! Wait for key press
  PRINT
  PRINT "Press any key..."
  GET KEY Before_continuing

! All done
  END

  FUNCTION Combination(N,R)
      DECLARE FUNCTION Factorial
      LET Combination = Factorial(N) / Factorial(N-R) / Factorial(R)
  END FUNCTION

  FUNCTION Permutation(N,R)
      DECLARE FUNCTION Factorial
      LET Permutation = Factorial(N) / Factorial(N-R)
  END FUNCTION

  FUNCTION Factorial(X)
      IF X < 0 OR X <> Int(X) THEN
          CAUSE ERROR 1,"Factorial of negative or non-integer."
      ELSEIF X > 170 THEN
          CAUSE ERROR 1000    ! (Overflow)
      ELSEIF X > 1 THEN
          LET Factorial = X * Factorial(X-1)
      ELSE
          LET Factorial = 1
      END IF
  END FUNCTION
```

Example: What is the probability of randomly selecting two red marbles when 10 marbles are drawn without replacement from a bag containing 20 marbles, 5 of which are red? This problem is typical of those solved with the hypergeometric distribution. Figure 6-1 shows the complete dialogue for this calculation. The code appears in Listing 6-2.

FACT

This program demonstrates a recursive function for finding the factorial of a positive integer. Several details in this short program are worth discussion. The **IF-ELSEIF-ELSE-ENDIF** structure is used here effectively, showing how a variety of possible conditions can be tested in an organized manner. Two different types of errors are generated. This first error is completely defined, error message and all, in the **CAUSE ERROR 1** statement. The second error condition causes error number 1000, which is True BASIC's predefined "overflow" condition. This error is generated if an attempt is made to calculate the factorial of any number greater than 170, because the answer is bigger than the largest possible number that True BASIC can handle.

This function is *recursive*, which means that it calls itself for part of its calculations. The factorial of X is exactly the same as X times the factorial of X–1, which is the same as X time X–1 times the factorial of X–2, and so on. The factorial of 1 is just 1—all of which leads to an interesting design for the factorial function. We define the factorial of X to return 1 if X is 1; otherwise it will return X times the returned value

```
 * DISTRIBU *

 Which distribution function ?

 <B>inomial
 <H>ypergeometric
 <N>ormal
 <P>oisson

 Press the key for your choice...

 Hypergeometric distribution function

 Sampling successes X ?   2
 Sample size ?   10
 Number of success in lot ?   5
 Lot size ?   20

 Hypergeometric distribution = .348297

 Press any key...
```

Fig. 6-1. Menu and data entry for distribution calculations.

Listing 6-2. Program to calculate probability distributions (continued to page 150).

```
 ! **********************************
 ! **   File:       DISTRIBU.TRU    **
 ! **   Date:       7/21/85         **
 ! **   Author:     John Craig      **
 ! **   Language:   True BASIC      **
 ! **********************************
 !
 ! This program calculates one of four types of
 ! probability distributions.

 ! Declare external functions
   DECLARE FUNCTION Binomial
   DECLARE FUNCTION Hypergeometric
   DECLARE FUNCTION Normal
   DECLARE FUNCTION Poisson

 ! Start with a clean slate
   CLEAR

 ! Display program name
   PRINT "* DISTRIBU *"
   PRINT
```

```
! Shake up the bag of random numbers
  RANDOMIZE

! Ask user for the computation choice
  PRINT "Which distribution function ?"
  PRINT                          .
  PRINT "<B>inomial"
  PRINT "<H>ypergeometric"
  PRINT "<N>ormal"
  PRINT "<P>oisson"
  PRINT
  PRINT "Press the key for your choice..."
  PRINT

! Wait until one of the keys is pressed
  DO

     ! Wait for any key press
       DO
       LOOP UNTIL KEY INPUT

     ! Grab the key and check for appropriate choice
       GET KEY Keycode
       LET Choice = Pos("BHNP",Ucase$(Chr$(Keycode)))

     ! Keep trying for an appropriate key press
  LOOP UNTIL Choice > Ø

! Ask user for required parameters and do the calculations
  SELECT CASE Choice
  CASE 1     ! Binomial distribution
      PRINT "Binomial distribution function"
      PRINT
      INPUT PROMPT "Number of successes X ? ": X
      INPUT PROMPT "Number of trials ? ": N
      INPUT PROMPT "Probability of single success ? ": P
      PRINT
      PRINT "Binomial distribution =",Binomial(X,N,P)
  CASE 2     ! Hypergeometric distribution
      PRINT "Hypergeometric distribution function"
      PRINT
      INPUT PROMPT "Sampling successes X ? ": X
      INPUT PROMPT "Sample size ? ": S
      INPUT PROMPT "Number of successes in lot ? ": A
      INPUT PROMPT "Lot size ? ": N
      PRINT
      PRINT "Hypergeometric distribution =",Hypergeometric(X,S,A,N)
  CASE 3     ! Normal distribution
      PRINT "Normal distribution function"
      PRINT
      INPUT PROMPT "Enter Z ? ": Z
      PRINT
      PRINT "Area of normal distribution =",Normal(Z)
  CASE 4     ! Poisson distribution
      PRINT "Poisson distribution function"
      PRINT
      INPUT PROMPT "Enter X ? ": X
      INPUT PROMPT "Enter Lambda ? ": Lambda
      PRINT
```

```
            PRINT "Poisson distribution =",Poisson(X,Lambda)
     END SELECT

  ! Wait for key press
     PRINT
     PRINT "Press any key..."
     GET KEY Before_continuing

  ! All done
     END

     FUNCTION Binomial(X,N,P)
         DECLARE FUNCTION Factorial
         LET Tmp = Factorial(N) * P^X * (1-P)^(N-X)
         LET Binomial = Tmp / Factorial(X) / Factorial(N-X)
     END FUNCTION

     FUNCTION Hypergeometric(X,S,A,N)
         DECLARE FUNCTION Factorial
         LET Tmp1 = Factorial(A) * Factorial(N-A)
         LET Tmp2 = Factorial(S) * Factorial(N-S)
         LET Tmp3 = Factorial(X) * Factorial(N) * Factorial(A-X)
         LET Tmp4 = Factorial(S-X) * Factorial(N-A-S+X)
         LET Hypergeometric = Tmp1 * Tmp2 / Tmp3 / Tmp4
     END FUNCTION

     FUNCTION Normal(Z)
         DECLARE FUNCTION Poly
         DIM Coef(5)
         FOR I = 1 TO 5
             READ Coef(I)
         NEXT I
         DATA .31938153, -.356563782, 1.781477937
         DATA -1.821255978, 1.330274429
         LET Tmp = 1 / (.2316419 * Z + 1)
         LET Normal = .5 - Poly(Coef,Tmp) * Exp(-(Z^2)/2) / Sqr(2*Pi)
     END FUNCTION

     FUNCTION Poisson(X,Lambda)
         DECLARE FUNCTION Factorial
         LET Poisson = Lambda^X * Exp(-Lambda) / Factorial(X)
     END FUNCTION

     FUNCTION Factorial(X)
         IF X < 0 OR X <> Int(X) THEN
             CAUSE ERROR 1,"Factorial of negative or non-integer."
         ELSEIF X > 170 THEN
             CAUSE ERROR 1000    ! (Overflow)
         ELSEIF X > 1 THEN
             LET Factorial = X * Factorial(X-1)
         ELSE
             LET Factorial = 1
         END IF
     END FUNCTION

  ! This function calculates polynomials of the form
  ! AX + BX^2 + CX^3 + ... out to N terms, where N
  ! is the size of the array of coefficients (A,B,C...)
  !
```

```
FUNCTION Poly(Array(),X)
    FOR I = Size(Array) TO 1 STEP -1
        LET Sum = (Sum + Array(I)) * X
    NEXT I
    LET Poly = Sum
END FUNCTION
```

of the factorial of X–1. The result of this multiplication is "put on hold" until the result of the next call to the factorial function is returned. These pending multiplications stack up, until finally the factorial of 1 is found. Quickly, the returned values are multiplied, satisfying each of the waiting multiplications.

Example: What is the factorial of 9? Here is a complete run of **FACT**.

* FACT *

Number, please ? 9

The factorial of 9 is 362880

Press any key to continue . . .

Listing 6-3 shows the program code.

Listing 6-3. Demonstration program for a recursive factorial function.

```
! ********************************
! ** File:       FACT.TRU       **
! ** Date:       2/28/85        **
! ** Author:     John Craig     **
! ** Language:   True BASIC     **
! ********************************
!
! Function to recursively calculate the factorial of a positive integer
  FUNCTION Factorial(X)
      IF X < 0 OR X <> Int(X) THEN
          CAUSE ERROR 1,"Factorial argument must be a positive integer."
      ELSEIF X > 170 THEN
          CAUSE ERROR 1000   ! (Overflow)
      ELSEIF X > 1 THEN
          LET Factorial = X * Factorial(X-1)
      ELSE
          LET Factorial = 1
      END IF
  END FUNCTION

! Start with a clean slate
  CLEAR

! Print the program name
  PRINT "* FACT *"
  PRINT
```

```
! Let's try it out
  INPUT PROMPT "Number, please ? ":N
  PRINT
  PRINT "The factorial of";N;"is";Factorial(N)

! Wait for a key press
  PRINT
  PRINT "Press any key to continue..."
  GET KEY Before_quitting

! All done
  END
```

FACT_BIG

This program finds the factorial of number greater than normally allowed. The returned result can be a number larger than **MAXNUM**, which is defined to be the largest number possible in True BASIC on any given computer. How is this possible? The technique used is to keep the intermediate results of each multiplication in the form of base-10 logarithms of the actual number involved. The sum of these logarithms is equal to the logarithm of the products of the numbers. The final result is converted to a string in the same scientific format with which "normal" large numbers are displayed.

Notice that a short recursive function is called by the **Fact__big** function to find the sum of the logarithms of the numbers 1 to N. This provides a second example of recursion for your review. Refer to Listing 6-4 for the code.

Listing 6-4. Program to calculate factorials of large numbers.

```
! ***********************************
! ** File:       FACT_BIG.TRU    **
! ** Date:       2/28/85         **
! ** Author:     John Craig      **
! ** Language:   True BASIC      **
! ***********************************
!
! Function to calculate the factorial of a positive integer.  This
! function returns a string as the answer may be greater than MAXNUM.

  FUNCTION Factorial$(N)
      DECLARE FUNCTION Log_sum
      IF N < 0 OR N <> Int(N) THEN
          CAUSE ERROR 1,"Factorial argument must be a positive integer."
      ELSEIF N = 0 THEN
          LET Factorial$ = "1"
      ELSE
          CALL Divide(Log_sum(N),1,Quot,Rmdr)
          LET Factorial$ = Str$(10^Rmdr) & "e+" & Str$(Quot)
      END IF
  END FUNCTION

! Recursive function used by Fact_big function
  FUNCTION Log_sum(N)
```

```
      IF N = 1 THEN
          LET Log_sum = Ø
      ELSE
          LET Log_sum = Log1Ø(N) + Log_sum(N-1)
      END IF
  END FUNCTION

! Start with a clean slate
  CLEAR

! Print the program name
  PRINT "* FACT_BIG *"
  PRINT

! Let's try it out
  INPUT PROMPT "Number, please ? ":N
  PRINT
  PRINT "The factorial of";N;"is ";Factorial$(N)

! Wait for a key press
  PRINT
  PRINT "Press any key to continue..."
  GET KEY Before_quitting

! All done
  END
```

Example: What is the factorial of 1000? The run is shown below.

```
* FACT__BIG *

Number, please ? 1000

The factorial of 1000 is 4.02387e+2567

Press any key to continue . . .
```

MEANS

This program presents four functions for finding four types of means of a set of numbers. These means are various methods of measuring central tendency.

The *arithmetic mean* is calculated as the sum of the N numbers divided by N. The *geometric mean* is calculated as the Nth root of the product of the N numbers. The *harmonic mean* is calculated as the reciprocal of the sum of the reciprocals of N numbers divided by N. The *quadratic mean* is calculated as the square root of the result of the sum of the squares of N numbers divided by N.

Figure 6-2 shows a sample run of the program; Listing 6-5 is the code.

RANDOM

True BASIC provides the **RND** function and the **RANDOMIZE** statement for creating pseudorandom real numbers in the range 0 to 1. In almost every case where random

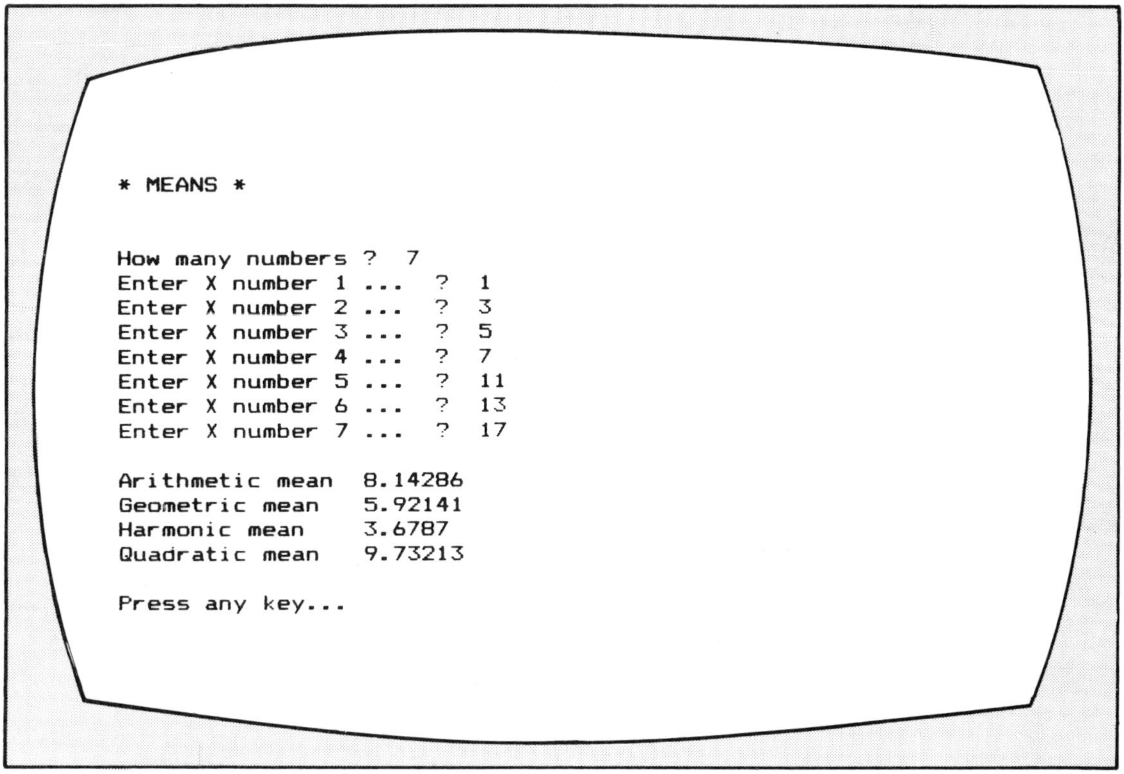

```
 *  MEANS  *

 How many numbers ?  7
 Enter  X  number  1  ...    ?   1
 Enter  X  number  2  ...    ?   3
 Enter  X  number  3  ...    ?   5
 Enter  X  number  4  ...    ?   7
 Enter  X  number  5  ...    ?   11
 Enter  X  number  6  ...    ?   13
 Enter  X  number  7  ...    ?   17

 Arithmetic mean    8.14286
 Geometric mean     5.92141
 Harmonic mean      3.6787
 Quadratic mean     9.73213

 Press any key...
```

Fig. 6-2. Calculating the means for a field of numbers.

Listing 6-5. MEANS.TRU calculates various types of means for any sequence of numbers.

```
!  *********************************
!  **   File:        MEANS.TRU      **
!  **   Date:        7/20/85        **
!  **   Author:      John Craig     **
!  **   Language:    True BASIC     **
!  *********************************
!
!  This program calculates the arithmetic, geometric,
!  harmonic, and quadratic means for a sequence of numbers.

!  Declare the functions
   DECLARE FUNCTION Arithmetic_mean
   DECLARE FUNCTION Geometric_mean
   DECLARE FUNCTION Harmonic_mean
   DECLARE FUNCTION Quadratic_mean

!  Start with a clean slate
   CLEAR

!  Display program name
   PRINT "* MEANS *"
   PRINT
```

```
! Create the array
  DIM X(1)

! Ask user for the quantity of numbers
  PRINT
  INPUT PROMPT "How many numbers ? ":N

! Redimension the array
  MAT X = Zer(N)

! Input data from the user for all the number pairs
  FOR I = 1 TO N
      PRINT "Enter X number";I;"... ";
      INPUT X(I)
  NEXT I

! Display the means
  PRINT
  PRINT "Arithmetic mean",Arithmetic_mean(X)
  PRINT "Geometric mean",Geometric_mean(X)
  PRINT "Harmonic mean",Harmonic_mean(X)
  PRINT "Quadratic mean",Quadratic_mean(X)

! Wait for key press
  PRINT
  PRINT "Press any key..."
  GET KEY Before_continuing

! All done
  END

  FUNCTION Arithmetic_mean(X())
      FOR I = Lbound(X) TO Ubound(X)
          LET Sum = Sum + X(I)
      NEXT I
      LET Arithmetic_mean = Sum / Size(X)
  END FUNCTION

  FUNCTION Geometric_mean(X())
      LET Product = 1
      FOR I = Lbound(X) TO Ubound(X)
          LET Product = Product * X(I)
      NEXT I
      LET Geometric_mean = Product ^ (1/Size(X))
  END FUNCTION

  FUNCTION Harmonic_mean(X())
      FOR I = Lbound(X) TO Ubound(X)
          LET Sum = Sum + 1/X(I)
      NEXT I
      LET Harmonic_mean = Size(X) / Sum
  END FUNCTION

  FUNCTION Quadratic_mean(X())
      FOR I = Lbound(X) TO Ubound(X)
          LET Sum = Sum + X(I)^2
      NEXT I
      LET Quadratic_mean = Sqr(Sum / Size(X))
  END FUNCTION
```

numbers are used in programming, though, it is necessary to generate either random integers or random reals in a different range than just 0 to 1. This program (Listing 6-6) demonstrates functions for generating four different types of random numbers, for just about every common random number requirement.

Listing 6-6. Random number generation program.

```
!  ************************************
!  **  File:       RANDOM.TRU     **
!  **  Date:       7/20/85        **
!  **  Author:     John Craig     **
!  **  Language:   True BASIC     **
!  ************************************
!
!  This program demonstrates several random
!  number generators.

!  Declare external functions
   DECLARE FUNCTION Random_integer
   DECLARE FUNCTION Random_real
   DECLARE FUNCTION Random_normal
   DECLARE FUNCTION Random_exponential

!  Start with a clean slate
   CLEAR

!  Display program name
   PRINT "* RANDOM *"
   PRINT

!  Shake up the bag of random numbers
   RANDOMIZE

!  Ask user about random integers
   INPUT PROMPT "How many random integers to create ? ": N
   IF N > 0 THEN
        INPUT PROMPT "Minimum, maximum integer range ? ": A,B
        PRINT
        FOR I = 1 TO N
             PRINT Random_integer(A,B),
        NEXT I
   END IF
   PRINT

!  Ask user about random real numbers
   INPUT PROMPT "How many random real numbers to create ? ": N
   IF N > 0 THEN
        INPUT PROMPT "Minimum, maximum real range ? ": X,Y
        PRINT
        FOR I = 1 TO N
             PRINT Random_real(X,Y),
        NEXT I
   END IF
   PRINT

!  Ask user about normal distribution random numbers
   INPUT PROMPT "How many normal distribution randoms ? ": N
```

155

```
      IF N > Ø THEN
          INPUT PROMPT "Mean, standard deviation ? ": Mean,Stdev
          PRINT
          FOR I = 1 TO N
              PRINT Random_normal(Mean,Stdev),
          NEXT I
      END IF
      PRINT

    ! Ask user about exponential distribution random numbers
      INPUT PROMPT "How many exponential distribution randoms ? ": N
      IF N > Ø THEN
          INPUT PROMPT "Mean ? ": Mean
          PRINT
          FOR I = 1 TO N
              PRINT Random_exponential(Mean),
          NEXT I
      END IF
      PRINT

    ! Wait for key press
      PRINT
      PRINT "Press any key..."
      GET KEY Before_continuing

    ! All done
      END

    ! Function to create random integers in range A to B
      FUNCTION Random_integer(A,B)
          LET Random_integer = Int(Rnd * (B - A + 1)) + A
      END FUNCTION

    ! Function to create random reals in range X to Y
      FUNCTION Random_real(X,Y)
          LET Random_real = Rnd * (Y - X) + X
      END FUNCTION

    ! Function to create normal distribution randoms
      FUNCTION Random_normal(Mean,Stdev)
          DO
              LET A = 2 * Rnd - 1
              LET B = A^2 + (2 * Rnd - 1)^2
          LOOP UNTIL B < 1
          LET Random_normal = Mean + A * Stdev * Sqr(-2 * Log(B)/B)
      END FUNCTION

    ! Function to create exponentially distributed randoms
      FUNCTION Random_exponential(Mean)
          LET Random_exponential = -Mean * Log(Rnd)
      END FUNCTION
```

The function **Random__integer (A,B)** returns a random integer in the range A to B inclusive. For example,

    Random__integer (1,2)

will randomly return either a 1 or a 2.

The function Random__real (X,Y) returns a real number somewhere in the range X to Y. For example,

$$\text{Random\_real (0,1)}$$

returns the same type of random numbers as the built in RND function, whereas

$$\text{Random\_real } (-1,1)$$

returns negative numbers about half the time.

The function Random__normal (Mean,Stdev) returns random numbers with a density distribution forming the bell curve shape of the normal distribution. Mean defines the center of the bell curve, and the Stdev (standard deviation) defines its width.

The Random__exponential (Mean) function returns random real numbers with a density distribution forming an exponential distribution curve. The Mean is the average of an infinite number of these numbers.

Example: Generate four random numbers of each type. Figure 6-3 shows the result.

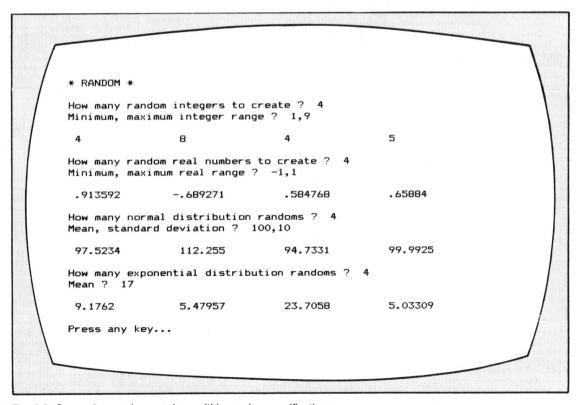

Fig. 6-3. Generating random numbers within varying specifications.

STAT

This program (Listing 6-7) demonstrates several functions useful for statistical analysis and for other programs that work with arrays of numbers. You are asked to input pairs of numbers, which are stored in the arrays named X and Y. When all the numbers have been entered, each of the various functions is called and the results are tabulated for your review.

Many of the functions use some of the other functions during their analysis. If you borrow any function for inclusion in a different program, be sure to check for **DECLARE FUNCTION** statements that indicate other functions that must also be included.

Example: Process these numbers and display the results:

(12,34), (56,78), and (98,76).

Figure 6-4 shows the sample run.

Listing 6-7. General-purpose statistical program (continued to page 161).

```
!  *********************************
!  **   File:       STAT.TRU       **
!  **   Date:       7/20/85        **
!  **   Author:     John Craig     **
!  **   Language:   True BASIC     **
!  *********************************
!
!  This program demonstrates use of the statistics functions

!  Declare external functions
   DECLARE FUNCTION Sum
   DECLARE FUNCTION Mean
   DECLARE FUNCTION Sum_2
   DECLARE FUNCTION Sum_xy
   DECLARE FUNCTION Sum_x2_y
   DECLARE FUNCTION Sum_xn_y
   DECLARE FUNCTION Correlation
   DECLARE FUNCTION Correlation_2
   DECLARE FUNCTION Covariance
   DECLARE FUNCTION Population_covariance
   DECLARE FUNCTION Standard_dev
   DECLARE FUNCTION Population_std_dev

!  Start with a clean slate
   CLEAR

!  Display program name
   PRINT "* STAT *"
   PRINT

!  Create the arrays
   DIM X(1),Y(1)

!  Ask user for the quantity of number pairs
   PRINT
   INPUT PROMPT "How many X,Y number pairs ? ":N
```

```
! Redimension the arrays
  MAT X = Zer(N)
  MAT Y = Zer(N)

! Input data from the user for all the number pairs
  FOR Pair = 1 TO N
      PRINT "Enter X,Y pair number";Pair;"... ";
      INPUT X(Pair),Y(Pair)
  NEXT Pair

! Display the statistics
  PRINT
  PRINT "Sum of  X",,Sum(X)
  PRINT "Sum of  Y",,Sum(Y)
  PRINT "Mean of  X",,Mean(X)
  PRINT "Mean of  Y",,Mean(Y)
  PRINT "Sum of X^2",,Sum_2(X)
  PRINT "Sum of Y^2",,Sum_2(Y)
  PRINT "Sum X * Y",,Sum_xy(X,Y)
  PRINT "Sum of X^2 * Y",,Sum_x2_y(X,Y)
  PRINT "Sum of X^3 * Y",,Sum_xn_y(X,Y,3)
  PRINT "Sum of X^4 * Y",,Sum_xn_y(X,Y,4)
  PRINT "Correlation",,Correlation(X,Y)
  PRINT "Correlation squared", Correlation_2(X,Y)
  PRINT "Covariance",,Covariance(X,Y)
  PRINT "Population covariance",Population_covariance(X,Y)
  PRINT "Standard deviation of  X",Standard_dev(X)
  PRINT "Standard deviation of  Y",Standard_dev(Y)
  PRINT "Population std dev of  X",Population_std_dev(X)
  PRINT "Population std dev of  Y",Population_std_dev(Y)

! Wait for key press
  PRINT
  PRINT "Press any key..."
  GET KEY Before_continuing

! All done
  END

!----------------------------------------------------

! Function to sum elements of a one dimensional array
  FUNCTION Sum(X())
      FOR I = Lbound(X) TO Ubound(X)
          LET Temporary_sum = Temporary_sum + X(I)
      NEXT I
      LET Sum = Temporary_sum
  END FUNCTION

! Function to find mean of an array
  FUNCTION Mean(X())
      DECLARE FUNCTION Sum
      LET Mean = Sum(X) / Size(X)
  END FUNCTION

! Function to find sum of the squares
  FUNCTION Sum_2(X())
      FOR I = Lbound(X) TO Ubound(X)
          LET Temporary_sum = Temporary_sum + X(I)^2
```

```
        NEXT I
        LET Sum_2 = Temporary_sum
    END FUNCTION

  ! Function to find sum of Xi * Yi products
    FUNCTION Sum_xy(X(),Y())
        FOR I = Lbound(X) TO Ubound(X)
            LET Temporary_sum = Temporary_sum + X(I) * Y(I)
        NEXT I
        LET Sum_xy = Temporary_sum
    END FUNCTION

  ! Function to find sum of Xi^2 * Yi
    FUNCTION Sum_x2_y(X(),Y())
        FOR I = Lbound(X) TO Ubound(X)
            LET Temporary_sum = Temporary_sum + X(I)^2 * Y(I)
        NEXT I
        LET Sum_x2_y = Temporary_sum
    END FUNCTION

  ! Function to find sum of Xi^N * Yi
    FUNCTION Sum_xn_y(X(),Y(),N)
        FOR I = Lbound(X) TO Ubound(X)
            LET Temporary_sum = Temporary_sum + X(I)^N * Y(I)
        NEXT I
        LET Sum_xn_y = Temporary_sum
    END FUNCTION

  ! Function to find correlation coefficient
    FUNCTION Correlation(X(),Y())
        DECLARE FUNCTION Standard_dev
        DECLARE FUNCTION Covariance
        LET Tmp = Standard_dev(X) * Standard_dev(Y)
        IF Tmp <> 0 THEN
            LET Correlation = Covariance(X,Y) / Tmp
        ELSE
            LET Correlation = 0
        END IF
    END FUNCTION

  ! Function to find correlation coefficient squared
    FUNCTION Correlation_2(X(),Y())
        DECLARE FUNCTION Correlation
        LET Correlation_2 = Correlation(X,Y)^2
    END FUNCTION

  ! Function to find covariance
    FUNCTION Covariance(X(),Y())
        DECLARE FUNCTION Mean
        DECLARE FUNCTION Sum_xy
        LET Tmp = Sum_xy(X,Y)-Size(X)*Mean(X)*Mean(Y)
        IF Size(X) > 1 THEN
            LET Covariance = Tmp / (Size(X)-1)
        ELSE
            LET Covariance = 0
        END IF
    END FUNCTION

  ! Function to find the population covariance
```

```
FUNCTION Population_covariance(X(),Y())
    DECLARE FUNCTION Mean
    DECLARE FUNCTION Sum_xy
    LET Tmp = Sum_xy(X,Y)-Size(X)*Mean(X)*Mean(Y)
    LET Population_covariance = Tmp / Size(X)
END FUNCTION

! Function to find the standard deviation
FUNCTION Standard_dev(X())
    DECLARE FUNCTION Sum
    DECLARE FUNCTION Sum_2
    LET Tmp = Sum_2(X)-Sum(X)^2/Size(X)
    LET Standard_dev = Sqr(Tmp/(Size(X)-1))
END FUNCTION

! Function to find the population standard deviation
FUNCTION Population_std_dev(X())
    DECLARE FUNCTION Standard_dev
    LET Tmp = Sqr((Size(X)-1)/Size(X))
    LET Population_std_dev = Standard_dev(X) * Tmp
END FUNCTION
```

```
* STAT *

How many X,Y number pairs ?   3
Enter X,Y pair number 1 ...   ?   12,34
Enter X,Y pair number 2 ...   ?   56,78
Enter X,Y pair number 3 ...   ?   98,76

Sum of X                      166
Sum of Y                      188
Mean of X                     55.3333
Mean of Y                     62.6667
Sum of X^2                    12884
Sum of Y^2                    13016
Sum X * Y                     12224
Sum of X^2 * Y                979408
Sum of X^3 * Y                85287392
Sum of X^4 * Y                7777793728
Correlation                   .852299
Correlation squared           .726414
Covariance                    910.667
Population covariance         607.111
Standard deviation of X       43.0039
Standard deviation of Y       24.8462
Population std dev of X        35.1125
Population std dev of Y        20.2868
```

Fig. 6-4. Screen display for STAT.TRU statistics program.

Chapter 7

DO Utilities

This chapter introduces the very powerful and useful "DO files" of True BASIC.

True BASIC provides a very powerful method for modifying any text residing in the Editing Window. DO files may be created to process BASIC programs or any other text. A DO file is simply an external subroutine that assumes an array of strings has been passed to it by a main program. In this very special case, you are the "main program," and the text residing in the Editing Window comprises the array of strings. When the **END SUB** statement is reached, control passes back to you, and any changes to the array of strings instantly appear in the Editing Window.

This chapter presents several examples of the powerful DO file concept. Perhaps the most important and useful progam is **FMT.DO**, which was used to format all the programs in this book. The **LET.DO** program automates the process of adding the key word **LET** where missing in assignment statements (we all forget at first!). The **THREE__D.DO** program presents an example of how a DO file can help you effectively create a special-purpose interpretive language!

Creating a DO-type program is very easy. Notice that all the programs in this book start out in much the same way. The first program unit is an external subroutine with several parameters defined, including the strong array containing all the text currently in the Editing window workspace. Generally, each string in the array is processed as desired, and the subroutine terminates. Command line parameters may be typed in when the **DO** command is given; refer to the **FMT.DO** program for an example case.

The True BASIC manual states that a DO file must be compiled. However, the preliminary version of True BASIC for the IBM PC used to write this book appears to allow the use of uncompiled files as well. To avoid confusion, all uncompiled DO programs in this book were saved with the extension .DO, and the compiled versions were saved with the default extension of .TRU. This allowed the **DO** command to be given without having to specify a compiled file's extension.

For example, the program named **FMT** was typed in and then saved using this command:

save fmt.do

To reload this file for further editing I typed

old fmt.do

To try out the program I first compiled it:

compile

and then saved the compiled version with this command:

save fmt.tru

Later, when I wanted to process a program, I typed

do fmt

The default extension was assumed by the system and the compiled **FTM.TRU** file was used.

There are many other possible uses for DO files. The True BASIC editor is excellent for progam editing and can be used for general text editing. DO files could be built to format, justify, or otherwise process the text, turning the True BASIC editor into an even more powerful editing system. The possibilities are limitless.

DETAB

This DO-type program solved a problem encountered while this book was being written; it could be modified easily for other, similar tasks. Before my copy of True BASIC arrived, I wrote a few programs following the guidelines in the draft proposal for the ANSI BASIC. I used my favorite text editor, which allowed me to indent the structured statements with tabs. When I later loaded these files into the Editing Window of True BASIC, the tab characters were displayed as strange little circular symbols, and the lines were not indented as desired. Hand editing the listings using the very nice editing capabilities of the built in True BASIC editor worked OK, but I tended to miss some tab characters, and the work involved was tedious. This program (Listing 7-1) is the product of my frustration.

When this program is run, all tab character residing in the Editing Window are replaced with spaces. It's that simple. To correct for indentation of lines, you can use the **FMT** utility program immediately after using the program. This program then serves

Listing 7-1. Program to remove Tab characters from text files such as True BASIC programs.

```
!   ************************************
! **   File:        DETAB.DO        **
! **   Date:        7/21/85         **
! **   Author:      John Craig      **
! **   Language:    True BASIC      **
!   ************************************
!
! This is a "DO" type program that replaces tab characters
! with spaces in the current program.
!
! Syntax:   DO DETAB

  EXTERNAL

! This is the main process
  SUB Main (Prog_line$(),Arg$)
      FOR Ptr = 1 TO Ubound(Prog_line$)
          CALL Process_each_line(Prog_line$(Ptr))
      NEXT Ptr
  END SUB
! This is where we return to the Editing Window

! Work on one line at a time here
  SUB Process_each_line(A$)

    ! Search for tab characters, but not in a remark
    FOR I = 1 TO Len(A$)
        IF A$(I:I) = Chr$(9) THEN
            LET A$(I:I) = " "
        END IF
    NEXT I

    ! Finished processing this line
  END SUB
```

as an example and framework from which to develop any other text-modifying utility routines desired.

To use this program, enter the command **DO DETAB** in the History Window.

DOC

This program prints out a program residing in the Editing Window in a neat format, suitable for three-hole punching and placing in a three-ring binder. As set up, the title of the program and a page number are printed at the top of each page, 70 lines are printed in a compressed mode (132 character per line) at 8 lines per inch, and a form feed is sent to start each new page.

Several escape code sequences are used to put the printer in a compressed mode at 1/8 inch per line. I used an Epson MX-80 printer while developing this program, and I believe that most Epson and IBM PC printers will respond as expected to these commands. If your printer behaves a little radically when this program is run, check your printer manual and change the escape code sequences as necessary.

True BASIC keeps track of the number of characters transmitted to your printer and inserts a CR/LF (carriage return and line feed) after 80 characters have been sent following the last CR/LF. Actually, the current setting of **MARGIN** is what determines how often an extra CR/LF will be sent; 80 is just the default value of **MARGIN**. This program resets **MARGIN** to 132 because lines longer than 80 characters in length will be printed on two lines if the default is not changed.

The program title is extracted from the second line in the Editing Window and assumes that the heading is in exactly the format that is followed throughout this book. If you prefer to place the program title at a different location in your heading, change the program line that follows this comment line

> ! Grab a title from the title line

to extract your title correctly.

You may wish to experiment with several important parameters that are defined near the start of the program. In particular, the number of lines per page and the indentation count may be altered to suit your taste.

To use this DO-type program, load your program to be listed into the Editing Window and type **DO DOC**. The code for **DOC** is shown in Listing 7-2.

Listing 7-2. Documentation formatting program DOC.DO.

```
! ************************************
! **   File:       DOC.DO          **
! **   Date:       3/1/85          **
! **   Author:     John Craig      **
! **   Language:   True BASIC      **
! ************************************
!
! This "DO" type program prints the current program in a format
! suitable for documentation purposes.
!
! Note that the printer control codes assume that an EPSON or IBM
! printer is being used.  Substitute similar code for other printers.
!
! Usage:   DO DOC
!

EXTERNAL

SUB Main(Prog_line$(),Arg$)

   ! Define important parameters
   LET Lines_per_page = 70
   LET Page_tab = 105
   LET Indentation = 18
   LET Esc$ = Chr$(27)
   LET Formfeed$ = Chr$(12)

   ! Get the printer ready
   OPEN #1: PRINTER
```

```
    ! What is the current MARGIN setting?
      ASK #1: MARGIN Marg

    ! Reset printer to power up state
      PRINT #1: Esc$ & "@";

    ! Turn on compressed mode
      PRINT #1: Chr$(15);

    ! Set the printer's MARGIN to 132
      SET #1: MARGIN 132

    ! Set line spacing to 1/8 inch
      PRINT #1: Esc$ & "0";

    ! Grab a title from the title line
      LET Title$ = (Trim$(Prog_line$(2)(15:35))&Repeat$(" ",12))(1:12)

    ! Main processing loop
      FOR Ptr = 1 TO Ubound(Prog_line$)

         ! Check for full page of printout
           LET Line_count = Line_count + 1
           IF Line_count = 1 OR Line_count = Lines_per_page THEN
                LET Line_count = 1
                LET Page = Page + 1
                IF Page > 1 THEN PRINT #1: Formfeed$;
                PRINT #1: Repeat$(" ",Page_tab);
                PRINT #1: Title$;"  Page ";Page
                PRINT #1
           END IF

         ! Print each line of the program
           PRINT #1: Repeat$(" ",Indentation); Prog_line$(Ptr)
      NEXT Ptr

    ! Kick out the last page
      PRINT #1: Formfeed$;

    ! Reset to power up state
      PRINT #1: Esc$ & "@";

    ! Reset the printer's MARGIN
      SET #1: MARGIN Marg

    ! All done, so exit back to Editing Window
  END SUB
```

FMT

This DO-type program (Listing 7-3) reformats and indents a program currently residing in the Editing Window; it is perhaps the most useful program presented in this book. All of the programs presented here were processed with this utility, allowing a consistent style and providing enhanced readability.

The program performs several operations on the program lines being edited. All keywords are converted to uppercase, and all function, subroutine, and variable names are converted to a leading uppercase character followed by lowercase characters. Key-

Listing 7-3. Deluxe formatting program FMT.DO (continued to page 172).

```
!  ****************************************
!  **  File:      FMT.DO         **
!  **  Date:      2/27/85        **
!  **  Author:    John Craig     **
!  **  Language:  True BASIC     **
!  ****************************************
!
!  This is a "DO" type program that reformats the program currently
!  residing in the Editing Window.  All key words are converted to
!  upper case, all variables and function names are converted to a
!  leading upper case character followed by lower case, and indentation
!  is performed with steps of 4 character spaces per level (default).
!
!  Syntax:  DO FMT [,N]     The optional value N defaults to 4 and is
!                           the number of spaces per indentation level.
!

    EXTERNAL

!  This is the main process
    SUB Main (Prog_line$(),Arg$)
        IF Len(Arg$) > 0 THEN
            LET Indent_amt = Val(Arg$)
        ELSE
            LET Indent_amt = 4
        END IF
        LET Indent_level = 1
        FOR Ptr = 1 TO Ubound(Prog_line$)
            IF Ptr = Ubound(Prog_line$) THEN
                LET Last_flag = 1
            ELSE
                LET Last_flag = 0
            END IF
            CALL Upper_and_lower(Prog_line$(Ptr))
            CALL Indent(Prog_line$(Ptr),Indent_level,Indent_amt,Last_flag)
        NEXT Ptr
    END SUB
!  This is where we return to the Editing Window

!  Convert key words to upper case, and others to mostly lower case
    SUB Upper_and_lower(A$)
        LET I,J,Comment_flag,Quote_flag = 0
        LET Separator$ = "  :;)(,/*+-[]=&$!""@#%^"
        DO
            CALL Next_word
            LET Word$ = A$(I:J)
            IF Comment_flag=0 AND Quote_flag=0 THEN CALL Process_word(Word$)
            LET A$(I:J) = Word$
        LOOP UNTIL Word$ = ""

        !  Find the next word, I and J will point to each end of it
        SUB Next_word
            FOR I = J+1 TO Len(A$)
                CALL Check_flags
                IF Pos(Separator$,A$(I:I)) = 0 THEN EXIT FOR
            NEXT I
            FOR J = I+1 TO Len(A$)
```

167

```
                    CALL Check_flags
                    IF Pos(Separator$,A$(J:J)) <> Ø THEN EXIT FOR
               NEXT J
               LET J = J-1
          END SUB


          ! Check if we're looking at REMarks, strings, or DATA statements
          SUB Check_flags
               LET T$ = Ucase$(A$(I:I+3))
               IF T$(1:1) = "!" OR T$ = "REM " OR T$ = "DATA" THEN
                    IF Quote_flag = Ø THEN
                         LET Comment_flag = 1
                         IF T$(1:1) <> "!" THEN LET A$(I:I+3) = T$
                    END IF
               END IF
               IF A$(I:I) = """" THEN
                    IF Comment_flag = Ø THEN
                         IF Quote_flag = Ø THEN
                              LET Quote_flag = 1
                         ELSE
                              LET Quote_flag = Ø
                         END IF
                    END IF
               END IF
          END SUB

     ! End of "Upper_and_lower" and it's nested subroutines
     END SUB

! Is the current word one of the known key words?
  SUB Process_word(W$)
       LET W$ = Ucase$(W$)
       SELECT CASE(W$)
       CASE "ACCESS"
       CASE "AND"
       CASE "ANGLE"
       CASE "AREA"
       CASE "ASK"
       CASE "AT"
       CASE "BACK"
       CASE "BACKGROUND"
       CASE "BASE"
       CASE "BEGIN"
       CASE "BOX"
       CASE "CALL"
       CASE "CASE"
       CASE "CAUSE"
       CASE "CHAIN"
       CASE "CIRCLE"
       CASE "CLEAR"
       CASE "CLOSE"
       CASE "COLOR"
       CASE "CREATE"
       CASE "CURSOR"
       CASE "DATA"
       CASE "DECLARE"
       CASE "DEF"
       CASE "DEGREES"
       CASE "DIM"
```

```
CASE "DO"
CASE "DRAW"
CASE "ELLIPSE"
CASE "ELSE"
CASE "ELSEIF"
CASE "END"
CASE "ERASE"
CASE "ERROR"
CASE "EXCEPTION"
CASE "EXIT"
CASE "EXTERNAL"
CASE "FILESIZE"
CASE "FLOOD"
CASE "FOR"
CASE "FUNCTION"
CASE "GET"
CASE "HANDLER"
CASE "IF"
CASE "IN"
CASE "INPUT"
CASE "IS"
CASE "KEEP"
CASE "KEY"
CASE "LET"
CASE "LIBRARY"
CASE "LINE"
CASE "LINES"
CASE "LOOP"
CASE "MARGIN"
CASE "MAT"
CASE "MAX"
CASE "MODE"
CASE "MORE"
CASE "MOUSE"
CASE "NAME"
CASE "NEXT"
CASE "NOT"
CASE "OPEN"
CASE "OPTION"
CASE "OR"
CASE "ORGANIZATION"
CASE "PAUSE"
CASE "PICTURE"
CASE "PLAY"
CASE "PLOT"
CASE "POINT"
CASE "POINTS"
CASE "POINTER"
CASE "PRINT"
CASE "PRINTER"
CASE "PROGRAM"
CASE "PROMPT"
CASE "RADIANS"
CASE "RANDOMIZE"
CASE "READ"
CASE "RECORD"
CASE "RECSIZE"
CASE "REM"
CASE "RESTORE"
```

```
        CASE "RETURN"
        CASE "SAME"
        CASE "SCREEN"
        CASE "SELECT"
        CASE "SET"
        CASE "SHOW"
        CASE "SOUND"
        CASE "STEP"
        CASE "STOP"
        CASE "SUB"
        CASE "TEXT"
        CASE "THEN"
        CASE "TO"
        CASE "UNSAVE"
        CASE "UNTIL"
        CASE "USE"
        CASE "USING"
        CASE "WHEN"
        CASE "WHILE"
        CASE "WINDOW"
        CASE "WITH"
        CASE "WRITE"
        CASE "ZONEWIDTH"
        CASE ELSE
            LET W$ = Ucase$(W$(1:1)) & Lcase$(W$(2:Len(W$)))
        END SELECT
    END SUB

! Determine the indentation for each line
    SUB Indent(A$,Indent_level,Indent_amt,Last_flag)
        CALL Split_up(A$,Number$,Comment$)
        LET Word_one$ = A$(1:Pos(A$," ")-1)
        IF Word_one$ = "" THEN LET Word_one$ = A$
        WHEN EXCEPTION IN
            IF Trim$(Word_one$) <> "" THEN
                ! Check for words that affect indentation level
                SELECT CASE Word_one$
                CASE "CASE"
                    LET Code = -2
                CASE "DEF"
                    IF Pos(A$,"=") = 0 THEN
                        LET Code = +1
                    ELSE
                        LET Code = 0
                    END IF
                CASE "DO"
                    LET Code = +1
                CASE "ELSE"
                    LET Code = -2
                CASE "ELSEIF"
                    LET Code = -2
                CASE "END"
                    IF A$ <> "END" THEN LET Code = -1
                CASE "FOR"
                    LET Code = +1
                CASE "FUNCTION"
                    IF Pos(A$,"=") = 0 THEN
                        LET Code = +1
```

170

```
                    ELSE
                        LET Code = 0
                    END IF
                CASE "IF"
                    IF A$(Len(A$)-3:Maxnum) = "THEN" THEN LET Code = +1
                CASE "LOOP"
                    LET Code = -1
                CASE "NEXT"
                    LET Code = -1
                CASE "PICTURE"
                    LET Code = +1
                CASE "SELECT"
                    LET Code = +1
                CASE "SUB"
                    LET Code = +1
                CASE "USE"
                    LET Code = -2
                CASE "WHEN"
                    LET Code = +1
                CASE ELSE
                    LET Code = 0
                END SELECT

                ! Build a string of spaces for the indicated indentation
                SELECT CASE Code
                CASE -2
                    LET A$ = Repeat$(" ",Indent_amt*(Indent_level-1)) & A$
                CASE -1
                    LET Indent_level = Indent_level - 1
                    LET A$ = Repeat$(" ",Indent_amt*Indent_level) & A$
                CASE 0
                    LET A$ = Repeat$(" ",Indent_amt*Indent_level) & A$
                CASE +1
                    LET A$ = Repeat$(" ",Indent_amt*Indent_level) & A$
                    LET Indent_level = Indent_level + 1
                CASE ELSE
                END SELECT
            ELSE
                LET Backstep = Min(2,Indent_amt)
                LET A$ = Repeat$(" ",Indent_amt*Indent_level-Backstep)
            END IF

         ! Check for structure syntax errors
            IF Indent_level < 1 THEN CAUSE EXCEPTION 1
            IF Last_flag = 1 AND Indent_level <> 1 THEN CAUSE EXCEPTION 1
      USE
            SOUND 555,.1
            SOUND 333,.5
            LET A$ = Number$ & A$ & Comment$
            CAUSE ERROR 1, "Nesting error detected"
      END WHEN
      LET A$ = Number$ & A$ & Comment$
END SUB

! Split the line into line number, statement, and REMArks
SUB Split_up(A$,Number$,Comment$)
    LET A$ = Trim$(A$)
    IF A$(1:1) >= "0" AND A$(1:1) <= "9" THEN
        FOR I = 1 TO Len(A$)
```

```
            IF A$(I:I) < "0" OR A$(I:I) > "9" THEN EXIT FOR
        NEXT I
        LET Number$ = A$(1:I-1) & " "
        LET A$ = Ltrim$(A$(I:Maxnum))
    ELSE
        LET Number$ = ""
    END IF
    LET Quote_flag = 0
    FOR I = Len(A$) TO 0 STEP -1
        IF A$(I:I) = """" THEN
            IF Quote_flag = 0 THEN
                LET Quote_flag = 1
            ELSE
                LET Quote_flag = 0
            END IF
        END IF
        IF A$(I:I) = "!" OR A$(I:I+2) = "REM" THEN
            IF Quote_flag = 0 THEN EXIT FOR
        END IF
    NEXT I
    IF I > 0 THEN
        FOR J = I-1 TO 0 STEP -1
            IF A$(J:J) <> " " THEN EXIT FOR
        NEXT J
        LET Comment$ = A$(J+1:Maxnum)
        LET A$ = A$(1:J)
    ELSE
        LET Comment$ = ""
    END IF
END SUB
```

words on each line are checked and indentation is performed accordingly. Remarks, data statements, and quoted string constants are left undisturbed. If line numbers are present they are retained.

This program automatically checks for incorrect nesting of structures. Each indentation level represents a matching pair of statements, such as **DO-LOOP**, or **IF-END IF**. At the end of any program listing the indentation level should return to zero, unless an error in the structure is present. For example, if an **END SELECT** statement was inadvertently left off the end of a **SELECT CASE** structure, the indentation level will not return to zero by the end of the program listing. A beep would be produced and a warning message displayed to catch your attention.

One optional command line parameter controls the number of spaces for each level of indentation. The default is four, but any reasonable number may be used. For example, type

DO FMT,3

if you prefer each level of indentation to move only three spaces. To use the default of four, simply type **DO FMT**. The program code is shown in Listing 7-1.

Example: Let's create a short program to generate prime numbers, demonstrating the operation of the **FMT** program. Figure 7-1 shows the "before" and "after."

```
┌─────────────────────────────────────────────────┐
│                                                 │
│  Before...                                      │
│                                                 │
│  ! Prime number generator                       │
│  DO                                             │
│  LET I = I + 1                                  │
│  LET PRIMEFLAG = 1                              │
│  FOR J = 2 TO SQR(I)                            │
│  IF MOD(I,J) = 0 THEN                           │
│  LET PRIMEFLAG = 0                              │
│  EXIT FOR                                       │
│  END IF                                         │
│  NEXT J                                         │
│  IF PRIMEFLAG = 1 THEN PRINT I,                 │
│  LOOP UNTIL KEY INPUT                           │
│  END                                            │
│                                                 │
│                                                 │
│  After...                                       │
│                                                 │
│  ! Prime number generator                       │
│    DO                                           │
│        LET I = I + 1                            │
│        LET Primeflag = 1                        │
│        FOR J = 2 TO Sqr(I)                      │
│            IF Mod(I,J) = 0 THEN                  │
│                LET Primeflag = 0                │
│                EXIT FOR                          │
│            END IF                               │
│        NEXT J                                   │
│        IF Primeflag = 1 THEN PRINT I,           │
│  LOOP UNTIL KEY INPUT                           │
│  END                                            │
│                                                 │
└─────────────────────────────────────────────────┘
```

Fig. 7-1. Before-and-after views of a True BASIC
program processed by FMT.DO.

LET

When you first start writing True BASIC programs it's easy to forget the **LET**
keywords for assignment statements. This DO-type program was created to add the
LET to lines where it was inadvertently forgotten. Listing 7-4 is the code.

Listing 7-4. LET.DO helps you correct habits engendered by the "other" BASIC.

```
!  ********************************
!  **   File:      LET.DO         **
!  **   Date:      5/28/85        **
!  **   Author:    John Craig     **
!  **   Language:  True BASIC     **
!  ********************************
!
!  This is a "DO" type program that adds the key word "LET" to lines
!  in the current program where it is missing.
!
!  Syntax:  DO LET

   EXTERNAL
```

```
! This is the main process
  SUB Main (Prog_line$(),Arg$)
      FOR Ptr = 1 TO Ubound(Prog_line$)
          CALL Process_each_line(Prog_line$(Ptr))
      NEXT Ptr
  END SUB
! This is where we return to the Editing Window

! Work on one line at a time here
  SUB Process_each_line(A$)

    ! Search for first alpha character, but not in a remark
    FOR I = 1 TO Len(A$)
        SELECT CASE Ucase$(A$(I:I))
        CASE "!"
            LET I = Maxnum
            EXIT FOR
        CASE "A" TO "Z"
            EXIT FOR
        CASE ELSE
        END SELECT
    NEXT I

    ! Search for next space or "="
    FOR J = I+1 TO Len(A$)
        IF A$(J:J) = " " OR A$(J:J) = "=" THEN EXIT FOR
    NEXT J

    ! Finally, check if next non-space is "="
    FOR K = J TO Len(A$)
        IF A$(K:K) <> " " THEN
            IF A$(K:K) = "=" THEN
                LET A$(I:0) = "LET "
            END IF
            EXIT FOR
        END IF
    NEXT K

    ! Finished processing this line
  END SUB
```

THREE__D

This program uses the powerful DO program concept of True BASIC to create three-dimensional graphics. In effect, this program creates a simple language that allows you to create, edit, and draw three-dimensional objects interactively.

First, let's take a look at a sample image as shown in Fig. 7-2. Run True BASIC and load in the file named **CUBE1.TRU** (Fig. 7-3) Type

old cube

To process this information and create the graphics, type

do three__d

174

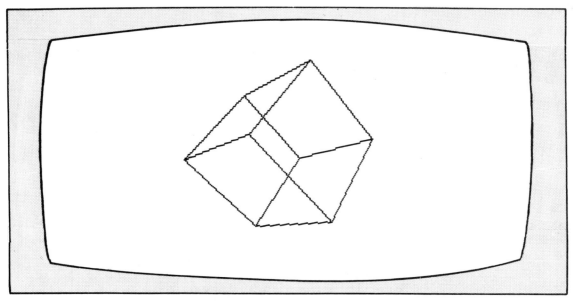

Fig. 7-2. CUBE1 display produced by THREE__D program.

Fig. 7-3. Contents of the file CUBE1.TRU.

```
! CUBE1

universe
perspective 45
translate Ø,Ø,-4

! Cube
object
rotatex 25
rotatey 35
rotatez 45

! Outline of the cube
move 1,1,1
draw 1,-1,1
draw 1,-1,-1
draw 1,1,-1
draw 1,1,1
draw -1,1,1
draw -1,1,-1
draw -1,-1,-1
draw -1,-1,1
draw 1,-1,1
move -1,-1,-1
draw 1,-1,-1
move -1,1,-1
draw 1,1,-1
move -1,1,1
draw -1,-1,1

end
```

The information residing in the Editing Window for drawing the three-dimensional cube will be interpreted by the program named **THREE__D** to create the cube image on your screen. When done, press any key to return to the True BASIC editing environment. Load and process the files **CUBE2** (Fig. 7-4, 7-5), **PLANE1** (Fig. 7-6, 7-7), and **PLANE2** (Fig. 7-8, 7-9) to see the other sample images.

Creating your own three-dimensional graphics is easy. Use True BASIC's excellent built-in text editor to create a file of statements as defined below. Type

do three__d

to experiment with your images, and edit the **rotate, translate,** and other commands as desired to create the view you want. When you're satisfied with the results, use the **SAVE** statement to place your commands in a file, in the same way that BASIC programs are saved.

There are just a few commands to master; in just minutes you'll be creating your own three-dimensional graphics objects! Let's discuss these commands now.

The **universe** command resets all parameters and starts a fresh scene. Normally, only one **universe** command is given, at the start of the list, but you may use two or more of these commands to effectively superimpose images.

The **perspective** or **othogonal** command declares the type of view. An *orthogonal*

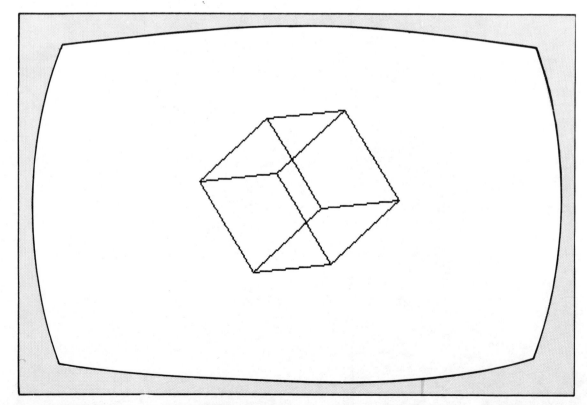

Fig. 7-4. CUBE2 display produced by THREE__D program.

Fig. 7-5. Contents of the file CUBE2.TRU.

```
! CUBE2

universe
orthogonal 5
translate 0,0,-4

! Cube
object
rotatex 25
rotatey 35
rotatez 45

! Outline of the cube
move 1,1,1
draw 1,-1,1
draw 1,-1,-1
draw 1,1,-1
draw 1,1,1
draw -1,1,1
draw -1,1,-1
draw -1,-1,-1
draw -1,-1,1
draw 1,-1,1
move -1,-1,-1
draw 1,-1,-1
move -1,1,-1
draw 1,1,-1
move -1,1,1
draw -1,-1,1

end
```

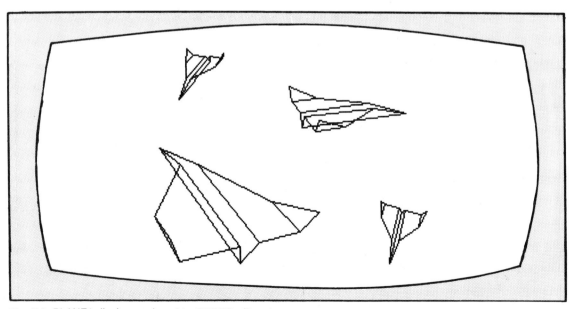

Fig. 7-6. PLANE1 display produced by THREE__D program.

177

```
universe
perspective 50
translate 0,0,-10

! First paper airplane
object
rotatex -55
rotatey 45
translate -3,-1,0

! Left leading edge
move 0,5,-1
draw -.4,2,0
draw -2.5,-1,0
draw -3,-3,1

! Across the trailing edge
draw -2.5,-3,0
draw -.4,-3,0
draw 0,-3,-1
draw .4,-3,0
draw 2.5,-3,0
draw 3,-3,1

! Right leading edge
draw 2.5,-1,0
draw .4,2,0
draw 0,5,-1

! Center fold line
draw 0,-3,-1

! Left wing tip fold
move -2.5,-1,0
draw -2.5,-3,0

! Right wing tip fold
move 2.5,-1,0
draw 2.5,-3,0

! Left wing main fold
move -.4,2,0
draw -.4,-3,0

! Right wing main fold
move .4,2,0
draw .4,-3,0

! Second paper airplane
object
rotatex -90
rotatey -75
rotatex 35
translate 4,4,-9
```

```
! Left leading edge
move 0,5,-1
draw -.4,2,0
draw -2.5,-1,0
draw -3,-3,1

! Across the trailing edge
draw -2.5,-3,0
draw -.4,-3,0
draw 0,-3,-1
draw .4,-3,0
draw 2.5,-3,0
draw 3,-3,1

! Right leading edge
draw 2.5,-1,0
draw .4,2,0
draw 0,5,-1

! Center fold line
draw 0,-3,-1

! Left wing tip fold
move -2.5,-1,0
draw -2.5,-3,0

! Right wing tip fold
move 2.5,-1,0
draw 2.5,-3,0

! Left wing main fold
move -.4,2,0
draw -.4,-3,0

! Right wing main fold
move .4,2,0
draw .4,-3,0

! Third paper airplane
object
rotatey 180
rotatex 150
rotatey -20
rotatez -15
translate -12,14,-30

! Left leading edge
move 0,5,-1
draw -.4,2,0
draw -2.5,-1,0
draw -3,-3,1
```

Fig. 7-7. Contents of the file PLANE1.TRU.

```
! Across the trailing edge          ! Left leading edge
draw -2.5,-3,0                      move 0,5,-1
draw -.4,-3,0                       draw -.4,2,0
draw 0,-3,-1                        draw -2.5,-1,0
draw .4,-3,0                        draw -3,-3,1
draw 2.5,-3,0
draw 3,-3,1                         ! Across the trailing edge
                                    draw -2.5,-3,0
! Right leading edge                draw -.4,-3,0
draw 2.5,-1,0                       draw 0,-3,-1
draw .4,2,0                         draw .4,-3,0
draw 0,5,-1                         draw 2.5,-3,0
                                    draw 3,-3,1
! Center fold line
draw 0,-3,-1                        ! Right leading edge
                                    draw 2.5,-1,0
! Right leading edge                draw .4,2,0
draw 2.5,-1,0                       draw 0,5,-1
draw .4,2,0
draw 0,5,-1                         ! Center fold line
                                    draw 0,-3,-1
! Center fold line
draw 0,-3,-1                        ! Left wing tip fold
                                    move -2.5,-1,0
! Left wing tip fold                draw -2.5,-3,0
move -2.5,-1,0
draw -2.5,-3,0                      ! Right wing tip fold
                                    move 2.5,-1,0
! Right wing tip fold               draw 2.5,-3,0
move 2.5,-1,0
draw 2.5,-3,0                       ! Left wing main fold
                                    move -.4,2,0
! Left wing main fold               draw -.4,-3,0
move -.4,2,0
draw -.4,-3,0                       ! Right wing main fold
                                    move .4,2,0
! Right wing main fold              draw .4,-3,0
move .4,2,0
draw .4,-3,0
                                    ! That's all folks
! Fourth paper airplane             end
object
rotatey 180
rotatex 150
rotatey -20
rotatez -15
translate 15,-9,-30
```

view can be thought of as though the camera were at a nearly infinite distance from the scene peering through a telescope. All parallel lines in space will be drawn as parallel lines on the screen. The **CUBE2** image is an example of the use of an orthogonal view. Notice how all edges are parallel to other edges. Technically speaking, the orthogonal view results from projecting all points on the object to the closest point in the X,Y plane of the screen. The number following the **orthogonal** command declares the width of the view as is used to determine the parameters for a **WINDOW** statement.

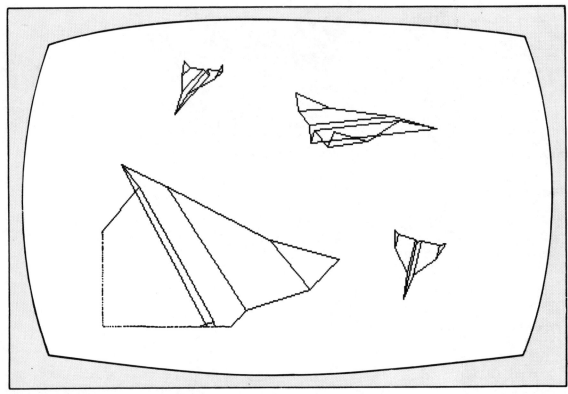

Fig. 7-8. PLANE2 display produced by THREE__D program.

```
universe                          ! Right leading edge
perspective 50                    draw 2.5,-1,0
translate 0,0,-6                  draw .4,2,0
                                  draw 0,5,-1
! First paper airplane
object                            ! Center fold line
rotatex -55                       draw 0,-3,-1
rotatey 45
translate -3,-1,0                 ! Left wing tip fold
                                  move -2.5,-1,0
! Left leading edge               draw -2.5,-3,0
move 0,5,-1
draw -.4,2,0                      ! Right wing tip fold
draw -2.5,-1,0                    move 2.5,-1,0
draw -3,-3,1                      draw 2.5,-3,0

! Across the trailing edge        ! Left wing main fold
draw -2.5,-3,0                    move -.4,2,0
draw -.4,-3,0                     draw -.4,-3,0
draw 0,-3,-1
draw .4,-3,0                      ! Right wing main fold
draw 2.5,-3,0                     move .4,2,0
draw 3,-3,1                       draw .4,-3,0
```

Fig. 7-9. Contents of the file PLANE2.TRU.

```
! Second paper airplane
object
rotatex -90
rotatey -75
rotatex 35
translate 4,4,-9

! Left leading edge
move 0,5,-1
draw -.4,2,0
draw -2.5,-1,0
draw -3,-3,1

! Across the trailing edge
draw -2.5,-3,0
draw -.4,-3,0
draw 0,-3,-1
draw .4,-3,0
draw 2.5,-3,0
draw 3,-3,1

! Right leading edge
draw 2.5,-1,0
draw .4,2,0
draw 0,5,-1

! Center fold line
draw 0,-3,-1

! Left wing tip fold
move -2.5,-1,0
draw -2.5,-3,0

! Right wing tip fold
move 2.5,-1,0
draw 2.5,-3,0

! Left wing main fold
move -.4,2,0
draw -.4,-3,0

! Right wing main fold
move .4,2,0
draw .4,-3,0

! Third paper airplane
object
rotatey 180
rotatex 150
rotatey -20
rotatez -15
translate -12,14,-30

! Left leading edge
move 0,5,-1
draw -.4,2,0
draw -2.5,-1,0
draw -3,-3,1

! Across the trailing edge
draw -2.5,-3,0
draw -.4,-3,0
draw 0,-3,-1
draw .4,-3,0
draw 2.5,-3,0
draw 3,-3,1

! Right leading edge
draw 2.5,-1,0
draw .4,2,0
draw 0,5,-1

! Center fold line
draw 0,-3,-1

! Left wing tip fold
move -2.5,-1,0
draw -2.5,-3,0

! Right wing tip fold
move 2.5,-1,0
draw 2.5,-3,0

! Left wing main fold
move -.4,2,0
draw -.4,-3,0

! Right wing main fold
move .4,2,0
draw .4,-3,0

! Fourth paper airplane
object
rotatey 180
rotatex 150
rotatey -20
rotatez -15
translate 15,-9,-30

! Left leading edge
move 0,5,-1
draw -.4,2,0
draw -2.5,-1,0
draw -3,-3,1

! Across the trailing edge
draw -2.5,-3,0
draw -.4,-3,0
draw 0,-3,-1
draw .4,-3,0
draw 2.5,-3,0
draw 3,-3,1

! Right leading edge
draw 2.5,-1,0
draw .4,2,0
draw 0,5,-1
```

```
! Center fold line            ! Left wing main fold
draw 0,-3,-1                  move -.4,2,0
                             draw -.4,-3,0
! Left wing tip fold
move -2.5,-1,0               ! Right wing main fold
draw -2.5,-3,0               move .4,2,0
                             draw .4,-3,0
! Right wing tip fold
move 2.5,-1,0                ! That's all folks
draw 2.5,-3,0                end
```

The **CUBE**1 image uses the **perspective** command, which declares that the view will be created by projecting all points on the image through the X,Y plane towards a single point on the Z axis. *Perspective* means that closer objects will look larger than further objects, and is more like how we normally see the world around us. The number following the **perspective** command declares the angle of view, in degrees. A 45- to 50-degree perspective view produces images similar in appearance to a normal camera. Larger angles produce strange "fisheye" effects, and very small angles create views similar to orthogonal views.

The **translate** command, if placed after the **universe** command but before an **object** command, causes all points on all objects to be translated (i.e., shifted) the indicated amounts in the X, Y, and Z directions. If this command appears after an **object** command, then only the points on the indicated object are translated that particular amount. Multiple translation commands are allowed; in fact, it is common to translate objects individually and as a **universe** grouping. Objects viewed in the perspective mode must reside in the negative Z hemisphere to be seen. The **translate** command allows you to define objects around a local origin before shifting the entire object to a location in space where it will be viewable.

The **object** commands define the start of individual object definitions. Each object is actually created by a group of **move** and **draw** commands, but may be translated and rotated as a complete entity. This allows objects to be created around a local origin, and then manipulated in space to the desired orientation and location.

Following the **object** command are the **translate** and various rotation commands. The translate command was described above. The **rotatex, rotatey,** and **rotatez** commands cause all points on the object to be rotated around one of the three axes in space. The positive X axis runs off the right hand edge of your screen, the positive Y axis runs off the top edge of your screen, and the positive Z axis runs out of the screen towards you. The screen can be thought of as a window residing in the X,Y plane. The rotation commands follow the "right-hand rule" and assume that all angles are expressed in degrees.

The right-hand rule for rotation can be remembered by picturing the thumb of your right hand following the positive direction of an axis. If you curl your fingers slightly toward your palm, they point in the direction of a positive rotation around that axis. For example, the command

rotatex 25

causes the object to rotate 25 degrees around the X axis. Point your thumb to the right, in line with the positive X axis, and notice that points above the center of the screen will follow your fingers and be rotated towards you, while points in the bottom half of the screen will rotate away.

The **move** and **draw** commands are used to create lines in space, which are then projected onto the two dimensional screen. Each of these commands is followed by three numbers: the X,Y,Z coordinates of a point in space. A **move** command moves an imaginary graphics cursor to the indicated point, and a **draw** command creates a visible line while moving to the given coordinates.

The subroutine named **Parse** can be quite useful for many different programmming tasks. Pass a string to this routine, and it passes back a string array of the individual words. "Words" are defined as any group of characters separated by one or more spaces or commas. This can be useful for analyzing command lines entered by a user.

The best way to learn how to create three-dimensional graphics is by experimenting with the various commands. Try changing the order of the translation and rotation commands for an object. Each command is acted upon in the order presented. Because the rotation commands are all referenced to the origin, translating an object before rotating it will affect the rotation. Try changing the order of some of the commands and this will become clearer.

Listing 7-5 shows the program code for **THREE__D.DO**.

Listing 7-5. Three-dimensional graphics program THREE__D.DO (continued through page 188).

```
!   *********************************
!   **   File:        THREE_D.DO      **
!   **   Date:        8/2/85          **
!   **   Author:      John Craig      **
!   **   Language:    True BASIC      **
!   *********************************
!
!   This is a "DO" type program that creates three dimensional
!   graphics using commands residing in the Editing Window.
!
!   Syntax:   DO THREE_D

    EXTERNAL

!   This is the main process
    SUB Main (Prog_line$(),Arg$)

        ! Draw a border around the edges
        SET WINDOW -1,1,-1,1
        SET COLOR "white"
        BOX LINES -1,1,-1,1

        ! Arrays for storing commands
        DIM Universe(9,4),Object(9,4)

        ! For each line in the Editing Window
        FOR Ptr = 1 TO Ubound(Prog_line$)
            CALL Process(Lcase$(Prog_line$(Ptr)))
        NEXT Ptr
```

```
! Process each line from the Editing Window
  SUB Process(A$)

    ! Create an array of strings for parsing each line
      DIM Parm$(9)

    ! Parse the line into an array of strings
      CALL Parse(A$,Parm$)

    ! Check for move or draw first
      IF Parm$(1) = "move" OR Parm$(1) = "draw" THEN
          LET X = Val(Parm$(2))
          LET Y = Val(Parm$(3))
          LET Z = Val(Parm$(4))

        ! Check for object operations
          IF Cmdlevel = 2 THEN
              FOR I = 1 TO 9
                  LET Cmd = Object(I,1)
                  IF Cmd = Ø THEN EXIT FOR
                  LET ANGLE = Object(I,2)
                  LET Tx = Object(I,2)
                  LET Ty = Object(I,3)
                  LET Tz = Object(I,4)
                  SELECT CASE Cmd
                  CASE 1
                      CALL Rotate_x(X,Y,Z,ANGLE)
          CASE 2
              CALL Rotate_y(X,Y,Z,ANGLE)
          CASE 3
              CALL Rotate_z(X,Y,Z,ANGLE)
          CASE 4
              CALL Translate(X,Y,Z,Tx,Ty,Tz)
          CASE ELSE
          END SELECT
      NEXT I
  END IF

! Check for universe operations
  IF Cmdlevel >= 1 THEN
      FOR I = 1 TO 9
          LET Cmd = Universe(I,1)
          IF Cmd = Ø THEN EXIT FOR
          LET ANGLE = Universe(I,2)
          LET Tx = Universe(I,2)
          LET Ty = Universe(I,3)
          LET Tz = Universe(I,4)
          SELECT CASE Cmd
          CASE 1
              CALL Rotate_x(X,Y,Z,ANGLE)
          CASE 2
              CALL Rotate_y(X,Y,Z,ANGLE)
          CASE 3
              CALL Rotate_z(X,Y,Z,ANGLE)
          CASE 4
              CALL Translate(X,Y,Z,Tx,Ty,Tz)
          CASE ELSE
          END SELECT
      NEXT I
```

```
        END IF

    ! Are we in perspective mode?
      IF Orthoflag = Ø THEN
         LET Zterm = Z / Eyez
         LET X = X / (1-Zterm)
         LET Y = Y / (1-Zterm)

         ! Ignore points behind us if perspective view
         IF Z > Ø THEN LET Parm$(1) = "move"
      END IF

    ! Update the current line endpoints
      LET Xold = Xnew
      LET Yold = Ynew
      LET Xnew = X
      LET Ynew = Y

    ! Was this a draw?
      IF Parm$(1) = "draw" THEN
         PLOT LINES: Xold,Yold ; Xnew,Ynew
      END IF

ELSE

! Wasn't a "move" or "draw", check other commands
  SELECT CASE Parm$(1)

    ! Is this a universe command?
  CASE "universe"
      CALL ERASE(Universe)
      CALL ERASE(Object)
      LET Cmdlevel = 1

    ! Is this an object command?
  CASE "object"
      CALL ERASE(Object)
      LET Cmdlevel = 2

    ! Is this a rotatex command?
  CASE "rotatex"
      SELECT CASE Cmdlevel
      CASE 1
         CALL Command_set(Universe,1,Val(Parm$(2)),Ø,Ø)
      CASE 2
         CALL Command_set(Object,1,Val(Parm$(2)),Ø,Ø)
      CASE ELSE
      END SELECT

    ! Is this a rotatey command?
  CASE "rotatey"
      SELECT CASE Cmdlevel
      CASE 1
         CALL Command_set(Universe,2,Val(Parm$(2)),Ø,Ø)
      CASE 2
         CALL Command_set(Object,2,Val(Parm$(2)),Ø,Ø)
      CASE ELSE
      END SELECT

    ! Is this a rotatez command?
```

```
    CASE "rotatez"
        SELECT CASE Cmdlevel
        CASE 1
            CALL Command_set(Universe,3,Val(Parm$(2)),0,0)
        CASE 2
            CALL Command_set(Object,3,Val(Parm$(2)),0,0)
        CASE ELSE
        END SELECT

      ! Is this a translate command?
    CASE "translate"
        LET X = Val(Parm$(2))
        LET Y = Val(Parm$(3))
        LET Z = Val(Parm$(4))
        SELECT CASE Cmdlevel
        CASE 1
            CALL Command_set(Universe,4,X,Y,Z)
        CASE 2
            CALL Command_set(Object,4,X,Y,Z)
        CASE ELSE
        END SELECT

      ! Is this an orthogonal command?
    CASE "orthogonal"
        LET Vertical = Val(Parm$(2)) / 2
        LET Horizontal = 4 * Vertical / 3
        SET WINDOW -Horizontal,Horizontal,-Vertical,Vertical
        LET Orthoflag = 1
                    ! Is this a perspective command?
                CASE "perspective"
                    LET Ang = Rad(Val(Parm$(2)))
                    LET Eyez = 1 / Tan(Ang / 2)
                    SET WINDOW -4/3,4/3,-1,1
                    LET Orthoflag = 0

                    ! Must have been a comment line
                CASE ELSE
                END SELECT

            END IF

        ! Finished processing each line
        END SUB

    ! (This is where we return to the Editing Window)
    END SUB

! Subroutine, rotation around x axis
  SUB Rotate_x(X,Y,Z,DEGREES)
      LET Ang = Rad(DEGREES)
      LET Ca = Cos(Ang)
      LET Sa = Sin(Ang)
      LET T = Y*Ca-Z*Sa
      LET Z = Z*Ca+Y*Sa
      LET Y = T
  END SUB

! Subroutine, rotation around y axis
  SUB Rotate_y(X,Y,Z,DEGREES)
```

```
        LET Ang = Rad(DEGREES)
        LET Ca = Cos(Ang)
        LET Sa = Sin(Ang)
        LET T = X*Ca+Z*Sa
        LET Z = Z*Ca-X*Sa
        LET X = T
    END SUB

! Subroutine, Rotation Around Z Axis
    SUB Rotate_z(X,Y,Z,DEGREES)
        LET Ang = Rad(DEGREES)
        LET Ca = Cos(Ang)
        LET Sa = Sin(Ang)
        LET T = X*Ca-Y*Sa
        LET Y = Y*Ca+X*Sa
        LET X = T
    END SUB

! Subroutine, translate x,y,z by adding tx,ty,tz
    SUB Translate(X,Y,Z,Tx,Ty,Tz)
        LET X = X + Tx
        LET Y = Y + Ty
        LET Z = Z + Tz
    END SUB

! Subroutine, erase the passed command array
    SUB ERASE(Array(,))
        FOR I = 1 TO Size(Array,1)
            LET Array(I,1) = 0
        NEXT I
    END SUB

! Subroutine, place command in proper place
    SUB Command_set(Array(,),Cmd,X,Y,Z)
        FOR I = 1 TO Size(Array,1)
            IF Array(I,1) = 0 THEN
                LET Array(I,1) = Cmd
                LET Array(I,2) = X
                LET Array(I,3) = Y
                LET Array(I,4) = Z
                EXIT FOR
            END IF
        NEXT I
    END SUB

! Subroutine to parse a string into individual words.
! Words are separated by spaces or commas.
!
    SUB Parse(A$,Parm$())

        ! Change all commas to spaces
        DO
            LET Position = Pos(A$,",")
            IF Position > 0 THEN LET A$(Position:Position) = " "
        LOOP UNTIL Position = 0

        ! Extract each word
        DO
            LET Ptr = Ptr + 1
            LET A$ = Trim$(A$) & " "
```

```
            LET Position = Pos(A$," ")
            LET Parm$(Ptr) = A$(1:Position-1)
            LET A$ = Trim$(A$(Position:Maxnum))
        LOOP UNTIL A$ = ""

END SUB
```

Chapter 8

File Manipulations

The programs in this chapter demonstrate the use of files using True BASIC. Techniques are presented for converting binary files to ASCII, enciphering any type of file, and for saving the entire contents of a graphics screen in a file.

BIN2HEX

With this program we can convert any file to a file consisting of standard ASCII characters. There are several possible uses for such a program. Suppose, for example, that you've written a handy utility program in assembly language and want to publish the program in a magazine, but you don't want to print the long assembly language listing. This program converts your binary program file into a file suitable for printing out with your printer, and which may be easily typed into a reader's computer using any standard text editor. By running the sister program named **HEX2BIN**, also presented in this book, the reader can then convert the file back to a copy of the original binary utility file.

Some communications packages don't support full 8-bit binary data transfer. Another use of this program is to convert any file into a format suitable for 7-bit transmission. This can solve some sticky communications problems for some people.

The program works by reading in one byte at a time from the file to be converted, and then writing out two hexadecimal character bytes as determined by a look-up table created in the string named **Hex$**. The use of a look-up table is faster and more efficient than other techniques that I tried.

The file processed in this manner can be any type of binary or ASCII file when using the PC-DOS operating system on an IBM PC. If you're using a different computer, be aware that it might be illegal to open a file in binary mode if it was originally created in a different mode. You might have to figure out a "work-around" if you run into this situation.

Let's process the short file named **PIETEST.TRU** with this program and call the output **PIETEST.HEX**. Here's what you should see on your display:

* BIN2HEX*

```
Name of input file ............... ? pietest.tru
Name of output file.............. ? pietest.hex
```

After the program finishes, you may load each into True BASIC's Editing Window to see the "before and after" contents of the files. Here's what the **PIETEST.TRU** file should look like:

```
TITLE Granny's Pie Company

    ITEM 17 Apple
    ITEM 12 Banana cream
    ITEM 9  Peach
    ITEM 9  Plum
    ITEM 21 Strawberry
    ITEM 10 Blueberry
    END
```

The resulting PIETEST.HEX file is shown in Fig. 8-1.

To double-check things, run the **HEX2BIN** program on this hexadecimal-format file, using a third filename for the output of that program. The final resulting file should be identical in content to the original **PIETEST.TRU** file.

The program code for **BIN2HEX** is shown in Listing 8-1.

HEX2BIN

This program (Listing 8-2) reconstructs binary files that have been converted to hexademical character files by the **BIN2HEX** program. This program actually will convert any hexadecimal characters in a file to the equivalent binary bytes. This provides

```
5449544C452020204772616E6E792773
2050696520436F6D70616E790D0A0D0A
4954454D20313720417070C650D0A49
54454D2031322042616E616E61206372
65616D0D0A4954454D20392020506561
63680D0A4954454D20392020506C756D
0D0A4954454D2032312053747261776276
657272790D0A4954454D20313020426C
75656265727279790D0A0D0A454E440D0A
```

Fig. 8-1. Typical hexadecimal output file of the BIN2HEX program.

Listing 8-1. Program to convert files to hexadecimal format.

```
!   **********************************
!   **   File:        BIN2HEX.TRU     **
!   **   Date:        7/16/85         **
!   **   Author:      John Craig      **
!   **   Language:    True BASIC      **
!   **********************************
!
!   This program converts any file, either ASCII or binary, to
!   an ASCII file of hexadecimal characters, suitable for
!   processing with a text editor or sending over a modem.
!   Use HEX2BIN.TRU to convert the file back to it's original
!   form.

!   Clean slate
    CLEAR

!   Name of program
    PRINT "* BIN2HEX *"
    PRINT

!   Ask user for input file name
    PRINT
    INPUT PROMPT "Name of input file ...   ? ":Filein$
    OPEN #1: NAME Filein$, ACCESS "input", ORGANIZATION "byte"

!   Ask user for output file name
    INPUT PROMPT "Name of output file...   ? ":Fileout$
    OPEN #2: NAME Fileout$, ACCESS "output", CREATE "new", ORGANIZATION "byte"

!   Build a table of hexadecimal characters
    LET Hex$ =         "000102030405060708090A0B0C0D0E0F"
    LET Hex$ = Hex$ & "101112131415161718191A1B1C1D1E1F"
    LET Hex$ = Hex$ & "202122232425262728292A2B2C2D2E2F"
    LET Hex$ = Hex$ & "303132333435363738393A3B3C3D3E3F"
    LET Hex$ = Hex$ & "404142434445464748494A4B4C4D4E4F"
    LET Hex$ = Hex$ & "505152535455565758595A5B5C5D5E5F"
    LET Hex$ = Hex$ & "606162636465666768696A6B6C6D6E6F"
    LET Hex$ = Hex$ & "707172737475767778797A7B7C7D7E7F"
    LET Hex$ = Hex$ & "808182838485868788898A8B8C8D8E8F"
    LET Hex$ = Hex$ & "909192939495969798999A9B9C9D9E9F"
    LET Hex$ = Hex$ & "A0A1A2A3A4A5A6A7A8A9AAABACADAEAF"
    LET Hex$ = Hex$ & "B0B1B2B3B4B5B6B7B8B9BABBBCBDBEBF"
    LET Hex$ = Hex$ & "C0C1C2C3C4C5C6C7C8C9CACBCCCDCECF"
    LET Hex$ = Hex$ & "D0D1D2D3D4D5D6D7D8D9DADBDCDDDEDF"
    LET Hex$ = Hex$ & "E0E1E2E3E4E5E6E7E8E9EAEBECEDEEEF"
    LET Hex$ = Hex$ & "F0F1F2F3F4F5F6F7F8F9FAFBFCFDFEFF"

!   Process each character of the file
    DO WHILE MORE #1

        !  Get each byte
        READ #1, Bytes 1: Byte$

        !  Process each byte
        IF Len(Byte$) = 1 THEN
            LET Ptr = Ord(Byte$) * 2 + 1

            !  Output the two hexadecimal characters to the file
```

```
            WRITE #2: Hex$(Ptr:Ptr+1)

        ! Every 16 bytes start a new string
          LET Count = Count + 1
          IF Count = 16 THEN
              WRITE #2: Chr$(13)   ! Carriage return
              WRITE #2: Chr$(10)   ! Line feed
              LET Count = 0
          END IF

      END IF

    ! Do all the bytes until the end of the file
  LOOP

! Add final CR/LF if string has been partially written
  IF Count > 0 THEN
      WRITE #2: Chr$(13)   ! Carriage return
      WRITE #2: Chr$(10)   ! Line feed
  END IF

! Close up the files
  CLOSE #1
  CLOSE #2

! End of the conversion process
  END
```

Listing 8-2. HEX2BIN reconverts files processed through the BIN2HEX program.

```
! *********************************
! **  File:      HEX2BIN.TRU     **
! **  Date:      7/16/85         **
! **  Author:    John Craig      **
! **  Language:  True BASIC      **
! *********************************
!
! This program reconverts any file back to it's original
! form after having been converted by the BIN2HEX program.
! Or, this can be a convenient method of building a binary
! file if you are given a hexadecimal list of the bytes.

! Clean slate
  CLEAR

! Name of program
  PRINT "* HEX2BIN *"
  PRINT

!  Ask user for input file name
  PRINT
  INPUT PROMPT "Name of input file ...  ? ":Filein$
  OPEN #1: NAME Filein$, ACCESS "input", ORGANIZATION "byte"

! Ask user for output file name
  INPUT PROMPT "Name of output file...  ? ":Fileout$
  OPEN #2: NAME Fileout$, ACCESS "output", CREATE "new", ORGANIZATION "byte"
```

```
! Process each character of the file
  DO WHILE MORE #1

    ! Get each byte
      READ #1, Bytes 1: Byte$

    ! Process each byte
      IF Len(Byte$) = 1 THEN
          IF Byte$ >= "Ø" AND Byte$ <= "9" THEN
              LET X = Ord(Byte$)-48
          ELSEIF Byte$ >= "A" AND Byte$ <= "F" THEN
              LET X = Ord(Byte$) - 55
          ELSE
              LET X = -1
          END IF

          ! Combine two nibbles at a time
          IF X >= Ø THEN
              LET Count = Count + 1
              IF Count = 1 THEN
                  LET Byte = X
              ELSE
                  LET Byte = Byte * 16 + X
                  LET Count = Ø
                  WRITE #2: Chr$(Byte)
              END IF
          END IF
      END IF

    END IF

    ! Do all the bytes until the end of the file
  LOOP

! Close up the files
  CLOSE #1
  CLOSE #2

! End of the conversion process
  END
```

a convenient way to build .**COM** files from the listings in popular magazines.

Use any editor (don't overlook the excellent text-editing capabilities of the True BASIC editor!) and create an ASCII file containing just the hexadecimal characters representing the resultant .**COM** file. Extra spaces are ignored, so feel free to include them between pairs of hexadecimal characters if desired. Save the file on disk and process it with this program to create the desired binary .**COM** file.

CIPHER

This program enciphers and deciphers any file, for securing sensitive data. The method used can probably be broken by the National Security Agency if they so desire, but it definitely will protect your data from most prying eyes.

The method used is fairly simple and straightforward. Each byte of the file to be ciphered is XORed with pseudorandom byte generated sequentially as a function of a key string you enter. The exclusive-or operation generates a one bit wherever the corresponding bits in the two bytes differ from each other and a zero bit if they are the same. A neat feature of this exclusive-or process is the ability to extract the original byte simply by doing the XOR with the same pseudorandom byte a second time. In other words, your ciphered file can be deciphered by processing it with the same key string that was originally used to encipher it.

To be able to decipher a ciphered file you must remember the key string used for enciphering it. This key string can be any string of your choice, so don't be lulled into using the fairly obvious keys such as your name, initials, Social Security number, etc. Think of some short, wacky phrase that you're not likely to forget; don't write it down anywhere, and don't tell it to anyone else if possible.

This is one of the few programs in this book that uses the History Window for interaction with the user, rather than the Editing Window. The **CLEAR** statement in the other programs causes the entire screen to erase, and all printed messages to appear there. This program doesn't have a **CLEAR** statement, and by default all **PRINT** statements send their output to the last line of the History Window.

Listing 8-3 is the code for the **CIPHER** program.

Listing 8-3. Encryption/decryption program CIPHER.TRU.

```
!  ***********************************
!  **  File:       CIPHER.TRU     **
!  **  Date:       3/8/85         **
!  **  Author:     John Craig     **
!  **  Language:   True BASIC     **
!  ***********************************
!
!  This program allows you to encipher or decipher any file.
!  By using the same key twice on the same file, the contents
!  are restored to their original condition.

!  Function to bitwise XOR two strings together
   FUNCTION Xor$(A$,B$)
       FOR I = 1 TO 8 * Min(Len(A$),Len(B$))
           CALL Packb(C$,I,1,Unpackb(A$,I,1)+Unpackb(B$,I,1))
       NEXT I
       LET Xor$ = C$
   END FUNCTION

!  Ask user for input file name
   PRINT
   INPUT PROMPT "Name of input file ...  ? ":Filein$
   OPEN #1: NAME Filein$, ACCESS "input", ORGANIZATION "byte"

!  Ask user for output file name
   INPUT PROMPT "Name of output file...  ? ":Fileout$
   OPEN #2: NAME Fileout$, ACCESS "output", CREATE "new", ORGANIZATION "byte"

!  Ask user for the key string
   PRINT
   PRINT "Type in the key (Any string of characters)..."
   LINE INPUT Key_string$
```

```
     LET Key_string$ = Key_string$ & "Default key string"

! Scroll the key string out of site
  FOR I = 1 TO 25
      PRINT
  NEXT I

! Create the starting random seed number
  FOR I = 1 TO Len(Key_string$)
      LET Seed = Mod((Seed+1/Ord(Key_string$(I:I)))*997+Pi,1)
  NEXT I

! Process each character of the file
  DO WHILE MORE #1

     ! Get each byte
     READ #1, Bytes 1: Byte$

     ! Process each byte
     IF Len(Byte$) = 1 THEN
         LET Seed = Mod(Seed*997+Pi,1)
         LET Seed$ = Chr$(Int(Seed*256))
         WRITE #2: Xor$(Byte$,Seed$)
     END IF

     ! Do all the bytes until the end of the file
  LOOP

! End of the ciphering process
  END
```

IMGFILES

The main purpose of this program is to demonstrate subroutines for saving to and reloading from a disk file the contents of a graphics screen image. Two other subroutines are also shown: The **Frame** subroutine draws a line box frame around the edges of any window, and the **Arc** subroutine draws an arc, or part of a circle, as desired.

When you run this program a "happy face" image (Fig. 8-2) will first be created, demonstrating the **Frame** and **Arc** subroutines. The entire 16,000 bytes comprising video memory are then copied into a string which is saved in a file named **IMGTEST.TRU**. (Make sure you have enough room on the disk in the default drive for this file to be created.) Finally, the screen is cleared and the file is reloaded into the video memory.

These two subroutines, **Save__screen** and **Load__screen**, would be prime candidates for placing in a "library" file, ready to be used by other programs you create. Listing 8-4 shows the program code.

LOADPIC

This program (Listing 8-5) is a general-purpose program for loading into video memory any image file created by use of the **Save__screen** function, as demonstrated in the **IMGFILES** and **MANDEBR** programs.

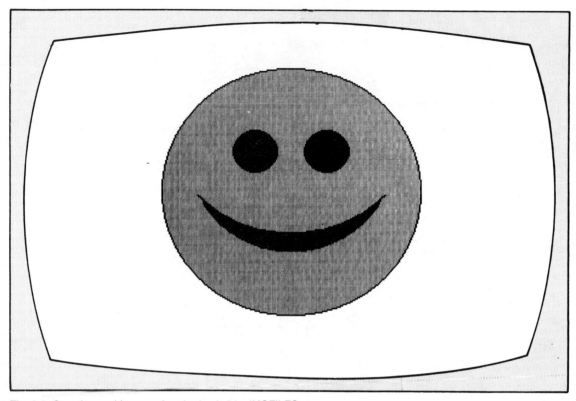

Fig. 8-2. Sample graphics saved and reloaded by IMGFILES.

Listing 8-4. Program to save and retrieve screen graphics (continued to page 198).

```
! ************************************
! **  File:       IMGFILES.TRU    **
! **  Date:        8/12/85        **
! **  Author:     John Craig      **
! **  Language:   True BASIC      **
! ************************************
!
! This program demonstrates subroutines for saving and
! reloading graphics screen images.  This program is designed
! for the IBM PC 320 X 200 medium resolution graphics mode.

! Start with a clean slate
  CLEAR

! Display program name
  PRINT "* IMGFILES *"
  PRINT

! Explain the operation to the user
  PRINT "A medium resolution graphics image will be created,"
  PRINT "stored in a file named IMGTEST.TRU, and then loaded"
  PRINT "back onto the screen."
```

```
  PRINT
  PRINT "Press the space bar when you are ready..."

! Wait for the space bar
  DO
      IF KEY INPUT THEN GET KEY Keycode
  LOOP UNTIL Keycode = Ord(" ")

! Create some "art"
  CALL Happy_face

! Store copy of screen to disk file
  CALL Save_screen("IMGTEST")

! Clear the screen
  CLEAR

! Load the image back onto the screen
  CALL Load_screen("IMGTEST")

! All done
  END

! Subroutine to save copy of IBM PC medium resolution screen image
  SUB Save_screen(File$)

    ! Copy screen bytes into a string
      FOR Location = 1 TO 8000
          LET Img$ = Img$ & Chr$(Peek(753663+Location))
          LET Img$ = Img$ & Chr$(Peek(761855+Location))
      NEXT Location

    ! Open the file
      OPEN #1: NAME File$, CREATE Newold, ORGANIZATION Byte

    ! Store string in file
      WRITE #1: Img$

    ! Close the file
      CLOSE #1

  END SUB

! Subroutine to load copy of IBM PC medium resolution screen image
  SUB Load_screen(File$)

    ! Open the file
      OPEN #1: NAME File$, ORGANIZATION Byte

    ! Load string from file
      READ #1, Bytes 16000: Img$

    ! Close the file
      CLOSE #1

    ! Copy string bytes onto screen
      FOR Location = 1 TO 8000
          LET Ptr = Ptr + 1
          CALL Poke(753663+Location,Ord(Img$(Ptr:Ptr)))
          LET Ptr = Ptr + 1
```

```
            CALL Poke(761855+Location,Ord(Img$(Ptr:Ptr)))
        NEXT Location

    ! Wait for a key press
        GET KEY Before_quitting

END SUB

! Subroutine to draw a "happy face"
  SUB Happy_face
      SET WINDOW -4/3,4/3,-1,1
      SET COLOR "yellow"
      CALL Arc(0,.6,.9,224,316)
      CALL Arc(0,.27,.7,206,334)
      BOX ELLIPSE -.4,-.1,.15,.45
      BOX ELLIPSE .1,.4,.15,.45
      BOX ELLIPSE -.9,.9,-.9,.9
      FLOOD -.3,.2
      FLOOD .3,.2
      FLOOD 0,-.4
      SET COLOR "green"
      FLOOD 0,0
      SET COLOR "red"
      CALL Frame
  END SUB

! Subroutine to draw an arc
! X,Y    are center point of circle defining the arc
! R      is the radius of the circle
! A1,A2  are the starting and ending angles, in degrees
!
  SUB Arc(X,Y,R,A1,A2)
      OPTION ANGLE DEGREES
      DO WHILE A2 < A1
          LET A2 = A2 + 360
      LOOP
      FOR Ang = Mod(A1,360) TO Mod(A2,360) STEP 2
          PLOT LINES: X + R * Cos(Ang), Y + R * Sin(Ang);
      NEXT Ang
      PLOT LINES: X + R * Cos(A2), Y + R * Sin(A2)
  END SUB

! Subroutine to draw a frame around a window
  SUB Frame
      ASK WINDOW Left,Right,Bottom,Top
      BOX LINES Left,Right,Bottom,Top
  END SUB
```

Listing 8-5. Program to load screen image files.

```
! ********************************
! **   File:      LOADPIC.TRU   **
! **   Date:      8/12/85       **
! **   Author:    John Craig     **
! **   Language:  True BASIC     **
! ********************************
!
```

```
! This program loads in image files created by the
! Save_screen subroutine as demonstrated in the MANDELBR program.

! Start with a clean slate
  CLEAR

! Display program name
  PRINT "* LOADPIC *"
  PRINT

! Ask for the image file name
  INPUT PROMPT "Enter the file name ? ": File$

! Set graphics window
  SET WINDOW 0,1,0,1

! Load in the image
  CALL Load_screen(File$)

! All done
  END

! Subroutine to load copy of IBM PC medium resolution screen image
  SUB Load_screen(File$)

     ! Open the file
       OPEN #1: NAME File$, ORGANIZATION Byte

     ! Load string from file
       READ #1, Bytes 16000: Img$

     ! Close the file
       CLOSE #1

     ! Copy string bytes onto screen
       FOR Location = 1 TO 8000
           LET Ptr = Ptr + 1
           CALL Poke(753663+Location,Ord(Img$(Ptr:Ptr)))
           LET Ptr = Ptr + 1
           CALL Poke(761855+Location,Ord(Img$(Ptr:Ptr)))
       NEXT Location

     ! Wait for any key press
       GET KEY Before_quitting

     ! All done
  END SUB
```

Chapter 9

Graphics Analysis

Tables of numbers can be boring or confusing. This chapter livens things up by allowing you to generate a quick barchart or piechart of a table of numbers, or a quick sketch of a numerical function.

PIECHART

This DO-type program demonstrates how data can be entered, edited, and graphically analyzed while residing in the Editing Window. This technique provides quick interaction with your data; it's a snap to add new or delete old information and see the resulting graph.

To see this program in action, load or type in the file named **PIETEST.TRU**. This short list of statements provides the title and data necessary to create a quick piechart:

```
TITLE Granny's Pie Company

ITEM 17 Apple
ITEM 12 Banana cream
ITEM 9  Peach
ITEM 9  Plum
ITEM 21 Strawberry
ITEM 10 Blueberry

END
```

There are three types of lines in this file (four if you want to count the blank lines, which are ignored by the PIECHART program). The TITLE line provides a string that will be centered at the top of the chart. The ITEM lines provide the raw ingredients for making our pie. Notice that these lines contain a quantity and a label defining each wedge of the pie. The END statement tells the PIECHART program that we're finished. Edit these lines to change the piechart as desired.

To create the pie chart, simply type "do piechart." Figure 9-1 shows the chart generated by the sample data, and Listing 9-1 is the program code.

QUICKBAR

This program demonstrates the use of one of the libraries of routines provided with True BASIC. The LIBRARY statement, used near the beginning of this program, patches in all of the subroutines and/or functions contained in the indicated library file. In this case we are interested in calling the subroutine named Bars, contained in the library file named graphlib.

The DATA statement in program QUICKBAR contains a collection of numbers. The program generates a simple bar chart for these numbers, providing a quick intuitive grasp of the relative magnitudes and patterns of the numbers. Feel free to edit the numbers in the DATA statement; the program was designed to accommodate a variable quantity of numbers of any size.

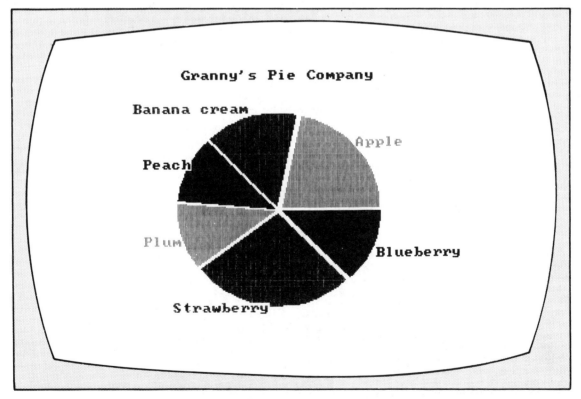

Fig. 9-1. Pie chart created using the PIETEST.TRU file.

Listing 9-1. Pie chart creation program (continued to page 204).

```
! ********************************
! **   File:        PIECHART.DO      **
! **   Date:        8/14/85          **
! **   Author:      John Craig       **
! **   Language:    True BASIC       **
! ********************************
!
! This is a "DO" type program that creates a piechart using
! information currently residing in the Editing Window.
!
! Syntax:   DO PIECHART

  EXTERNAL

! This is the main process
  SUB Main (Prog_line$(),Arg$)

    ! Save room for info on each slice of pie
      DIM Item$(20),Qnty(20)

    ! Draw a border around the edges
      SET WINDOW 0,1,0,1
      SET COLOR "green"
      BOX LINES 0,1,0,1

    ! Process each line in the Editing Window
      FOR Ptr = 1 TO Ubound(Prog_line$)
          CALL Process_each_line(Prog_line$(Ptr),Item$,Qnty)
      NEXT Ptr

    ! Wait for any key press
      GET KEY Before_quitting

  END SUB
! This is where we return to the Editing Window

! Work on one line at a time here
  SUB Process_each_line(String$,Item$(),Qnty())

    ! Create an array of strings for parsing each line
      DIM Parm$(20)

    ! Parse the line into an array of strings
      CALL Parse(String$,Parm$)

    ! Check for a "title" command
      IF Ucase$(Parm$(1)) = "TITLE" THEN
          LET Label$ = Parm$(2)
          FOR I = 3 TO 20
              IF Parm$(I) = "" THEN EXIT FOR
              LET Label$ = Label$ & " " & Parm$(I)
          NEXT I
          SET COLOR "yellow"
          SET CURSOR 3,2
          PRINT USING Repeat$("#",38): Label$
      END IF
```

```
        ! Check for an "item" command
        IF Ucase$(Parm$(1)) = "ITEM" THEN
            LET Amount = Val(Parm$(2))
            LET Thing$ = Parm$(3)
            FOR I = 4 TO 20
                IF Thing$ = "" THEN EXIT FOR
                LET Thing$ = Thing$ & " " & Parm$(I)
            NEXT I
            FOR I = 1 TO 20
                IF Item$(I) = "" THEN
                    LET Item$(I) = Thing$
                    LET Qnty(I) = Amount
                    EXIT FOR
                END IF
            NEXT I
        END IF

        ! Check for "END" command
        IF Ucase$(Parm$(1)) = "END" THEN
            CALL Serve_pie(Item$,Qnty)
        END IF

    END SUB

! Subroutine to parse a string into individual words.
! Words are separated by spaces or commas.
!
    SUB Parse(String$,Parm$())

        ! Work on a copy of the passed string
        LET A$ = String$

        ! Extract each word
        DO
            LET Ptr = Ptr + 1
            LET A$ = Trim$(A$) & " "
            LET Position = Pos(A$," ")
            LET Parm$(Ptr) = A$(1:Position-1)
            LET A$ = Trim$(A$(Position:Maxnum))
        LOOP UNTIL A$ = ""

        ! Set parameter after the last one to a null string
        LET Parm$(Ptr + 1) = ""

    END SUB

! Subroutine to draw the main piechart
    SUB Serve_pie(Item$(),Qnty())

        ! Determine number of pie slices and total weight of pie
        FOR Slice = 0 TO 19
            LET Weight = Weight + Qnty(Slice+1)
            IF Qnty(Slice+1) = 0 THEN EXIT FOR
        NEXT Slice

        ! Scale the window for drawing the pie
        LET Scale = .5
        LET Left = -Scale * 4
        LET Right = Scale * 4
```

```
      LET Bottom = -Scale * 2.5
      LET Top = Scale * 3.5
      SET WINDOW Left,Right,Bottom,Top


      Define how far from center to slide each slice
      LET Shift = .05

      Do each wedge (slice)
      FOR I = 1 TO Slice

         ! Rotate through colors 1, 2 and 3
         LET Clr = Mod(Clr,3) + 1
         SET COLOR Clr

         ! Calculate angles for each edge of the slice
         LET Ang1 = Ang2
         LET Ang2 = Ang1 + 2 * Pi * Qnty(I) / Weight

         ! Calculate the center, or averaged slice angle
         LET Avang = (Ang1 + Ang2) / 2

         ! Calculate the sliding distance for the slice
         LET Xc = Shift * Cos(Avang)
         LET Yc = Shift * Sin(Avang)

         ! Draw the curved "crust" edge
         FOR J = Ang1 TO Ang2 STEP (Ang2-Ang1)/20
             PLOT LINES: Xc + Cos(J), Yc + Sin(J);
         NEXT J

         ! Connect the crust to the center
         PLOT LINES: Xc + Cos(Ang2), Yc + Sin(Ang2);
         PLOT LINES: Xc,Yc;
         PLOT LINES: Xc + Cos(Ang1), Yc + Sin(Ang1)

         ! Pour in some quick setting filling
         FLOOD Xc + .5 * Cos(Avang), Yc + .5 * Sin(Avang)

         ! Put a label on each slice
         LET X1 = Xc + Cos(Avang)
         LET Y1 = Yc + Sin(Avang)
         LET Down = 25 * (Y1 - Top) / (Bottom - Top)
         IF Y1 < 0 THEN LET Down = Down + 1
         LET Across = 40 * (X1 - Left) / (Right - Left)
         IF X1 < 0 THEN
             LET Across = Across - Len(Trim$(Item$(I))) + 1
         ELSE
             LET Across = Across + 1
         END IF
         SET CURSOR Down,Across
         PRINT Trim$(Item$(I));

      ! Ready for another slice ?
      NEXT I

   ! We drew the whole thing
END SUB
```

Figure 9-2 shows the bar chart generated with the numbers given, and Listing 9-2 is the True BASIC code.

QUICKPLT

This program demonstrates the use of one of the libraries of routines provided with True BASIC. The **LIBRARY** statement, used near the beginning of this program, patches in all of the subroutines and/or functions contained in the indicated library file. In this case we are interested in calling the subroutine named **Fplot**, contained in the library file named **graphlib**.

The **QUICKPLT** program first prompts you for the starting and ending values of X to define the sketch:

```
* QUICKPLT *

Starting value of X ?    – 17
Ending value of X ?      17
```

The program then generates a simple plot of the function you've defined as F, providing a quick intuitive grasp of the function. Feel free to redefine the function F as desired.

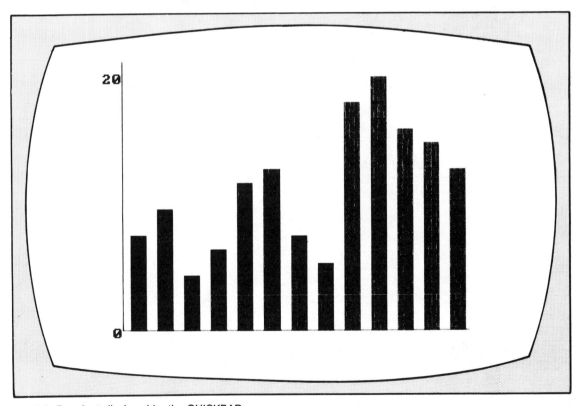

Fig. 9-2. Bar chart displayed by the QUICKBAR program.

Listing 9-2. Bar chart creation program.

```
! ********************************
! ** File:        QUICKBAR.TRU   **
! ** Date:        8/10/85        **
! ** Author:      John Craig     **
! ** Language:    True BASIC     **
! ********************************
!
! This program generates a quick bar graph of a table of numbers
! entered by the user in DATA statements.

! Grab the graphics library routines
  LIBRARY "\tbfiles\graphlib"

! Prepare array space
  DIM Array(1000)

! Grab the data
  WHEN EXCEPTION IN
       DO
            READ Array(Count + 1)
            LET Count = Count + 1
       LOOP
  USE
       CALL Bars(Array,Count)
  END WHEN

! Here's the sample data, edit these for your data
  DATA 7,9,4,6,11,12,7,5,17,19,15,14,12

! Wait for a key press
  GET KEY Before_continuing

! All done
  END
```

Listing 9-3. Program to plot graphs of functions.

```
! ********************************
! ** File:        QUICKPLT.TRU   **
! ** Date:        8/10/85        **
! ** Author:      John Craig     **
! ** Language:    True BASIC     **
! ********************************
!
! This program generates a quick sketch of any function F(x)
! that is defined by the user as an external function.

! Grab the graphics library routines
  LIBRARY "\tbfiles\graphlib"

! Declare external function
  DECLARE FUNCTION F
  CLEAR

! Display program name
  PRINT "* QUICKPLT *"
```

```
    PRINT

! Ask user for the plot range
  INPUT PROMPT "Starting value of X ? ": X1
  INPUT PROMPT "Ending value of X ?   ": X2

! Generate the quick sketch
  CALL Fplot(X1,X2)

! Wait for any key press
  GET KEY Before_quitting

! All done
  END

! User defined function F(x)
! In this example, we will sketch Y = SIN(X) / X
!
  FUNCTION F(X)
      IF X <> Ø THEN
          LET F = Sin(X) / X
      ELSE
          LET F = 1
      END IF
  END FUNCTION
```

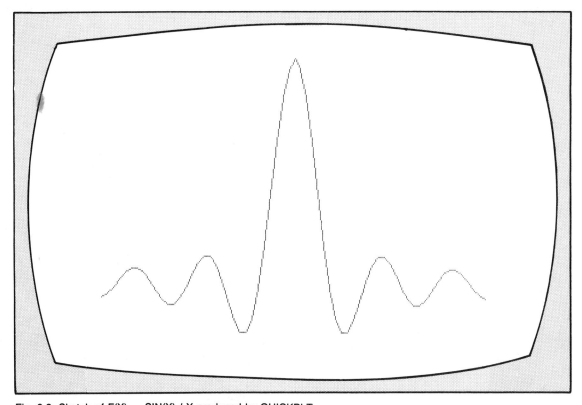

Fig. 9-3. Sketch of F(X) = SIN(X) / X produced by QUICKPLT.

Figure 9-3 shows the plot of the function

F(X) = SIN(X) /X

for X values from − 17 to + 17. Listing 9-3 is the code.

Appendix

A few of the illustrations in this book were created by short programs written just for this purpose. For those who are interested, here are the program listings.

BRIDGE.FIG

```
OPTION ANGLE DEGREES

PICTURE Element
    PLOT LINES: 0,0; 1,0; 1,.2; 2,.2; 2,-.2; 1,-.2; 1,0
    PLOT LINES: 2,0; 3,0
END PICTURE

PICTURE Ground
    PLOT LINES: 0,0; 0,-3
    PLOT LINES: -2,-3; 2,-3
    PLOT LINES: -1.5,-4; 1.5,-4
    PLOT LINES: -1,-5; 1,-5
END PICTURE

SET WINDOW 0,8,0,8
SET COLOR "white"
BOX LINES 0,8,0,8

DRAW Element WITH Rotate(-60) * Shift(2.5,4)
DRAW Element WITH Rotate(-120) * Shift(5.5,4)
DRAW Element WITH Rotate(60) * Shift(2.5,4)
```

```
DRAW Element WITH Rotate(120) * Shift(5.5,4)
DRAW Ground WITH Scale(.2) * Shift(4,1.4)

PLOT LINES: 2.5,4; 3.5,4
PLOT LINES: 5.5,4; 4.5,4
PLOT TEXT, AT 3.7,4: "0 V"

PLOT LINES: 4,6.6; 2,6.6
PLOT TEXT, AT 1.4,6.3: "V+"

PLOT TEXT, AT 2,7.5: "Balanced Bridge Network"

END
```

CIRCLE3P.FIG

```
LIBRARY "\tbfiles\graphlib"

SET WINDOW -8,15,-3,15
SET COLOR "yellow"

CALL Ticks(1,1)

CALL Arc(.684211,7.34211,6.34996,0,360)

BOX ELLIPSE .8,1.2,.8,1.2
BOX ELLIPSE 6.8,7.2,7.8,8.2
BOX ELLIPSE 4.8,5.2,11.8,12.2

PLOT TEXT, AT 1,2: "(1,1)"
PLOT TEXT, AT 8,8: "(7,8)"
PLOT TEXT, AT 6,12: "(5,12)"

CALL Frame

END
```

RCTIMING.FIG

```
PICTURE Resistor
    PLOT LINES: 0,0; 2,1; -2,2; 2,3; -2,4; 0,5; 0,6
END PICTURE

PICTURE Capacitor
    PLOT LINES: 0,0; 0,2
    PLOT LINES: -2,2; 2,2
    PLOT LINES: -2,3; 2,3
    PLOT LINES: 0,3; 0,5
END PICTURE

PICTURE Ground
    PLOT LINES: 0,0; 0,-3
    PLOT LINES: -2,-3; 2,-3
    PLOT LINES: -1.5,-4; 1.5,-4
    PLOT LINES: -1,-5; 1,-5
```

```
END PICTURE

SET WINDOW 0,30,0,25
SET COLOR "white"
BOX LINES 0,30,0,25

DRAW Ground WITH Shift(15,10)
DRAW Capacitor WITH Shift(15,10)
DRAW Resistor WITH Scale(.5,1) * Shift(15,15)

PLOT LINES: 15,21; 10,21
PLOT LINES: 15,14; 20,14

PLOT TEXT, AT 4,20: "V1 " & Chr$(26) & " V2"
PLOT TEXT, AT 12,17: "R"
PLOT TEXT, AT 11,12: "C"
PLOT TEXT, AT 21,14: "Vi"
PLOT TEXT, AT 11,23: "RC TIMING"

END
```

DELWYE.FIG

```
OPTION ANGLE DEGREES

PICTURE Element
    PLOT LINES: 0,0; 1,0; 1,.2; 2,.2; 2,-.2; 1,-.2; 1,0
    PLOT LINES: 2,0; 3,0
END PICTURE

SET WINDOW 0,9,0,6
SET COLOR "white"
BOX LINES 0,9,0,6

DRAW Element WITH Shift(1,4)
DRAW Element WITH Rotate(-60) * Shift(1,4)
DRAW Element WITH Rotate(-120) * Shift(4,4)

DRAW Element WITH Rotate(30) * Scale(.6,1.1) * Shift(6.5,3.1)
DRAW Element WITH Rotate(150) * Scale(.6,1.1) * Shift(6.5,3.1)
DRAW Element WITH Rotate(270) * Scale(.6,1.1) * Shift(6.5,3.1)

PLOT TEXT, AT 2,5: "Delta              Wye"

END
```

Index

212

Other Bestsellers From TAB

☐ **MACINTOSH™ PROGRAMMING USING MS-BASIC™ 2.0**

Go beyond the constraints of ordinary BASIC and discover how MS-BASIC 2.0 can turn your Mac into a high-powered programming machine! Now this unprecedented manual takes off where the users manual leaves off and shows how you can make the most of the special interactive features of MA-BASIC 2.0. With an emphasis on learning-by-doing, expert programmer Richard Vile guides you confidently through techniques for using the menus, windows, buttons, edit fields, dialog boxes, mouse, quickdraw graphics, and other conveniences. And most importantly, he demonstrates these features in action using more than 20 ready-to-run programs. Once you discover how to build upon the unique features of the Macintosh, the applications available to you are wide open. 288 pp., 117 illus. Large Format (7″ × 10″).

Paper $16.95   **Book No. 2621**
Hard $24.95

☐ **MACINTOSH™ ASSEMBLY LANGUAGE PROGRAMMING**

Delve below the surface-level capabilities of your Macintosh and discover the incredible power that assembly language can unlock. You'll learn all about the fundamentals of machine code . . . gain an understanding of editors and assemblers . . . and tap into the 68000's addressing modes and instruction set. It's a book no Mac owner can afford to miss! 208 pp., 31 illus. 7″ × 10″.

Paper $16.95   **Book No. 2611**
Hard $24.95

☐ **TRUE BASIC® A COMPLETE MANUAL**

Have you heard about the new, improved version of BASIC that's taking the microcomputer industry by storm? Now, this groundbreaking guide makes it possible for you to understand and even start programming in True BASIC. Written by microcomputer programmer and consultant Henry Simpson, *True BASIC—A Complete Manual* covers all the main features of True BASIC including commands/statements and functions, program control, input/output, file-handling, and even graphics. 208 pp., 53 illus. Large Format (7″ × 10″).

Paper $14.95   **Book No. 1970**
Hard $22.95

☐ **SERIOUS PROGRAMMING FOR THE IBM® PC™/XT™/AT®**

Here's your key to learning how programs can be developed and designed for your own specific purposes to really do the job you need accomplished. You'll cover different aspects of program design, including using subroutines to build an effective subroutine library of your own, get special tips on learning to write a user's guide and creating help screens. 208 pp., 113 illus. 7″ × 10″.

Paper $14.95   **Book No. 1921**
Hard $21.95

☐ **THE DOSTALK SCRAPBOOK**

Take advantage of Apple DOS 3.3's outstanding capabilities with this practical handbook by Tom Weishaar, and Apple expert and publisher of the *Open Apple* newsletter and Bert Kersey, founder of Beagle Bros. Micro Software, Inc.! They show you how to master everything from booting your system and creating invisible filenames to assembly language programming with DOS and "inside" techniques for using DOS utility programs . . . they even touch on ProDOS! 280 pp.

Paper $14.95   **Book No. 2615**
Hard $21.95

☐ **469 PASCAL PROBLEMS WITH DETAILED SOLUTIONS—Veklerov**

Now this unique self-teaching guide makes it amazingly easy even for a novice programmer to master Pascal. With a total of 469 problems ranging from the most basic to advanced applications, the guide provides a unique learning opportunity for anyone who wants hands-on understanding of the Pascal language and its programming capabilities. 224 pp., 23 illus. 7″ × 10″.

Paper $14.95   **Book No. 1997**
Hard $21.95

☐ **SERIOUS PROGRAMMING FOR YOUR APPLE® II/IIe/IIc**

Here's your opportunity to advancing far beyond ineffective trial and error programming methods and learn the secrets of writing programs that accomplish exactly what you want them to—for business, educational, and other practical purposes. Taking a simple and straightforward approach, this guide leads you through the process of program development, step-by-step. Author Henry Simpson provides all the guidelines and techniques to give you the understanding needed to develop your own serious applications programs. 192 pp., 104 illus. Large Format (7″ × 10″).

Paper $12.95   **Book No. 1960**
Hard $18.95

☐ **PERFECT PASCAL PROGRAMS—Washington Apple Pi**

Much more than just another collection of programs, this is a compilation of articles by Pascal experts who are members of Washington Apple Pi—the nation's second largest Apple® user's group. Covering a wide variety of applications from simple utility routines to advanced programming techniques, it's the perfect tool for Apple users *and* for Pascal programmers using almost any micro (one of Pascal's unique features is its easy transportability between machines). 288 pp., 13 illus., 7″ × 10″.

Paper $16.95   **Book No. 1894**
Hard $22.95

Other Bestsellers From TAB